GOSPEL JESUSES AND
OTHER NONHUMANS

SEMEIA STUDIES

Steed V. Davidson, General Editor

Editorial Board:
Pablo R. Andiñach
Fiona Black
Denise K. Buell
Masiiwa Ragies Gunda
Jacqueline Hidalgo
Monica Jyotsna Melanchthon
Yak-Hwee Tan

Number 89

GOSPEL JESUSES AND OTHER NONHUMANS

Biblical Criticism Post-poststructuralism

Stephen D. Moore

SBL PRESS

Atlanta

Copyright © 2017 by Stephen D. Moore

All rights reserved. No part of this work may be reproduced or transmitted in any form or by any means, electronic or mechanical, including photocopying and recording, or by means of any information storage or retrieval system, except as may be expressly permitted by the 1976 Copyright Act or in writing from the publisher. Requests for permission should be addressed in writing to the Rights and Permissions Office, SBL Press, 825 Houston Mill Road, Atlanta, GA 30329 USA.

Library of Congress Cataloging-in-Publication Data

Names: Moore, Stephen D., 1954– , author.
Title: Gospel Jesuses and other nonhumans : Biblical criticism post-poststructuralism / by Stephen D. Moore.
Description: Atlanta : SBL Press, 2017. | Series: Semeia studies ; number 89 | Includes bibliographical references and index.
Identifiers: LCCN 2017037011 (print) | LCCN 2017039331 (ebook) | ISBN 9780884142515 (ebook) | ISBN 9781628371901 (paperback) | ISBN 9780884142522 (hardcover)
Subjects: LCSH: Jesus Christ—Person and offices. | Poststructuralism. | Bible—Hermeneutics.
Classification: LCC BT205 (ebook) | LCC BT205 .M656 2017 (print) | DDC 232/.8—dc23
LC record available at https://lccn.loc.gov/2017037011

Printed on acid-free paper.

Contents

Acknowledgments vii
Abbreviations ix

1. Introduction (and Conclusion): Posts Passed, Turns Taken 1

2. Why the Risen Body Weeps 15

3. The Messiah Who Screamed 41

4. The Dog-Woman of Canaan and Other Animal Tales 61

5. The Inhuman Acts of the Holy Ghost 85

6. What a (Sometimes Inanimate) Divine Animal and Plant
   Has to Teach Us about Being Human 107

Bibliography 127
Index of Modern Authors 147

Acknowledgments

This little book bears large debts of gratitude. It was on research leave granted by Drew Theological School that much of it was written. I am grateful to Javier Viera, dean among deans, for his receptivity and responsiveness to my work; to my ever-supportive biblical studies colleagues; to my doctoral students, who provide my research with its first raison d'être; and to Catherine Keller, whose various enthusiasms fuel my own and whose students are such vital additions to my doctoral seminars.

Chapter 2, "Why the Risen Body Weeps," began life as a paper commissioned by F. Scott Spencer for the Society of Biblical Literature program unit, "The Bible and Emotion." In addition to Scott, its original implied readers were the other presenters in that session, all of whose work with affect theory has been an inspiration to me: Maia Kotrosits, Jennifer Knust, Jennifer L. Koosed, Erin Runions, and Amy C. Cottrill. Chapter 3, "The Messiah Who Screamed," was written in fear and trembling for the extrabiblical affect theorists who participated in the Fifteenth Drew Transdiciplinary Theological Colloquium, "Affectivity and Divinity"—Eugenie Brinkema, Mel Y. Chen, Patricia Ticineto Clough, Ann Cvetkovich, and Gregory J. Seigworth—and for my respondent, Jennifer Knust. Chapter 4, "The Dog-Woman of Canaan and Other Animal Tales," originally appeared in a Festschrift for Fernando F. Segovia. I rededicate the essay to him with gratitude and admiration. The names that leap most readily to mind in connection with chapter 5, "The Inhuman Acts of the Holy Ghost," and chapter 6, "What a (Sometimes Inanimate) Divine Animal and Plant Has to Teach Us about Being Human," as deserving of special mention and particular gratitude are Denise Kimber Buell, Joseph A. Marchal, Hannah M. Strømmen, Catherine Keller, and above all Maia Kotrosits, who first came up with the idea of applying object-oriented new materialism to the Gospel of John.

Thanks, finally, to Steed Davidson and the other members of the Semeia Studies editorial board for admitting my book into a series that has been important to me ever since I was a graduate student long ago; to Steed additionally for excellent editorial interventions from which the book has benefited greatly; and to Bob Buller, Nicole Tilford, Kathie Klein, and the other members of the SBL Press editorial team for the privilege of working with them yet again.

Abreviations

1 Esd	1 Esdras
AB	Anchor Bible
ABRL	Anchor Bible Reference Library
ADEBull	*ADE Bulletin*
BAGD	Bauer, Walter, William F. Arndt, F. Wilbur Gingrich, and Frederick W. Danker. *A Greek-English Lexicon of the New Testament and Other Early Christian Literature*. 3rd ed. Chicago: University of Chicago Press, 2001.
Bar	Baruch
BCCC	Blackwell Companions in Cultural Studies
BCT	*The Bible and Critical Theory*
BibInt	*Biblical Interpretation*
BibInt	Biblical Interpretation Series
BL	Bible and Liberation
BMW	The Bible in the Modern World
BP	The Bible and Postcolonialism
BRP	Brill Research Perspectives in Biblical Interpretation
BS	*Buffalo Studies*
C21	Center for 21st Century Studies
CC	*Cultural Critique*
CCS	Cambridge Classical Studies
CI	Continuum Impacts
CIB	A Critical Inquiry Book
CLMS	Clarendon Lectures in Management Studies
CLS	Critical Life Studies
Contraversions	Contraversions: Jews and Other Differences
CP	Cultural Politics
CPS	Critical Plant Studies
differences	*differences: A Journal of Feminist Cultural Studies*
Divinations	Divinations: Rereading Late Ancient Religion

DRB	Douay-Rheims Bible
EBC	Earth Bible Commentary
Ekstasis	Ekstasis: Religious Experience from Antiquity to the Middle Ages
EP	European Perspectives
ETP	Ecocritical Theory and Practice
Flac.	Cicero, *Pro Flacco*
GC	Gender and Culture
GLQ	*GLQ: A Journal of Lesbian and Gay Studies*
GNV	Geneva Bible
HBM	Hebrew Bible Monographs
Hermeneia	Hermeneia: A Critical and Historical Commentary on the Bible
Hom. Act.	John Chrysostom, *Homiliae in Acta apostolorum*
Hom. Matt.	John Chrysostom, *Homiliae in Matthaeum*
ICC	International Critical Commentary
ILS	International Library of Sociology
Inc.	Athanasius, *De incarnatione*
ISBL	Indiana Studies in Biblical Literature
JBL	*Journal of Biblical Literature*
JFSR	*Journal of Feminist Studies in Religion*
JRS	*Journal of Roman Studies*
JSHJ	*Journal for the Study of the Historical Jesus*
JSNT	*Journal for the Study of the New Testament*
JSNTSup	Journal for the Study of the New Testament Supplement Series
J. W.	Josephus, *Jewish War*
KJV	King James Version
LCL	Loeb Classical Library
LHBOTS	The Library of Hebrew Bible/Old Testament Studies
LNTS	The Library of New Testament Studies
LSJ	Liddell, Henry George, Robert Scott, and Henry Stuart Jones. *A Greek-English Lexicon*. 9th ed. with revised supplement. Oxford: Clarendon, 1996.
LXX	Septuagint
Marc.	Seneca, *Ad Marciam de consolatione*
Meridian	Meridian: Crossing Aesthetics
Next Wave	Next Wave: New Directions in Women's Studies
NIGTC	The New International Greek Testament Commentary

NKJV	New King James Version
NLH	*New Literary History*
NM	New Metaphysics
NPNF	*Nicene and Post-Nicene Fathers*
NRSV	New Revised Standard Version
Part. an.	Aristotle, *De partibus animalium*
PCI	Post-Contemporary Interventions
PCP	Perspectives in Continental Philosophy
PG	Migne, Jacques-Paul, ed. Patrologia Graeca [= *Patrologiae Cursus Completus*: Series Graeca]. 162 vols. Paris: Migne, 1857–1886.
PhiloSOPHIA	*PhiloSOPHIA: A Journal of Continental Feminism*
PM	Perverse Modernities
PMLA	*Publications of the Modern Language Association*
PR	Postcolonialism and Religions
Prov. cons.	Cicero, *De provinciis consularibus*
PT	Postmodern Theory
Pyrrh.	Sextus Empiricus, *Outlines of Pyrrhonism*
QI	Queer Interventions
RBS	Resources for Biblical Study
RC	Routledge Classics
RH	*Rethinking History*
RRCMS	Routledge Research in Cultural and Media Studies
RV	Revised Version
SBLDS	Society of Biblical Literature Dissertation Series
SBR	Studies of the Bible and Its Reception
SemeiaSt	Semeia Studies
Serm.	Augustine, *Sermones*
SerQ	Series Q
SESI	Studies in Emotion and Social Interaction
SJD	The Seminars of Jacques Derrida
SP	Sacra Pagina
Spec.	Philo, *De specialibus legibus*
SR	Speculative Realism
ST	Scriptural Traces
StBibLit	Studies in Biblical Literature
Sum. theol.	Aquinas, *Summa theologiae*
SV	Miller, Robert J., ed. *The Complete Gospels Annotated Scholars Version*. 4th ed. Salem, OR: Polebridge, 2010.

Synkrisis	Synkrisis: Comparative Approaches to Early Christianity in Greco-Roman Culture
T/C	Theory/Culture
Thinking C21	*Thinking C21: Center for 21st Century Studies*
THL	Theory and History of Literature
TIN	Theory and Interpretation of Narrative
TOB	Theory Out of Bounds
TTC	Transdisciplinary Theological Colloquia
USQR	*Union Seminary Quarterly Review*
ZNW	*Zeitschrift für die Neutestamentliche Wissenschaft*

1

Introduction (and Conclusion): Posts Passed, Turns Taken

> Perhaps the most important stake for me in the nonhuman turn is how it might help us live more sustainably, with less violence toward a variety of bodies.
> —Jane Bennett, "Systems and Things"

The What and the Why

The Jesuses invoked in the title of this book are those of the four canonical gospels together with the Acts of the Apostles. Explorations and defamiliarizations of these overly familiar texts, excavations of their incessantly erased strangeness, are the book's most prominent feature. The book refocuses the Jesuses that inhabit those texts, along with other consequential characters, through the lens of nonhuman theory, a term that names an eclectic confluence of several of the main theoretical currents that have issued forth since the heyday of high poststructuralism, preeminently the 1980s and 1990s.[1]

---

1. The expression *high poststructuralism* conjures up a congeries of interrelated projects: dismantlings of metaphysical concepts and hierarchical oppositions; demonstrations of how literary and philosophical arguments are destabilized by the figures and tropes they employ; examinations of the ways in which every text, independently of the conscious intentions of any author, invokes innumerable other texts, recycling and rewriting them; exposures of the exclusions, omissions, and systemic blind spots that enable texts, and entire societies, to function; unearthings of the constructedness of certain of the most solid-seeming features of our cultural landscapes; investigations of the ineluctable role of power in the fabrication of truth and knowledge; explorations of the internal heteronomy fissuring every human subject; and so on. For a recent introduction to biblical poststructuralism, see George Aichele, *The Play of Signifiers: Poststructuralism and Study of the Bible*, BRP (Leiden, Netherlands: Brill, 2016).

Those were also the decades when poststructuralism, especially deconstruction, construed as the most conspicuous manifestation of postmodernism, was sending at least minor shock waves through biblical studies,[2] and major shock waves through my own work. From my initial infatuation with poststructuralism in its pure French forms,[3] my passions gradually shifted to gender and sexuality, then to the postcolonial, and eventually to the ecological[4]—each successive shift, however, sweeping the previous phases along with it and (ideally, anyway) bringing them all into intersectional exchange.

The ecological is the most encompassing concern in the present book, explicitly so on occasion, implicitly so more often. The theoretical threads that intertwine in what I am calling nonhuman theory[5] combine to effect an unprecedented erosion of the Western conception of "the human" that has coalesced since the Enlightenment. As such, these theoretical threads pair well with early Christian texts that long precede that epochal amalgamation and that testify to other notions of the human in its relations with the nonhuman, notions other than the anthropocentric conceptions that have generated the Anthropocene, which is to say our current Age of Extinction.

---

2. The excitement around postmodernism, whether eager or anxious, has long subsided in biblical studies. I have reflected elsewhere on this development; see my "The Slight Rise and Precipitous Decline of Postmodernism in Biblical Studies," in *Simulating Aichele: Essays in Bible, Film, Culture and Theory*, ed. Melissa C. Stewart, BMW 69 (Sheffield: Sheffield Phoenix, 2015), 225–45.

3. See especially my *Mark and Luke in Poststructuralist Perspectives: Jesus Begins to Write* (New Haven: Yale University Press, 1992).

4. See Stephen D. Moore, *Poststructuralism and the New Testament: Derrida and Foucault at the Foot of the Cross* (Minneapolis: Fortress, 1994), 43–64. More particularly, see Moore, *God's Gym: Divine Male Bodies of the Bible* (New York: Routledge, 1996); Moore, *God's Beauty Parlor: And Other Queer Spaces in and around the Bible*, Contraversions (Stanford, CA: Stanford University Press, 2001); Moore, *Empire and Apocalypse: Postcolonialism and the New Testament*, BMW 12 (Sheffield: Sheffield Phoenix, 2006); Stephen D. Moore and Fernando F. Segovia, eds., *Postcolonial Biblical Criticism: Interdisciplinary Intersections*, BP 8 (New York: T&T Clark International, 2005); Moore, *Untold Tales from the Book of Revelation: Sex and Gender, Empire and Ecology*, RBS 79 (Atlanta: SBL Press, 2014); Moore, ed., *Divinanimality: Animal Theory, Creaturely Theology*, TTC (New York: Fordham University Press, 2014).

5. Not yet a term I have seen others use but one implicit in the recent "nonhuman turn" in theory, introduced below.

1. Introduction (and Conclusion)

The Cast

The principal actors in our theodrama, at once theoretical and theological, are:

- a nonhuman risen body that shudders violently and weeps bitterly on discovering its own inerasable mortality
- a Messiah who screams shatteringly in an attempt to exit his animal body through his own mouth as excruciating forces bear down on him to crush him
- a dog-woman who reveals to a Human One the ineluctable truth of his own animal condition, including his destiny to be devoured
- a Holy Ghost generated by intergenerational trauma and assembled from both human and nonhuman elements (it both is and is not the ghost of a dead Messiah)
- a god-man who is also and always a god-man-animal, as well as a god-man-animal-plant and a god-man-animal-plant-thing

The Turn Away, the Turn Toward

The prime catalyst for the present book is a recent turn in "theory"—the latter a term that, within literary and cultural studies, is primarily a cipher for poststructuralism and, now additionally, post-poststructuralism (an inelegant but necessary term). Theory in the twenty-first century thus far is marked by a turn away from *language*, the preeminent preoccupation of classic poststructuralism, which is simultaneously a turn toward *the nonhuman* (epitomized by materiality and animality) and *affect* (emotion but also sensation and still more diffuse states).

Differently Put

Poststructuralism, notwithstanding its roots in postwar French antihumanism,[6] centered obsessively on the putative distinguishing

---

6. An antihumanism aphoristically channeled by Michel Foucault in the conclusion to the 1966 book that made him famous (and famous first and foremost as a structuralist): "Man is an invention of recent date. And one perhaps nearing its end" (*The Order of Things: An Archaeology of the Human Sciences*, trans. anon., RC [New York: Routledge, 2001], 422). The precise origins of the term poststructuralism are

feature of the human: *language*.[7] In contrast, the interrelated theoretical currents now seen as constituting a nonhuman turn in theory systematically interrogate human exceptionalism, classically expressed as a conceptual dualism of the human and the nonhuman (animals, plants, inorganic entities), and they also shift attention from human language and cognition to prepersonal and transpersonal affective processes and human/nonhuman assemblages.[8]

---

occluded (appropriately enough), but it began to appear in anglophone book and article titles in the late 1970s. Once the term started to circulate it came to be affixed to various French works that previously had been deemed structuralist, even archstructuralist, notably all of Jacques Derrida's and Julia Kristeva's publications, Jacques Lacan's publications from the late 1950s onward, and Michel Foucault's and Roland Barthes's publications from the late 1960s onward.

7. A blanket statement, of course, one that conceals any number of nuanced maneuvers within the general panlinguism of poststructuralism, such as Derrida's insistence that the structural elements that make human language possible—the elements his early work isolated, most famously *différance*—"*are themselves not only human*" since they also enable animal languages ("'Eating Well,' or the Calculation of the Subject," in *Points...: Interviews, 1974-1994*, ed. Elizabeth Weber, Meridian [Stanford, CA: Stanford University Press, 1995], 285, emphasis original). Nevertheless, as Karen Barad succinctly puts it in one of the theoretical interventions that will subsequently come to be seen as a decisive push beyond poststructuralism from within poststructuralism, "Language has been given too much power" ("Posthumanist Performativity: Toward an Understanding of How Matter Comes to Matter," *Signs* 28 [2003]: 801). She continues: "Language matters. Discourse matters. Culture matters. There is an important sense in which the only thing that does not seem to matter anymore is matter" (801).

8. Much more below on affect theory in this mode and also on assemblage theory (see esp. 15–20, 43–45, 113–16). Affect theory is provisionally defined later in this introduction; a preliminary definition of assemblages, therefore, is also in order. An assemblage is an ad hoc coalescence of heterogeneous elements and agencies, both human and nonhuman. Jane Bennett ventures a near-to-hand example: "The sentences of this book ... emerged from the confederate agency of many striving macro- and microactants: from 'my' memories, intentions, contentions, intestinal bacteria, eyeglasses, and blood sugar, as well as from the plastic computer keyboard, the bird song from the open window, or the air or particulates in the room, to name only a few of the participants" (*Vibrant Matter: A Political Ecology of Things* [Durham, NC: Duke University Press, 2010], 23).

From the Posthuman to the Nonhuman

The ultimate context and catalyst for much nonhuman theory—explicitly at times, implicitly at other times—is the current global ecological crisis. Introducing the nonhuman turn in twenty-first century theory, Richard Grusin distinguishes it from the posthuman turn:[9]

> Unlike the posthuman turn..., the nonhuman turn does not make a claim about teleology or progress in which we begin with the human and see a transformation from the human to the posthuman, after or beyond the human.... The nonhuman turn ... insists (to paraphrase Latour) that "we have never been human" but that the human has always coevolved, coexisted, or collaborated with the nonhuman—and that the human is characterized precisely by this indistinction from the nonhuman.[10]

Representative expressions of nonhuman theory, for Grusin, include animal studies, as one might expect, and affect theory, which one might not expect, together with assorted new materialisms and assemblage theory, to mention only the manifestations of nonhuman theory that are germane to the present book.[11] Grusin might also have included critical plant studies on his list, a blossoming field that is crucial for my final chapter.

---

9. For biblical-critical forays into the posthuman, see George Aichele, *Tales of Posthumanity: The Bible and Contemporary Popular Culture*, BMW 65 (Sheffield: Sheffield Phoenix, 2014); Jennifer L. Koosed, ed., *The Bible and Posthumanism*, SemeiaSt 74 (Atlanta: Society of Biblical Literature, 2014).

10. Richard Grusin, "Introduction," in *The Nonhuman Turn*, ed. Richard Grusin, C21 (Minneapolis: University of Minnesota Press, 2015), ix–x. Grusin is paraphrasing Bruno Latour's "we have never been modern," but it is Donna Haraway who explicitly insists "we have never been human"; that is the title of part 1 of her book *When Species Meet*, Posthumanities 3 (Minneapolis: University of Minnesota Press, 2008). Independently of Grusin, Jon Roffe and Hannah Stark's introduction to their own edited volume *Deleuze and the Non/Human* (New York: Palgrave Macmillan, 2015) contains a brief but cogent section titled "The Nonhuman Turn" (2–5). Their opening claim is sweeping: "At this present moment in intellectual history it is impossible to consider the human without contextualizing it with the nonhuman turn" (2). For yet another cogent framing of nonhuman theory, see Claire Colebrook, *Death of the Posthuman: Essays on Extinction*, vol. 1 (Ann Arbor, MI: Open Humanities, 2014), esp. the essay titled "Extinct Theory" (29–45).

11. Grusin, "Introduction," viii–ix. Grusin's bulleted list of theoretical developments signaling a nonhuman turn also includes: actor-network theory (à la Latour); new brain sciences "like neuroscience, cognitive science, and artificial intelligence";

Nonhuman Affect?

Why the emergence of the transdisciplinary field variously known as animal studies, human-animal studies, critical animal studies, animality studies, posthuman animality studies, and zoocriticism should be seen as a prominent sign of a nonhuman turn in theory is no mystery.[12] But

---

new media theory, "especially as it has paid close attention to technical networks, material interfaces, and computational analysis"; and systems theory "in its social, technical, and ecological manifestations" (viii–ix). Grusin adds: "As something of a theoretical and methodological assemblage, the nonhuman turn tries to make sense of what holds these various other 'turns' together, even while allowing for their divergent theoretical and methodological commitments and contradictions" (x). Jane Bennett, whose influential version of object-oriented new materialism is a vital ingredient of the present book, ventures the following generalization about the nonhuman turn: "All parties see the nonhuman turn as a response to an overconfidence about human power that was embedded in the postmodernism of the 1980s and 1990s" ("Systems and Things: On Vital Materialism and Object-Oriented Philosophy," in Grusin, *Nonhuman Turn*, 227). Or as Jeffrey Jerome Cohen phrases it in his introduction to yet another volume marking the nonhuman turn: "The human is not the world's sole meaning-maker, and never has been" ("Introduction: All Things," in *Animal, Vegetable, Mineral: Ethics and Objects*, ed. Cohen [Washington, DC: Oliphaunt, 2012], 7).

12. How might the current theoretical enchantment with the animal relate to the current theoretical disenchantment with language? Kari Weil has commented on that relationship, and in a register that is quasi-theological. Affirming a "counterlinguistic turn" in recent theory, one facet of which is fascination with an "ineffable animality," Weil writes: "If the linguistic turn insisted that we have no access to unmediated experience or knowledge, but only to representations that are themselves fraught with linguistic and ideological baggage, the turn to animals can be seen as responding to a desire for a way out of this 'prison-house of language.' It responds to a desire to know that there are beings or objects with ways of knowing and being that resist our flawed systems of language and who may know us and themselves in ways we can never discern" (*Thinking Animals: Why Animal Studies Now?* [New York: Columbia University Press, 2012], 11–12). For biblical and theological examples of animality studies, see several of the essays in both Koosed, *Bible and Posthumanism*, and Moore, *Divinanimality*, as well as Moore, "Why There Are No Humans or Animals in the Gospel of Mark," in *Mark as Story: Retrospect and Prospect*, ed. Kelly R. Iverson and Christopher W. Skinner, RBS 65 (Atlanta: Society of Biblical Literature, 2011), 71–94; Ken Stone, "Animating the Bible's Animals," in *The Oxford Handbook of Biblical Narrative*, ed. Danna Nolan Fewell (Oxford: Oxford University Press, 2016), 444–55; Stone, *Reading the Hebrew Bible with Animal Studies* (Stanford, CA: Stanford University Press, 2017); Hannah M. Strømmen, *Every Living Creature: The Question of the Animal in the Bible*, SemeiaSt (Atlanta: SBL Press, forthcoming).

why should affect theory—which, preliminarily and provisionally, may be defined as post-poststructuralist analysis of sensations, feelings, and/or emotions—also be seen as signaling such a turn? As Rebekah Sheldon explains, what the nonhuman turn problematizes, among other things, is any conception of the human "as consolidated, easily referenced, and transparent," the homogeneous obverse of the heterogenous nonhuman. "An account of the nonhuman turn," Sheldon insists, "must also include an understanding of the human as itself nonhuman, caught up in molecular flows of matter and force—rhythmic milieux, repeated refrains, gestural affordances, hormonal fluxes, audiovisual surround."[13] In other words, an account of the nonhuman turn must also include an apprehension of the human as caught up in *affect* as French philosopher Gilles Deleuze and theorists who take their lead from him employ the term.

A Philosopher of Flux

Deleuze looms large in this book. "Perhaps one day, this century will be known as Deleuzian," Michel Foucault once remarked.[14] Foucault may have had the century wrong. Just as he and Jacques Derrida were the towering theoretical eminences of the latter decades of the twentieth century, Deleuze is the thinker who, thus far, has most galvanized theory in the twenty-first century.[15]

---

13. Rebekah Sheldon, "Affect, Epistemology and the Nonhuman Turn," *Thinking C21*, 27 April 27 2012, https://tinyurl.com/SBL0691a. For a different set of reflections on nonhuman affect, see Bennett, *Vibrant Matter*, xi–xiii. On affect theory's relationship to poststructuralism, meanwhile, Patricia Ticineto Clough notes that the former impels "a substantial shift" in returning theory "to bodily matter, which had been treated in terms of various constructionisms under the influence of poststructuralism," whereas "the turn to affect points instead to a dynamism immanent to bodily matter and matter generally" (Clough, "The Affective Turn: Political Economy, Biomedia, and Bodies," in *The Affect Theory Reader*, ed. Melissa Gregg and Gregory J. Seigworth [Durham, NC: Duke University Press, 2010], 206–7); while Eugenie Brinkema characterizes "the turn to affect" as "part of a larger reawakening of interest in problematics of embodiment and materiality in the wake of twentieth-century Western theory that, for many, was all semiotics and no sense, all structure and no stuff" (*The Forms of the Affects* [Durham, NC: Duke University Press, 2014], xi).

14. Michel Foucault, "Theatrum Philosophicum," in *Language, Counter-Memory, Practice: Selected Essays and Interviews*, ed. Donald F. Bouchard, trans. Donald F. Bouchard and Sherry Simon (Ithaca, NY: Cornell University Press, 1977), 165.

15. The literature on Deleuze beggars footnoting. As an index of the number of

Deleuze rejected the panlinguism and hypertextualism of both structuralism and poststructuralism. He was not a philosopher of language at base,[16] which is why he was always an anomalous poststructuralist at best; but it is also why his work is attracting unprecedented attention in the post-poststructuralist era in which theory now finds itself. Deleuze was a philosopher of becoming, of the event, of affect, of sensation. He was a philosopher of flux.

In consequence, when Deleuze explains, as he once did in a colloquium when quizzed about the relationship of his reading strategies to those of Derridean deconstruction, that a text for him "is merely a little cog in an extratextual practice," that "it is not a matter of commenting on the text through a method … of textual practice" but rather "a matter of seeing what use can be made of a text in the extratextual practice that extends the text,"[17] we should not imagine that we are being gently taken by the elbow and ushered back into a pretheoretical world that is reassuringly solid and familiar and in which literary authors, even biblical

---

fields his work is impacting, see Edinburgh University Press's Deleuze Connections series, currently at twenty-eight volumes: *Deleuze and Feminist Theory, Deleuze and Literature, Deleuze and Music, Deleuze and Space, Deleuze and the Social, Deleuze and Philosophy, Deleuze and Politics, Deleuze and Queer Theory, Deleuze and History, Deleuze and New Technology, Deleuze and the Postcolonial, Deleuze and Ethics, Deleuze and Film, Deleuze and Law, Deleuze and Race, Deleuze and Architecture, Deleuze and the Animal*, and so on. More than a dozen books on Deleuze and religion, including theology, have appeared. Biblical scholars have engaged little with Deleuze to date; the notable exceptions include B. H. McLean, *Biblical Interpretation and Philosophical Hermeneutics* (Cambridge: Cambridge University Press, 2012), 268–301; Brennan W. Breed, *Nomadic Text: A Theory of Reception History*, ISBL (Bloomington: Indiana University Press, 2014), esp. 116–206; Caroline Vander Stichele, "The Head of John and Its Reception or How to Conceptualize 'Reception History,'" in *Reception History and Biblical Studies: Theory and Practice*, ed. Emma England and William John Lyons, ST 6 (New York: Bloomsbury T&T Clark, 2015), 79–94; Moore, "A Bible That Expresses Everything While Communicating Nothing: Deleuze and Guattari's Cure for Interpretosis," in *Exegesis without Authorial Intentions?*, ed. Clarissa Breu, BibInt (Leiden: Brill, forthcoming); and periodic forays in George Aichele's copious writings, such as much of Aichele, *Simulating Jesus: Reality Effects in the Gospels*, BibleWorld (London: Equinox, 2011); Aichele, *Tales of Posthumanity*, 45–51.

16. He comes closest to being that in Gilles Deleuze, *The Logic of Sense*, trans. Mark Lester, 2nd ed. (New York: Columbia University Press, 1990).

17. Gilles Deleuze, "Discussion" following "Pensée nomade," in *Intensités*, vol. 1 of *Nietzsche aujourd'hui?*, ed. Maurice de Gandillac and Bernard Pautrat, Colloque de Cerisy (Paris: Union Générale d'Éditions, 1973), 186–87 (my translation).

authors, once again communicate their intentions commonsensically and successfully to their audiences. What the text effects, for Deleuze, how it functions, is, as we shall see, considerably more complex and immeasurably more unsettling than that.

A Juicy Irony

"Probably, when Guattari picks up an article whose first sentence has the words 'machine,' 'structure,' and 'determination,' he cathects it immediately. Great stuff. Juicy, terrific." So Jane Tompkins wrote in 1987 about Félix Guattari, best known for his remarkable collaborations with Deleuze, most notably *Anti-Oedipus* and *A Thousand Plateaus*, and her words make me smile.[18] My chance discovery of Tompkins's article the year it was published represented my own first encounter with post-poststructuralism (although that clumsy name was yet to be concocted then). I was laboring to become better acquainted with poststructuralism, to know it intimately, when I stumbled on Tompkins's disarmingly frank, thoroughly engaging, intra-poststructuralist, post-poststructuralist, feminist critique of what she sees as the alienating abstractness and implacable impersonality of the modes of poststructuralist theory that, by then, were saturating her field of literary studies.[19] But what makes me smile is not sentimentality so much as the sheer irony of Tompkins's pronouncement on Guattari whose book *Molecular Revolution* is one of three works of theory she has plucked from her bookshelf to illustrate what she alleges is theory's wooden inability to engage with feelings or the sensory saturatedness of being in a life—"noises, smells, aches and pains," as she puts it—an ironic pronouncement because the hypertheoretical team of Deleuze and Guattari are widely seen

---

18. Jane P. Tompkins, "Me and My Shadow," in *The Intimate Critique: Autobiographical Literary Criticism*, ed. Diane P. Freeman, Olivia Frey, and Frances Murphy Zauhar (Durham, NC: Duke University Press, 1993), 36, a piece first published in *NLH* 19 (1987): 169–78; Gilles Deleuze and Félix Guattari, *Anti-Oedipus: Capitalism and Schizophrenia*, trans. Robert Hurley, Mark Seem, and Helen R. Lane, CI (Minneapolis: University of Minnesota Press, 1983); Deleuze and Guattari, *A Thousand Plateaus: Capitalism and Schizophrenia*, trans. Brian Massumi, CI (Minneapolis: University of Minnesota Press, 1987).

19. I eventually wrote on Tompkins's article in a different context; it was by then seen as an originating instance of autobiographical criticism, which was beginning to seep into biblical studies. See my "True Confessions and Weird Obsessions: Autobiographical Interventions in Literary and Biblical Studies," *Semeia* 72 (1995): 19–51.

today as the most important resource for the most influential strand of affect theory, and affect theory, notionally at least, is supposed to engage the previously excluded dimensions of lived experience that Tompkins poignantly articulated in her posttheory article.[20]

This Will Hurt Only for a Moment

All the preceding scene-setting may have made this book sound like a particularly dense and deadly theoretical treatise, but theoretical exposition constitutes only a small portion of it. Most of the book is occupied with theoretically inflected close readings of specific texts and themes in the canonical gospels and Acts.

Chattering Chapters

The body of the book is bookended by two chapters on John. Clustered between these two chapters, and chattering compulsively with them and each other, are chapters on Mark, Matthew, and Luke-Acts.

The Book of Rot

Chapter 2, "Why the Risen Body Weeps," is an exploration of death, decay, and disgust in the Gospel of John. More precisely, it is a meditation on meat, the common condition of all animals, whether human or nonhuman, and that meditation is conducted through the medium of affect theory. What really causes the Johannine Jesus to weep at the tomb of Lazarus (11:35)? To ponder that question is to reckon with forces in the Fourth Gospel that only come to oblique expression in it. The Johannine narrative is suffused with unstated affect, one affect in particular: *disgust*. Disgust enacts exclusion. What the Fourth Gospel attempts to exclude is meat, or, to use its own term, *sarx* ("flesh"), insistently aligning it with death. Flesh is always

---

20. Tompkins, "Me and My Shadow," 33. See Félix Guattari, *Molecular Revolution: Psychiatry and Politics*, trans. Rosemary Sheed (Harmondsworth, UK: Peregrine, 1984). Another strand of affect theory emerges out of the kind of feminist work modeled by Tompkins in her essay—work Ann Cvetkovich has described as "engagement with the shifting fortunes of the feminist mantra that 'the personal is the political' as it has shaped theoretical and political practice and their relation to everyday life" (*Depression: A Public Feeling* [Durham, NC: Duke University Press, 2012], 8).

already rotting, even in life. The Johannine Jesus does not refuse his own death, but he does refuse his own decay. In raising Lazarus, he is refusing not only Lazarus's putrefaction but also his own. Even on the path to his own tomb, the Johannine Jesus is always already risen, but his resurrected body is an uncertain guarantor of its own incorruptibility. The marks of death, and hence of decomposition, persist indelibly on the still-mortally-wounded risen body. This is a risen body with bloody meat on its bones—which, more than anything else, is why it weeps at Lazarus's tomb.

The Book of Pain

Chapter 3, "The Messiah Who Screamed," stays with the theme of bloody meat. It is an examination of flayed flesh, raw sensation, and Mark's crucifixion. In the climactic moment of the climactic scene in Mark, the protagonist utters an animal shriek, a bestial roar, a death-scream. What in Deleuzian terms is the Markan crucifixion? Above all, perhaps, it is an *assemblage*, and like all assemblages, it combines human and nonhuman elements: the denuded, impaled man; the wood-and-metal torture device; the divine being erupting from the bowels of the bloody carcass. On the one hand, there is no incarnation in Mark, no preexistent divine being secondarily remade as meat. On the other hand, there is nothing *but* incarnation in Mark, nothing but a Christ who in his consummate moment of self-revelation is encountered only as sensate matter, as scoured flesh. Sacrificed flesh, which is to say butchered meat, is the sacred place in which the human encounters the divine in Mark, in which the human shudders before, and is affected by, the divine. It is not the omnipotent imperial Christ on his cloud but the tortured peasant Christ on his cross—not the throne assemblage, then, resplendent with radiant, glorious flesh, but the cross assemblage, laden with throbbing, suffering flesh—that has been the hyperaffective megamachine for the ages, as Christian piety has never stopped insisting.

The Book of Dogs and Sheep

Chapter 4, "The Dog-Woman of Canaan and Other Animal Tales," intensifies our engagement with metaphoric animality, this time in tandem with queer temporality.[21] Narrative time bends queerly in the ethnically

---

21. Queer theory has had much to say about history, historiography, historical

and colonially charged space that is the Matthean Jesus's encounter with "a Canaanite woman" (15:21–28). Slavish Canaan, represented as an animalized woman, debases herself before Israel, represented by the "Son of David" (15:22), submissively picking up the humiliating dog epithet hurled at her, a nationalistic fantasy that reinvents the archaic past. The dog-woman's exchange with the Human One (*ho huios tou anthrōpou*) participates in a larger Matthean discourse on human-animal relations. The humanity of the Human One is repeatedly thrown into question, but nowhere more acutely than in his words over the Passover cup (26:27–28) in which he implicitly identifies his impending slaughter as that of a sacrificial animal. This anthropophagic repast is anticipated by the Canaanite woman. The dog-woman's problem, the Human One would seem to be saying, is that she is not a sheep-woman. The more basic problem, she would seem to be replying, is that the sheep he has culled from the larger flock to follow him must soon morph into dogs so as to be able to heed his command to devour his flesh and drink his blood, while he himself must morph into a sheep in order that this abominable meal may occur.

The Haunted Books

Chapter 5, "The Inhuman Acts of the Holy Ghost," picks up queer temporality from the previous chapter and sets it in the center of the stage.

---

periodization, and time in general, as we shall see (chapter 5 below). The importance of queer theory for the nonhuman turn in theory is implicitly but effectively articulated by Jon Roffe and Hannah Stark: "Recently the category of the human has been besieged from all sides. Not only has it been revealed to have been complicit with the violent exclusions of those considered to be less-than-human, understood as a normative notion (women, nonheterosexuals, people of color, the disabled) but its metaphysical security has also been challenged by the flourishing of theoretical interest in the nonhuman: forces, animals, objects, and plants" ("Deleuze and the Nonhuman Turn: An Interview with Elizabeth Grosz," in Roffe and Stark, *Deleuze and the Non/Human*, 17). In her response to Roffe and Stark's remarks, Grosz observes: "The nonhuman turn, one of many 'turns' occurring at the moment, is one of the implications of a critique of the restriction of the human to the able-bodied, Western, white, civilized, masculine man, and forms of control exerted by the category 'human'" (18). See further Noreen Giffney and Myra J. Hird, eds., *Queering the Non/Human*, QI (Aldershot, UK: Ashgate, 2008); the editors note in their introduction to the volume: "Queering has the job of undoing 'normal' categories, and none is more critical than the human/nonhuman sorting operation" (xxiv).

There it is joined by affect theory, and in combination, they show Luke-Acts to be a consummate exercise in queer temporality and affective historiography as well as a precritical model for a postcritical history of proto-Christianity. The role of the nonhuman, meanwhile, is played by the ghost—or, better, the ghosts, most especially the ghost of Jesus and the Holy Ghost (that antiquated yet timely term). The unhuman spectral agent that is the Holy Ghost is a product of intergenerational trauma, as will be argued. It is also an assemblage of material and immaterial forces and human and nonhuman elements: a dead Jesus, a living God, a dove, a violent wind, tongues of fire, a liquid that is lavishly poured out. The Holy Ghost is a transhuman habitat. At once personal and impersonal, intimate and external, the Holy Ghost in its nonhuman register is akin to affect in the Deleuzian register. The Holy Ghost is a force, an intensity that impacts bodies, infiltrates them, circulates between them. It impels movement, emotion, and cognition. It flows incessantly but it does not seem to think. Rather, *it acts*—most of all in the Acts of the Holy Ghost, Luke's spectral second volume.

The Book of Inhuman Incarnations

Chapter 6, "What a (Sometimes Inanimate) Divine Animal and Plant Has to Teach Us about Being Human," lingers with the project of defamiliarizing the divine characters of the New Testament but shifts the analytic lens from the Holy Ghost to the preexistent Son of God. The Jesus of John's Gospel is not, or not solely, a human being. The god-man is also a nonhuman animal (a lamb), a vegetable (a vine), vegetable byproducts (bread and a door), and inorganic energy, namely, electromagnetic radiation (light)—all epithets no more or no less metaphoric than "Son of God." Of course, it is Son Christology that has commanded center stage since at least the fourth century. The nonhuman turn in theory, elicited in no small part by the global ecological crisis, impels a shift of attention from Son Christology to animal Christology, vegetal Christology, and inorganic Christology. This chapter seeks to stage that shift, arguing that the Fourth Gospel enacts a profound disturbance of what Mel Chen has termed *the animacy hierarchy*: the world-structuring human ranking of inorganic material, plant life, animal life, disabled life, "fully human" life—and, one might add, divine life—in terms of perceived intrinsic worth. The Johannine Jesus enacts animacy in multiple interpenetrating nonhuman ways that invite less anthropocentric modes of affective engagement than the

Christs of classic orthodoxy, Christs supposedly modeled on the Johannine Jesus.

A Confession and No Conclusion

I have been using the term *chapters* for the constituent units of this book and will continue to do so in the body of it, but let me come clean and confess what will be apparent anyway to the attentive reader. This book is a collection—I am tempted to say an assemblage—of five essays. Yes, the essays are ordered in something like a logical sequence, and yes, they are bound intimately to each other by any number of theoretical and thematic threads. Ultimately, however, each of the essays is a freestanding agent, upright if occasionally wobbly. What the first essay has to say about the Fourth Gospel, for example, cannot easily be reconciled with what the final essay has to say about it. Each of those essays plugs the Johannine text into a different theoretical apparatus and each apparatus causes the text to light up in a different configuration. More generally, there is no inexorably unfolding argument running through all five essays, molding them to its will and climaxing in a grand summative conclusion—which is why this book has no formal conclusion and why this introduction doubles as a conclusion. The ending is embedded in the beginning—and we are now at the end of the beginning. So let us begin again.

2
Why the Risen Body Weeps*

Nothing preexists rot.
—Eugenie Brinkema, *Forms of the Affects*

Jesus burst into tears.... Then Jesus, profoundly moved again, came to the tomb; but it was a cave and a stone lay upon it. Jesus said, "Lift the stone." Martha, the sister of the dead man, said to him, "Lord, by now he stinks because he has been dead four days."
—John 11:35–39

How does one read emotion in that thing we call a text? How does one make sense of tears when the entity that sheds them is not a human being but a god in a paper body? How and why does the Johannine Jesus weep at the tomb of Lazarus? What does fleshly decomposition do in this literary composition? What affects does it embody or engender? These are the questions that animate this chapter, an experiment in "applied" affect theory. A rudimentary recitation of the history of affect theory is first in order, then, together with an explication of the competing concepts of affect that have informed it.

Feeling Theory

The now canonical etiology of affect theory conjures up two incongruent origins. The earlier origin—including the coinage of the term *affect theory* itself—is associated with US psychologist Silvan S. Tomkins (1911–1991),

---

* An earlier version of this essay appears as "Why the Johannine Jesus Weeps at the Tomb of Lazarus," in *Mixed Feelings and Vexed Passions: Exploring Emotions in Biblical Literature*, ed. F. Scott Spencer, RBS 90 (Atlanta: SBL Press, 2017). Reused here with permission.

whose biologically based research distinguished nine allegedly innate affects: distress-anguish; interest-excitement; enjoyment-joy; surprise-startle; anger-rage; fear-terror; shame-humiliation; disgust; and, related to the latter but subtly distinct from it, "dismell."[1] An *affect*, in Tomkins's special sense of the term, is not an emotion. An affect is rather a physiological response to a stimulus, whether internal or external, and as such is the biological basis of *emotion*. But emotion proper, for Tomkins, also entails memory and biography, the layered intricacy of a multifaceted life unfolding in time. *Feeling*, meanwhile, in Tomkins's usage of the term, mediates between affect and emotion. Feeling is the incipient psychological processing of bodily affect—the conscious registering of affect—prior to its full assimilation as emotion.

Tomkins's pre-poststructuralist work on affect attained post-poststructuralist significance through its championing and channeling by revered queer theorist Eve Kosofsky Sedgwick.[2] In retrospect, her 1995 essay coauthored with Adam Frank, "Shame in the Cybernetic Fold: Reading Silvan Tomkins," may be said to have marked a significant early moment in the turning of poststructuralist attention from the linguistic to the extralinguistic—more specifically in this case, from the human body as discursive construction to the human body as extradiscursive agent. Sedgwick and Frank write: "'Theory' has become almost simply coextensive with the claim (you can't say it often enough) *It's not natural*," a stance they dub "reflexive antibiologism."[3] Consequently, Sedgwick and Frank's turn to Tomkins transgresses certain of theory's most cherished dogmas: "You don't have to be long out of theory kindergarten to make mincemeat

---

1. See Silvan S. Tomkins, *Affect, Imagery, Consciousness*, 4 vols. (New York: Springer, 1962–1992). Vol. 1: *The Positive Affects*; vol. 2: *The Negative Affects*; vol. 3: *The Negative Affects: Anger and Fear*; vol. 4: *Cognition: Duplication and Transformation of Information*. For a more accessible entrée to Tomkins's psychology, see Tomkins, *Exploring Affect: The Selected Writings of Silvan S. Tomkins*, ed. E. Virginia Demos, SESI (Cambridge: Cambridge University Press, 1995).

2. See Eve Kosofsky Sedgwick and Adam Frank, eds., *Shame and Its Sisters: A Silvan Tomkins Reader* (Durham, NC: Duke University Press, 1995). Still more important for the Tomkins trajectory of affect theory as it has impinged on literary and cultural studies has been Sedgwick's *Touching Feeling: Affect, Pedagogy, Performativity* (Durham, NC: Duke University Press, 2003).

3. Eve Kosofsky Sedgwick and Adam Frank, "Shame in the Cybernetic Fold: Reading Silvan Tomkins," in *Touching Feeling*, 109, emphasis original. This essay originally served as the introduction to Sedgwick and Frank, eds., *Shame and Its Sisters*.

of, let's say, a psychology that depends on the separate existence of eight (only sometimes it's nine) distinct affects hardwired into the human biological system."[4] Yet this biopsychology is, in their estimation, excellently equipped to take the precise measure of affect in situations in which classic poststructuralist theory (Derridean, Foucauldian, or Lacanian, say) would be a clumsy tool at best.

Yet it is not as though nothing pertinent to the analysis of affect has emerged from "French theory," broadly conceived. Affect theory's other point of origin is associated with French philosopher Deleuze (1925–1995). Even though Tomkins coined the term affect theory, it should not be imagined that his biopsychology is a major driver of this theory as it has developed in literary and cultural studies. Sedgwick's "discovery" of Tomkins has impelled many literary and cultural studies folk to dip into his work—to live "a theoretical moment not one's own," as she and Frank put it[5]—though relatively few have lingered there. Far more consequential for affect theory has been the para-poststructuralist oeuvre of Deleuze, including Deleuze's extraordinary thought experiments with Guattari.

Unlike Tomkins's biopsychology, Deleuze's philosophy developed in contiguity with structuralism and poststructuralism—but strategically to the side of them; for Deleuze was primarily interested in sensation and only secondarily in language. Like Baruch Spinoza, Henri Bergson, or Alfred North Whitehead, Deleuze was a philosopher of becoming, and his concept of affect was a concept of incessant, irreducible becoming.[6] More precisely, Deleuzian affect is the ineffable, preprocessed, visceral, visual, aural, tactile, olfactory, kinetic, rhythmic, chaotic encounter with the material world prior to structured sensory perception, prior to conscious cognition, prior to linguistic representation—and also prior to emotion or feeling. "Affects aren't feelings," Deleuze insisted in an interview; "they're becomings that spill over beyond whoever lives through them (thereby becoming someone else)."[7] Deleuzian affects are transpersonal but also prepersonal.

Just as the Tomkins brand of affect theory has been mediated and further elaborated by Sedgwick, so has the Deleuze brand of affect theory

---

4. Sedgwick and Frank, "Shame in the Cybernetic Fold," 94.
5. Ibid., 117.
6. "Affects are becomings" (Deleuze and Guattari, *A Thousand Plateaus*, 256).
7. Gilles Deleuze, "On Philosophy," in Deleuze, *Negotiations, 1972–1990*, trans. Martin Joughin (New York: Columbia University Press, 1995), 137.

been mediated and further elaborated by Brian Massumi, initially in a 1995 article, "The Autonomy of Affect" (in eerily symmetrical counterpoint to Sedgwick and Frank's "Shame in the Cybernetic Fold"), and subsequently in a significant book, *Parables for the Virtual*.⁸ Massumi's distinction between affect and emotion is often quoted:

> An emotion is a subjective content, the sociolinguistic fixing of the quality of an experience, which is from that point onward defined as personal. Emotion is qualified intensity [for Massumi, "intensity" is a synonym for "affect"], the conventional, consensual point of insertion of intensity into semantically and semiotically formed progressions, into narrativizable action-reaction circuits, into function and meaning. It is intensity owned and recognized. It is crucial to theorize the difference between affect and emotion.⁹

This second, Deleuzian trajectory we have been tracing makes for an implacably austere, immensely elusive concept of affect. Yet it is this construal that has been most influential for affect theory in recent literary and cultural studies. Deleuzian affect explicitly permeates much of Patricia Ticineto Clough's pivotal collection *The Affective Turn*, while it implicitly permeates Gregory Seigworth and Melissa Gregg's introduction to their field-consolidating volume *The Affect Theory Reader*.¹⁰ Deleuze is every-

---

8. Brian Massumi, "The Autonomy of Affect," *CC* 31 (1995): 83–109; Massumi, *Parables for the Virtual: Movement, Affect, Sensation*, PCI (Durham, NC: Duke University Press, 2002). Like Sedgwick and Frank's "Shame in the Cybernetic Fold," Massumi's "The Autonomy of Affect" also took aim at "the varieties of social constructivism currently dominant in cultural theory" (*Parables for the Virtual*, 38). A "common thread" running through this dominant strand of theory "holds that everything, including nature, is constructed in discourse. The classical definition of the human as the rational animal returns in new permutation: the human as the chattering animal. Only the animal is bracketed: the human as the chattering of culture. This reinstates a rigid divide between the human and the nonhuman.... Saying that nature is discursively constructed is not necessarily the same as saying that nature is *in* discourse.... It is meaningless to interrogate the relation of the human to the nonhuman if the nonhuman is only a construct of human culture" (38–39). Like "Shame in the Cybernetic Fold," "The Autonomy of Affect" marked a significant moment in the intra-poststructuralist critique of poststructuralism.

9. Massumi, *Parables for the Virtual*, 28. See also Massumi, *Politics of Affect* (Cambridge: Polity, 2015), 5: "An emotion is a very partial expression of affect."

10. Patricia Ticineto Clough, ed., with Jean Halley, *The Affective Turn: Theorizing the Social* (Durham, NC: Duke University Press, 2007); Gregory J. Seigworth and

where present even if nowhere named, for example, in Seigworth and Gregg's preliminary definition of affect:

> Affect is found in those intensities that pass body to body..., in those resonances that circulate about, between, and sometimes stick to bodies and worlds.... Affect ... is the name we give to those forces—visceral forces beneath, alongside, or generally *other than* conscious knowing, vital forces insisting beyond emotion—that can serve to drive us toward movement, toward thought.¹¹

Meanwhile, prominent affect theorists like Lauren Berlant, Kathleen Stewart, and Jasbir Puar also work with concepts of affect that are essentially Deleuzian.¹²

Affect theory is not a two-party system, however, as certain notable affect theorists, including Sara Ahmed and Ann Cvetkovich, fail to fit neatly into either the Tomkins or Deleuze camps.¹³ Indeed, Cvetkovich's comments on both "the affective turn" and the affect/emotion distinction problematize much of the (oversimplifying) tale I have been telling thus far. Cvetkovich questions the common notion that the affective turn in the humanities is a recent phenomenon, declaring it already implicit in "the [early] feminist mantra that 'the personal is the political.'"¹⁴ More broadly, Cvetkovich argues that many different domains of inquiry, few of them new, have been animated by an interest in affect: cultural memory studies; explorations of the role of emotions in political discourse; analyses

> of the politics of negative affects, such as melancholy and shame, inspired in particular by queer [theory]; new forms of historical inquiry ... that

---

Melissa Gregg, "An Inventory of Shimmers," in Gregg and Seigworth, *Affect Theory Reader*, 1–25.

11. Seigworth and Gregg, "Inventory of Shimmers," 1, emphasis original.

12. See, e.g., Lauren Berlant, *Cruel Optimism* (Durham, NC: Duke University Press, 2011); Kathleen Stewart, *Ordinary Affects* (Durham, NC: Duke University Press, 2007); Jasbir Puar, *Terrorist Assemblages: Homonationalism in Queer Times*, Next Wave (Durham, NC: Duke University Press, 2007); Ann Pellegrini and Jasbir Puar, "Affect," *Social Text* 27.3 (2009): 35–38.

13. See Sara Ahmed, *The Cultural Politics of Emotion*, 2nd ed. (London: Routledge, 2014); Ahmed, *The Promise of Happiness* (Durham, NC: Duke University Press, 2010); Ann Cvetkovich, *An Archive of Feelings: Trauma, Sexuality, and Lesbian Public Cultures*, SerQ (Durham, NC: Duke University Press, 2003); Cvetkovich, *Depression*.

14. Cvetkovich, *Depression*, 8.

emphasize the affective relations between past and present; the turn to memoir and the personal in criticism…; histories of intimacy, domesticity, and private life; the cultural politics of everyday life; histories and theories of sensation and touch informed by phenomenology and cultural geography

—and so on.[15] Cvetkovich also resists any rigid distinction between affect and emotion or affect and feeling: "I tend to use *affect* in a generic sense, rather than in the more specific Deleuzian sense, as a category that encompasses affect, emotion, and feeling, and that includes impulses, desires, and feelings that get historically constructed in a range of ways (whether as distinct specific emotions or as a generic category often contrasted with reason)."[16]

Ahmed, another influential thinker commonly associated with affect theory, is no less skeptical about "the affective turn" as a concept—arguing that it elides the feminist and queer work that made it possible[17]—and about the theoretical elevation of affect over emotion. "A contrast between a mobile impersonal affect and a contained personal emotion suggests that the affect/emotion distinction can operate as a gendered distinction," Ahmed contends. "It might even be that the very use of this distinction performs the evacuation of certain styles of thought (we might think of these as 'touchy feely' styles of thought, including feminist and queer thought) from affect studies."[18] Such objections to the dominance of Deleuzian affect within contemporary affect theory have prompted Pansy Duncan to propose the term *feeling theory* instead for the field "in order to encompass both work on affect and work on emotion."[19]

---

15. Ibid., 3.
16. Ibid., 4.
17. Sara Ahmed, "Afterword: Emotions and Their Objects," in Ahmed, *Cultural Politics of Emotion*, 205–6. This afterword, specially written for the second edition, provides a survey and critique of the field of affect theory whose emergence the first edition of the book in 2004 helped to catalyze.
18. Ibid., 207.
19. Pansy Duncan, *The Emotional Life of Postmodern Film: Affect Theory's Other*, RRCMS 81 (New York: Routledge, 2015), 3. See also Duncan, "Taking the Smooth with the Rough: Texture, Emotion, and the Other Postmodernism," *PMLA* 129 (2014): 205.

2. Why the Risen Body Weeps

Interpreting after the End of Interpretation

However renamed, affect theory remains a complex and conflicted field, not least because it is not one field but several intersecting fields, as we have seen. What might this heterogeneous field yield for biblical interpretation? Can affect theory yield strategies for analyzing biblical texts, even for close reading biblical texts? Apparently it can because it already has. Erin Runions, Maia Kotrosits, Amy Cottrill, Jennifer Knust, Jennifer Koosed, Alexis Waller, and I myself have all published exegetical analyses of biblical texts that draw on affect theory.[20] Our interpretive appropriations of affect theory were, however, highly anomalous in the larger interdisciplinary context. In relation specifically to the field called "literary studies," one mainly populated by denizens of modern language and comparative literature departments, our affective interpretations of biblical literature were doubly anomalous: not only were they affective interpretations of *biblical* literature, but they were affective *interpretations* of biblical literature. In the land of literary studies, literature is no longer king and interpretation is no longer queen.[21]

---

20. See Erin Runions, "From Disgust to Humor: Rahab's Queer Affect," in *Bible Trouble: Queer Reading at the Boundaries of Biblical Scholarship*, ed. Teresa J. Hornsby and Ken Stone, SemeiaSt 67 (Atlanta: Society of Biblical Literature, 2011), 45–74; Runions, "Prophetic Affect and the Promise of Change: A Response," in *Jeremiah (Dis)Placed: New Directions in Writing/Reading Jeremiah*, ed. A. R. Pete Diamond and Louis Stulman, LHBOTS 529 (New York: T&T Clark International, 2011), 235–42; Maia Kotrosits, "The Rhetoric of Intimate Spaces: Affect and Performance in the Corinthian Correspondence," *USQR* 62 (2011): 134–51; Kotrosis, "Romance and Danger at Nag Hammadi," *BCT* 8 (2012): 29–52; Kotrosis, *Rethinking Early Christian Identity: Affect, Violence, and Belonging* (Minneapolis: Fortress, 2015); Maia Kotrosits and Hal Taussig, *Re-reading the Gospel of Mark Amidst Loss and Trauma* (New York: Palgrave Macmillan, 2013); Jennifer L. Koosed and Stephen D. Moore, eds., *Affect Theory and the Bible*, BibInt 22.4 (2014), which has articles by Jennifer Knust, Jennifer Koosed, Amy Cottrill, Alexis Waller, Maia Kotrosits, and Stephen Moore. For an extensive and incisive survey of biblical-scholarly engagements with affect theory, see Kotrosits, *How Things Feel: Biblical Studies, Affect Theory, and the (Im)personal*, BRP (Leiden: Brill, 2016).

21. Reviewing the current literary studies scene, Jeffrey T. Nealon asks rhetorically, "when was the last time you heard a junior job candidate do an actual close reading of a poem?" and adds, "one could at this point begin multiplying anti-hermeneutic references"; his list, as it happens, begins with "critical theories invested in Deleuze and Guattari" (*Post-Postmodernism, or, the Cultural Logic of Just-in-Time Capitalism* [Stanford, CA: Stanford University Press, 2012], 132). Nealon continues: "While fac-

What has replaced literary interpretation in literary studies, in particular close reading? What has replaced it, mainly, is cultural studies. Close reading was the trademark practice of leading-edge literary studies from the 1930s through the 1980s, which is to say from the hegemony of the New Criticism, which invented and patented literary close reading, through the heyday of deconstructive criticism and reader-response criticism, with new historicism straddling the now and the not yet and foreshadowing the future of the discipline.[22] In the 1990s, literature began to slide altogether from the center of US literary studies. Now any high-cultural icon or low-cultural artifact was fair game for theory-infused analysis. We learned to stop saying "literary studies" and to say "literary and cultural studies" instead. But as literature slid to the side, so too did

---

ulty research surrounding the mechanics and production of meaning (and/or its flip side, undecidability) experienced a boom during the postmodern big theory years, it's almost impossible only a few years later to imagine a publishing future that consists of new and improved interpretations of [literary texts].... [T]he decisive conceptual difference separating the present from the era of big theory is not so much a loss of status for theoretical discourses (just look at any university press catalog and you'll be quickly disabused of that notion), but the waning of literary interpretation itself as a viable research (which is to say, publishing) agenda" (133). Nealon's argument is in line with "the significant negative conclusion" at which Andrew Goldstone and Ted Underwood arrive in their joint survey article on recent developments in literary studies: "Neither interpretation, nor criticism, nor form, nor texts, nor language itself can be thought of as the invariant core of the discipline of literary studies" ("The Quiet Transformations of Literary Studies: What Thirteen Thousand Scholars Could Tell Us," *NLH* 45 [2014]: 375).

22. Colonial discourse analysis (what would be termed postcolonial theory by the end of the 1980s) also played a bridging role, as Simon During notes. It was part of a "general restructuring" of literary studies that began in the 1980s, a restructuring that "has, perhaps, been insufficiently acknowledged by the profession," in which "literary criticism ceased to ground itself on its attention to its objects' literary qualities.... It turned rather to thinking about literature as, for instance, a vehicle of cultural-political identities, or as a resistance to ideology, or, more neutrally, as articulated into broader signifying or social structures" ("The Postcolonial Aesthetic," *PMLA* 129 [2014]: 498). As Rita Felski lyrically puts it: "The critic no longer dirties her hands by burrowing into the text, scrabbling through layers of soil in pursuit of buried treasure.... Instead of reading deep, she prefers to read wide, swapping the close-up view of the microscope for a wide-angle lens that offers a panoramic view of systems of discourse and grids of power" (*The Limits of Critique* [Chicago: University of Chicago Press, 2015], 70).

close reading.²³ To put it another way, contemporary literary studies is postliterary and postmethodological.²⁴ "Method" in the biblical studies sense—that is to say, a quasi-formulaic and easily repeatable interpretive procedure—began to hemorrhage from literary studies at precisely the same moment when close reading began to bleed from it.

Affect theory, too, has been notably uninterested in literature, by and large, in method narrowly defined (or as definable at all) or in close reading. Most affect theory huddles comfortably under the umbrella of "cultural studies" rather than "literary studies." Literary interpretation plays no significant role in *The Affect Theory Reader* or its predecessor *The Affective Turn*. Neither does literary interpretation play a prominent role, or any role whatsoever, in many of the most admired monographs of affect theory, ranging from Massumi's *Parables for the Virtual*, Teresa Brennan's *The Transmission of Affect*, and Sianne Ngai's *Ugly Feelings* to Denise Riley's *Impersonal Passion*, Kathleen Stewart's *Ordinary Affects*, and Nigel Thrift's *Non-representational Theory*.²⁵ The case need not be overstated. Berlant's *Cruel Optimism* does analyze some literary works alongside artistic works in other media, and the same can be said for Cvetkovich's *An Archive of*

---

23. Jane Gallop, hardly a stodgy traditionalist, complains: "When I started teaching, students would come into my classes knowing how to close read, but for more than a decade, many and, perhaps, even most students come into my classes not knowing how to close read at all. I'm talking about English majors and grad students in English. They show up having learned lots of valuable things, well stocked with knowledge of cultural and social history. But more often than not, … it falls to me to teach them the habit of literary reading.… These days I often find myself worrying about the fate of close reading. And sometimes about the fate of literary studies" ("Close Reading in 2009," *ADEBull* 149 [2010]: 15). See further Gallop, "The Historicization of Literary Studies and the Fate of Close Reading," *Profession* (2007): 181–86.

24. I wrote an article some years ago entitled "A Modest Manifesto for New Testament Literary Criticism: How to Interface with a Literary Studies Field That Is Postliterary, Post-theoretical, and Post-methodological," *BibInt* 15 (2007): 1–25. I was right about "Post-literary" and "Post-methodological," but wrong, it now seems, about "Post-theoretical."

25. Teresa Brennan, *The Transmission of Affect* (Ithaca, NY: Cornell University Press, 2004); Sianne Ngai, *Ugly Feelings* (Cambridge: Harvard University Press, 2005); Denise Riley, *Impersonal Passion: Language as Affect* (Durham, NC: Duke University Press, 2005); Nigel Thrift, *Non-representational Theory: Space, Politics, Affect*, ILS (New York: Routledge, 2008). Publication details for the other books listed have been provided in earlier footnotes.

Feelings, while Sedgwick's *Touching Feeling* devotes two chapters to Henry James and the Victorian novel.

Yet none of these literary analyses sent me scurrying excitedly to my Bible to reread a text or passage and have it mean more and other than before. This is a highly subjective judgment, I realize. Knust and Waller, for example, upon reading Sedgwick's *Touching Feeling* and Cvetkovich's *An Archive of Feelings*, respectively, saw sparks fly onto the dusty pages of Genesis and Mark and instantly set them alight.[26] That happened for me only when I read Ahmed's *The Cultural Politics of Emotion*: the book of Revelation began to smolder as I read Ahmed's dark chapters on pain, hate, fear, disgust, and shame and saw how Revelation was inflamed by all these feelings.[27] Yet even Ahmed is not reading literature, but rather "web sites, government reports, political speech, and newspaper articles,"[28] which is to say that *The Cultural Politics of Emotion* too is a work of cultural studies.

Jesus in the Shower

All of this brings me to Eugenie Brinkema's *The Forms of the Affects*, a book that sets out to model affect theory as close reading and to do so in critical dialogue with the Deleuzian trajectory of affect. The book's manifesto-like preface takes aim at Deleuze-driven versions of affect theory that privilege ineffable affect—affect that "cannot be written," affect that is only ever "visceral, immediate, sensed, embodied, excessive," affect that "as the capacity for movement or disturbance" can never settle or congeal as any specifiable textual operations or describable formal properties.[29] Such notions of affect, Brinkema complains, are incapable of accounting for "textual particularities."[30] Moreover, if affect is conceived as raw force, or unpro-

---

26. Jennifer Knust, "Who's Afraid of Canaan's Curse? Genesis 9:18–29 and the Challenge of Reparative Reading," *BibInt* 22 (2014): 388–413; Alexis G. Waller, "Violent Spectacles and Public Feelings: Trauma and Affect in the Gospel of Mark and *The Thunder: Perfect Mind*," *BibInt* 22 (2014): 450–72.

27. Stephen D. Moore, "Retching on Rome: Vomitous Loathing and Visceral Disgust in Affect Theory and the Apocalypse of John," *BibInt* 22 (2014): 503–28. Soon after, I had a similar epiphany when I read Gilles Deleuze, *Francis Bacon: The Logic of Sensation* (trans. Daniel W. Smith, CI [Minneapolis: University of Minnesota Press, 2003]) in tandem with the Gospel of Mark, as chapter 3 of the present book testifies.

28. To cite Ahmed's own list (*Cultural Politics of Emotion*, 14).

29. Brinkema, *Forms of the Affects*, xii–xiii.

30. Ibid., xiv.

cessed intensities, or the mere capacity for mutability or movement, then "why turn to affect at all?" she asks, since, "in the end, ethics, politics, aesthetics—indeed, lives—must be enacted in the definite particular."[31]

In response to this impasse, Brinkema calls for a coupling of affect theory and close reading. "There is a perversity to this," she admits; "if affect theory is what is utterly fashionable," the prescribed "corrective" of close reading is what is "utterly unfashionable."[32] Over against the formulaic, the predictable, the mechanical confirmation of prior theoretical models, close reading at its most effective, for Brinkema, offers "the vitality of all that is not known in advance" of the "hard tussle" with texts, along with "slow, deep attention" not just to the presence of formal features in texts but to "absences, elisions, ruptures, gaps, and points of contradiction" and to all the surprising, often unsettling complexity that is not simply "uncovered by interpretation but ... brought into being as its activity."[33]

Did I mention that Brinkema is a film theorist? Her "texts," then, are cinematic texts, and so the models of analysis she supplies are not applicable to biblical texts without a labor of translation. Her primary text is the shower scene in Hitchcock's *Psycho* (1960):

> The black-hole vacuum of the first scream; the striating diagonals of the shower spray; the cool white grid of the cold white tile against which Marion's hand, stretched out and spread, like a claw, grasps, scratches, in bent digitate branches.... And after that, so much water. It rushes, famously mixing with the darkened blood, filling the empty drain.... The liquid rush moves in a fast counterclockwise, delimiting the contours of the hungry aperture.[34]

The shuddering intensity of the *Psycho* shower scene is as good an indication as any of why affect theory, whether named as such or *avant la lettre*, has been at home in film theory in recent decades. The visual, aural, and emotional bombardment that is cinematic experience might have catalyzed the invention of affect theory even if Tomkins or Deleuze had never set pen to paper.[35]

---

31. Ibid., xv.
32. Ibid.
33. Ibid., xiv, 37–39.
34. Ibid., 1.
35. Not that film was unimportant to Deleuze; he devoted two singular books to it: *Cinema 1: The Movement-Image*, trans. Hugh Tomlinson and Barbara Habber-

But the *Psycho* shower scene also prompts medium-specific questions about affect and biblical texts, or affect and literature in general. Film is a bisensory medium, limited to sight and sound. So too is literature, which may be read silently or aloud. But whereas cinematic worlds are objects of *direct* visual and aural representation, literary worlds, including biblical worlds, are objects of *indirect* visual and aural representation.[36] Moreover, whereas a cinematic text like the *Psycho* shower scene is designed for maximum visceral impact, a biblical text seldom is—even such a text as the Johannine flogging or crucifixion scene, potentially no less horrific, no less shocking. We do not read of "the black-hole vacuum of the first scream" as the whistling scourge or the hammered nail strikes home, or of "the striating diagonals of the shower" of blood, or of the warm rough wood against which Jesus's hand, "stretched out and spread, like a claw, grasps, scratches, in bent digitate branches." The Johannine Jesus does not scream, and so neither do we on reading the bloodless account of his bloody demise.

Yet the Johannine Jesus does weep, even if not when the lash is descending or the nails are being driven home. It is actually Brinkema who reminds us of his tears, and so it is no accident that we stepped out of the *Psycho* shower only to find ourselves, naked and bewildered, in the Johannine torture chamber. Brinkema's analytic lens has come to rest on the final image of the shower scene: Marion's frozen face plastered to the bathroom floor and under her now dead but open eye an ambiguous water drop that may or may not be a "small, fat tear." This "small spherule" demands to be read, indeed close read, insists Brinkema, and read it she does, first situating it "in the long history of the philosophy of emotion" that stretches back at least to Aristotle's *Poetics*, and in which "the tear has been the supreme metonym for the expressivity of interior states." "It is fitting," she adds, "that the shortest verse in … the New Testament is … 'Jesus wept' (John 11:35), *and no more needed to be said.*"[37]

---

jam (London: Athlone, 1984); *Cinema 2: The Time-Image*, trans. Hugh Tomlinson and Robert Galeta (Minneapolis: University of Minnesota Press, 1989).

36. I am not purporting to offer a philosophically watertight distinction here. I am merely remarking that when we experience a film, our affective capacities are engaged by more than symbolic marks on a page or a voice decoding those marks.

37. Brinkema, *Forms of the Affects*, 2, emphasis original.

2. Why the Risen Body Weeps

As If the Ship Were a Folding of the Sea

Brinkema herself says no more about the Johannine Jesus weeping, but she provides tools that enable, indeed impel, us to reframe that affective display not as the expression of an internal state, self-sufficient in its signification and not requiring the supplement of speech, but rather as an external link in a causal chain that holds the text together, but so tightly as to rupture its delicate logic. Although Brinkema is scathingly dismissive of the way in which Deleuzian affect is deployed in contemporary affect theory—"every time the same model of vague shuddering intensity"[38]—Deleuze is nonetheless a crucial resource for the neoformalist model of affective criticism she is attempting to develop.

Brinkema is drawn to Deleuze's concept of *the fold*, a prominent facet of Deleuze's relentless critique of the notion of interiority in all its forms, including human subjectivity conceived as an internal self separate and distinct from an external body and an external world. Deleuze subsumes every concept of interiority into a depthless and unbounded exteriority. The inside, for Deleuze, can only ever be the inside of an outside, "an operation of the outside, ... merely the *fold* of an outside, as if the ship were a folding of the sea."[39]

How might the concept of the fold relate to the concept of character, whether cinematic or literary? For Brinkema, following Deleuze, the depthless counterepistemology of the fold forces a movement from emotion to affect in the analysis of character. The etymological trajectory of *emotion*—from Latin *emovere*, "move" or "move out"[40]—evokes expressive transmission from the interiority of a sender to the interiority of a receiver. The etymological trajectory of *affect*, however—at least for Deleuze—does not evoke transmission from depth to depth, internal subject to internal subject, but from surface to surface, body to body, action to action. *Affectus* for Deleuze, as glossed by Massumi, is "a prepersonal intensity corresponding to the passage from one experiential state of the body to

---

38. Ibid., xv.
39. Gilles Deleuze, *Foucault*, trans. Seán Hand, CI (Minneapolis: University of Minnesota Press, 1988), 97, quoted in Brinkema, *Forms of the Affects*, 23, emphasis added. Deleuze develops his concept of the fold in dialogue with Foucault, but even more so in dialogue with Leibniz. See Deleuze, *The Fold: Leibnitz and the Baroque*, trans. Tom Conley (Minneapolis: University of Minnesota Press, 1993).
40. As Ahmed also notes (*Cultural Politics of Emotion*, 11).

another,"⁴¹ which, as we saw earlier, is precisely the concept of affect that, in the hands of contemporary affect theorists, tends to dissolve into the unrepresentable, the ineffable, the apophatic. But Brinkema is having none of it. She is intent on locating Deleuzian affect in textual form, thereby rendering it readable, even close readable. She writes: "This book regards any individual affect as a self-folding exteriority that manifests in, as, and with textual form."⁴²

Deep Emotion, Flattened Affect

All of this also resonates with me. In recent years I have become fascinated with postclassical narratology, so called, and particularly with certain poststructuralist inflections of it that interrogate the traditional and still-prevalent concept of literary character as an unproblematized channeling of the Cartesian concept of interiorized human subjectivity.⁴³ Oceans of

---

41. Brian Massumi, translator's introduction to Deleuze and Guattari, *A Thousand Plateaus*, xvi. Deleuze in turn is glossing Spinoza, from whom he takes (and retools) the terms *affectus* and *affectio* (see especially the chapter titled "What Can a Body Do?," in Deleuze, *Expressionism in Philosophy: Spinoza*, trans. Martin Joughin [New York: Zone, 1990], 217–34). Deleuze's passage through *affectus* and *affectio* yields a concept of affect that Gregory Seigworth parses in part as follows: "Pure immanence at its most concrete abstraction from all becomings and states of things. The autonomy of affect as outside any distinction of interiority or exteriority" ("From Affection to Soul," in *Gilles Deleuze: Key Concepts*, ed. Charles J. Stivale [New York: Routledge, 2005], 167). Affect, for Deleuze, thus conceived, is in turn intimately bound up with what he terms *the plane of imminence*. Seigworth muses: "Locating the plane of immanence is not unlike discovering the intricate weave and meshings of a whole fabric of cloth, constantly moving, folding and curling back upon itself even as it stretches beyond and below the horizon of the social field (without ever separating from it or departing it). Trace out the story of affect and its encounters, and you will arrive at this plane of immanence: always there, always to be made, never still" ("From Affection to Soul," 168–69). The (overambitious) aim of the present chapter is to read the Johannine text as such an affective weave, such an intricate meshing, such a constantly folding fabric encompassing and exceeding the social—the plane of immanence in microcosm.

42. Brinkema, *Forms of the Affects*, 25. Brinkema also wants to detach Deleuzian affect from its tight attachment to the body (24–25), but I am not yet ready to follow her there. The body has established too tentative a toehold in biblical studies, all told, to be beaten back quite so quickly.

43. This narratological trajectory began in earnest with Patrick O'Neill, *Fictions of Discourse: Reading Narrative Theory*, T/C (Toronto: University of Toronto Press, 1994); Andrew Gibson, *Towards a Postmodern Theory of Narrative*, PT (Edinburgh:

ink have been spilled on the inner lives of paper people. Many of these paper personages have been biblical.⁴⁴ Turning to Stephen Voorwinde's *Jesus' Emotions in the Fourth Gospel*, for instance, we encounter repeated ascription of inner lives to biblical characters.⁴⁵ The adjective *deep* punctuates declarations about characters' emotional states in Voorwinde's study with a symptomatic repetitiveness. God experiences "deep sorrow," while Jesus experiences "deep distress" and "deep emotional disturbance."⁴⁶

University of Edinburgh Press, 1996); and Mark Currie, *Postmodern Narrative Theory*, 2nd ed., Transitions (New York: Palgrave, 2010). Postclassical narratology has many variants beyond the poststructuralist, however. For a sense of its breadth, see Jan Alber and Monika Fludernik, eds., *Postclassical Narratology: Approaches and Analyses*, TIN (Columbus: Ohio State University Press, 2010). For an attempt to assess its potential for biblical narrative analysis, see my "Biblical Narrative Analysis from the New Criticism to the New Narratology," in *The Oxford Handbook of Biblical Narrative*, ed. Danna Nolan Fewell (Oxford: Oxford University Press, 2016), 27–50.

44. For an incisive critique of biblical narrative criticism, most especially its prevailing concept of character, from the vantage point of postclassical narratology, see Scott S. Elliott, *Reconfiguring Mark's Jesus: Narrative Criticism after Poststructuralism*, BMW 41 (Sheffield: Sheffield Phoenix, 2011).

45. Stephen Voorwinde, *Jesus' Emotions in the Fourth Gospel: Human or Divine?*, JSNTSup 284 (New York: T&T Clark International, 2005). The Fourth Gospel also receives a chapter in Voorwinde, *Jesus' Emotions in the Gospels* (New York: T&T Clark International, 2011), 151–214. Historical-critical analysis of biblical emotions of the kind undertaken by Voorwinde has become increasingly difficult, as emerges, for example, from the recent thematic issue, Françoise Mirguet and Dominika Kurek-Comycz, eds., *Emotions in Ancient Jewish Literature*, BibInt 24.4-5 (2016) (which includes New Testament literature). Petra von Gemünden reflects the views of all the contributors when she states: "'Emotion' is a ... term that has no equivalent in Biblical Hebrew or Greek" ("Emotions and Literary Genres in the *Testaments of the Twelve Patriarchs* and the New Testament: A Contribution to Form History and Historical Psychology," *BibInt* 24 [2016]: 516). Mirguet is especially clear on why locating "'emotions' in Biblical Hebrew, at least in the sense that the concept has in English and other modern languages, is problematic," and on several levels. Hebrew words ordinarily translated by emotional terms, for instance, "exceed our emotional realm, as they also include actions, ritual gestures, and physical sensations.... Biblical Hebrew does not organize human experience by delimiting a strictly emotional dimension comparable to ours" ("What Is an 'Emotion' in the Hebrew Bible? An Experience That Exceeds Most Contemporary Concepts," *BibInt* 24 [2016]: 463). Reflecting on these conundrums, Mirguet suggests that "studies inspired by affect theories, with their attention to bodily sensations and affects prior to conceptualization, constitute a promising avenue of research" (465).

46. Voorwinde, *Jesus' Emotions in the Fourth Gospel*, 39; 51, n. 64; 177.

"Deep human emotions ... repeatedly come over [Jesus] on his way to the cross."[47] Deep pools of emotion collect in the Lazarus narrative in particular, as Voorwinde reads it.[48] There "Jesus is portrayed as a man of deep feeling."[49] Jesus holds "deep affection" for Lazarus and experiences "deep emotion" at Lazarus's death.[50] Jesus's affection for Mary and Martha is also "deep and close."[51] Martha in particular "arouse[s] very deep feelings in Jesus," while Mary, for her part, has a "deep devotion" to Jesus.[52] How does Voorwinde understand what, ostensibly at least, is the most emotionally fraught detail in the Fourth Gospel, *edakrysen ho Iēsous*, "Jesus burst into tears" (11:35)?[53] For Voorwinde, Jesus's tears well up from an assumed interiority, are expressed (in both senses of the term) as outward signs of a deep hidden pool of emotion. Jesus's tears are "the outward expressions of his sorrow," Voorwinde asserts. Jesus's grief "openly express[es] itself in the shedding of tears."[54]

Deleuze and Brinkema impel a different construal of the Johannine Jesus's emotions. They prompt us to see these apparent pockets of interiority as folds in the surface of the text, pockets of an exteriority that extends uninterruptedly to the horizon of the text. The ostensible inside becomes the fold of an outside, "as if the ship were a folding of the sea"[55]—the ship in question being a certain boat laboring strenuously across the Sea of Galilee but to which Jesus comes "walking on the sea" (John 6:19), which, after all, as a textual sea is surface without depth. Jesus himself folds and refolds

---

47. Ibid., 221, quoting Herman N. Ridderbos, *The Gospel According to John: A Theological Commentary*, trans. John Vriend (Grand Rapids: Eerdmans, 1997), 468.

48. Voorwinde is not alone in this regard. Many interpreters would concur with Dennis Sylva's pronouncement on the Lazarus episode: "The otherwise virtually implacable Johannine Jesus has his *deepest* emotions involved in the plight of Lazarus and his sisters (11.33, 35, 38)." Dennis Sylva, *Thomas—Love as Strong as Death: Faith and Commitment in the Fourth Gospel*, LNTS (New York: Bloomsbury T&T Clark, 2013), 132, emphasis added.

49. Voorwinde, *Jesus' Emotions in the Fourth Gospel*, 139.

50. Ibid., 152, 114.

51. Ibid., 155.

52. Ibid., 148, 169.

53. As Voorwinde notes, some lexicons translate *dakryō* in the aorist as an inceptive, hence "burst into tears" (BAGD, s.v. "δακρύω"). See Voorwinde, *Jesus' Emotions in the Fourth Gospel*, 182.

54. Voorwinde, *Jesus' Emotions in the Fourth Gospel*, 181.

55. Deleuze, *Foucault*, 97.

continuously in John, but not always as a human body. He—or, better, it—also refolds as a nonhuman animal ("Behold the lamb of God!" [1:36; cf. 1:29; 3:14]), as an inanimate object ("I am the door/gate [*hē thyra*]" [10:9; cf. 10:7]), as a plant ("I am the true vine" [15:1; cf. 15:5]), and so on. The Johannine Jesus is not merely or not quite a human being, then, and not only because he is also a divine being.[56] He or it is a nonhuman character as well as a paper person.

Jesus's tears, then, far from welling up expressively from a deep, hidden, internal pool of emotion—bursting up from imagined depths to splash the surface of the page—are better seen as yet further folds in the Johannine text, tiny but highly consequential pockets of insideness within its paper-thin, infinitely extensible outside. Each folding and refolding, each tear, sends forceful ripples across the surface of the text, impelling further folds and engendering further agents, events, and objects. Consider the consequential causal ripple that comes into view when we approach Jesus's tears not as an expressive outward sign of an abruptly unleashed (e)motion surging up from an imagined human interior but as an impersonal affective force impelling horizontal movement across the plane of the text. Jesus wept. Because Jesus wept, Lazarus lived. Because Lazarus lived, Jesus died (see 11:45–53).[57] Because Jesus died, all who believe in him will live. Why then does Jesus weep?[58]

Refusing Rot

To begin to ponder this question is to reckon with forces in the Fourth Gospel that only come to oblique expression in it. The Johannine narrative is replete with understated—indeed, unstated—affect, one affect in particular, as we are about to see. That affect is not love, I would argue, despite

---

56. In chapter 6, I explore the animality, vegetality, and inanimacy of the Johannine Jesus.

57. Structurally, Jesus's symbolic raising of Lazarus plays the same catalytic role in the Fourth Gospel that Jesus's symbolic action in the Jerusalem temple plays in the Synoptic Gospels: it consolidates the indigenous Judean elite's opposition to him (John 11:45–53) and so precipitates his arrest, trial, and execution.

58. Jesus is represented as intending to raise Lazarus from the dead even before Lazarus has managed to die (John 11:3–4; cf. 11:11–15), which suggests that factors other than an abrupt welling of grief felt by a suddenly human Jesus have conspired to produce his textual tears.

the frequency of love language in the narrative.[59] The benign face of the Johannine God, in particular ("God so loved the world" [3:16]), masks the real locus of affect in the narrative. "No one has ever seen [that] God" (1:18; cf. 5:37; 6:46; Exod 33:20), but they have seemed to see his compassionate smile, a Cheshire cat smile that is visible even though its owner is invisible.[60] Jesus's face, although equally undescribed in the narrative, eventually cracks. Something shatters its composure. The movement that creases Jesus's preternaturally serene countenance in John 11:38—"Jesus, … profoundly moved [*embrimōmenos en heautō*], came to the tomb" (see also 11:33; 12:27)[61]—a movement or disturbance that is a fold within the fold that is his face, together with his abrupt weeping in 11:35, fleetingly makes visible the electrifying affect that has been rippling across the surface of the narrative all along and generating its innumerable folds. That affect is *disgust*.

What makes Jesus's eyes water in 11:35 is a certain smell, indeed a certain unmistakable stench, as yet only wafted on the breeze, for he is still some distance from Lazarus's tomb. "Lord, by now he stinks [*ēdē ozei*] because he has been dead four days," Martha will demur when Jesus marches up to the tomb and demands that it be opened (11:39). The text, qua text, can represent this stench but not reproduce it. "Odor, and not blindness, is vision's true other," as Brinkema notes, and never more than in the case of literary odor. In literature as in cinema, smell is the absolutely excluded, a sensory prohibition intrinsic to the medium.[62] In the Fourth Gospel, the smell that is excluded, the stench that cannot be smelled except by the figures enfolded in the text, is that of rotting flesh. As literary smell it cannot properly be spoken. It is hermetically sealed up within the surface pockets of the text. It represents the ultimate unrepresentability of the object of disgust around which the Fourth Gospel is organized. Better put, putrescence is the adhesive that holds this moldering ancient text together.

---

59. On which, see Voorwinde, *Jesus' Emotions in the Fourth Gospel*, especially 150–61, 195–210, 222–23, and 232–52. Voorwinde takes love to be the dominant emotion in the narrative. See also Matthew A. Elliott, *Faithful Feelings: Rethinking Emotion in the New Testament* (Grand Rapids: Kregel, 2006), 149–53.

60. "Certain assemblages of power…require the production of a face, others do not," as Deleuze and Guattari argue (*A Thousand Plateaus*, 175).

61. Translations of John's Gospel in this chapter are my own. Otherwise I employ NRSV.

62. Brinkema, *Forms of the Affects*, 121, 144.

The Fourth Gospel, then, is structured by disgust, by its convulsive, heaving movements of revulsion, expulsion, and exclusion. For of all the objects that elicit disgust—bodily secretions and excretions, things that wriggle, squirm, and swarm—putrefaction and decay take pride of place.[63] Brinkema defines disgust as "the worse than the worst."[64] That is why putrefaction is the ultimate object of disgust. Death, while tragic, and even the worst, is not in itself disgusting. What is worse than the worst, and as such the quintessence of disgust, is that the corpse refuses to be still. "In death ... the body is furiously *too much*.... It churns, it moves, it froths" in a ghastly fecundity.[65] The ultimate, utterly obscene desecration of the flesh, even after death, is as certain as death itself.[66] Which is what causes the Johannine Jesus finally to weep—or, more precisely, causes the Johannine textual logic, a machinic logic operating independently of the intentions of any human textual producer,[67] to fold its protagonist so that he assumes the form of a weeping figure.

Brinkema quotes disgust theorist Winfried Menninghaus: "Every book about disgust is not least a book about the rotting corpse."[68] Conversely, every book about the rotting corpse is not least a book about dis-

---

63. So ibid., 164, following Aurel Kolnai, *On Disgust*, ed. Barry Smith and Carolyn Korsmeyer (Chicago: Open Court, 2004), 53–62.

64. Brinkema, *Forms of the Affects*, 130, here extrapolating from Jacques Derrida, "Economimesis," trans. Richard Klein, *Diacritics* 11.2 (1981): 23. Derrida's article gradually builds up, via Kant on "good taste," to an extended meditation on distaste and vomit, and hence disgust. Vomit also erupts in Brinkema's text, not surprisingly, since that text is, as much as anything, a book on disgust (*Forms of the Affects*, 141–45).

65. Brinkema, *Forms of the Affects*, 171, emphasis original. I am reminded once again of the harrowing journal entry that French historian Jules Michelet wrote in 1839 after witnessing the opening of his wife Pauline's grave forty-two days after her burial: "Exhumation: 8:00 a.m. Stormy morning, after the rain. Severe ordeal. Alas! I scarcely saw anything but worms. It is said: 'returned to the earth.' It is a figure of speech. The corpse's inanimate substance reanimates a living substance. That aspect is hideous to the eye, harsh as Christian humiliation." Jules Michelet, *Mother Death: The Journals of Jules Michelet, 1815–1850*, ed. and trans. Edward K. Kaplan (Amherst: University of Massachusetts Press, 1984), 89–90.

66. See Brinkema, *Forms of the Affects*, 177.

67. It is a machinic logic because a book "is a little machine" (Deleuze and Guattari, *A Thousand Plateaus*, 4). Further on this Deleuzoguattarian motif, see 43–45 below.

68. Brinkema, *Forms of the Affects*, 130, quoting Winfried Menninghaus, *Disgust: Theory and History of a Strong Sensation*, trans. Howard Eiland and Joel Golb (Albany: SUNY Press, 2003), 1.

gust. As we are beginning to see (and perhaps even to smell), the Fourth Gospel is a book about the rotting corpse—or, rather, a book about the *refusal* of the rotting corpse. Brinkema writes: "The form of disgust is the form of the excluded as such."[69] In the Fourth Gospel, the excluded as such is *flesh* as such. The Fourth Gospel insistently aligns flesh with death. Within the text's odorless folds, flesh is always already rotting, even in life. "It is the spirit that gives life; the flesh is worthless, worse than useless [*hē sarx ouk ōphelei ouden*]," declaims the Johannine Jesus (6:63), he who took on decaying flesh, encased himself in its fetid folds, to live among us. Life cannot come of death, he insists. "What is born of the flesh is flesh, and what is born of the Spirit is spirit" (3:6). To be reborn so as never to die, never to decay, is to be born "not of blood or of the will of the flesh" (1:13). The Johannine Jesus is that which *preexists* rotting flesh ("In the beginning was the Word" [1:1]), which *becomes* rotting flesh ("And the Word became flesh" [1:14]), and which *overcomes* rotting flesh ("'Lazarus, come out!' The dead man came out, his hands and feet wrapped with strips of cloth, and his face wrapped in a cloth" [11:44; cf. 5:25, 28–29]). With rotting flesh, however vehemently refused, the Johannine Jesus's entire existence is intimately interfused

Always Already Risen, Always Already Rotten

The Johannine Jesus does not refuse his own death, but he does refuse his own decay. In raising Lazarus, Jesus is refusing not only Lazarus's putrefaction but also his own. For although the worst does comes to pass for the Johannine Jesus—"Then Pilate took Jesus and had him scourged.... Then he handed him over to them to be crucified" (19:1, 16)—the worse than the worst does not come to pass for him. Jesus dies but apparently does not decay. Peter, the Beloved Disciple, and Mary Magdalene all boldly stick their heads into the tomb in which the shredded, perforated, blood-drained corpse of Jesus has been laid (20:3–12). There is no stench of putrefying flesh from which to recoil, but not because the corpse is still relatively fresh and has been cocooned in aromatic spices (19:39–40). There is, indeed, no flesh of any kind in the tomb.

The tomb of the Johannine Jesus is a pocket of insideness in the outsideness of the text, a concealing fold in its surface, into which flesh van-

---

69. Brinkema, *Forms of the Affects*, 131.

ishes and reemerges as something else. That something else is not simply spirit. The not-flesh—yet also not-spirit—that is the altogether anomalous body of the risen Johannine Jesus passes through physical barriers ("and the doors being shut…, Jesus came and stood among them" [20:19; see also 20:26]) but also bears physical wounds: "Put your finger here.… Put out your hand and stick it in my side" (20:27; cf. 19:34). The marks of a torturous death are now eternally inscribed on a body that, we are to assume, can no longer die and hence no longer decay. These unerased and unerasable marks, however, preclude any simple separation of the risen body and the rotting body in the Fourth Gospel—and not just on the other side of the peculiar pocket or portal that is Jesus's tomb. Even when Jesus is engaged in his long, meandering journey to that tomb, the flesh he has become ("And the Word became flesh …") is rotting flesh and rot-resistant flesh at one and the same time; for the pre-Easter Johannine Jesus is not yet risen, yet always already risen.

Flesh is the locus of intense and immense paradox in the Fourth Gospel.[70] Countervailing affective forces swirl around flesh in this text, producing convoluted folds in its narrative logic. Flesh is what must be renounced in the Fourth Gospel, as we have seen. It must be disowned and expelled as the ultimate object of disgust. It must be pushed outside. But the Fourth Gospel also spectacularly enacts *the paradox of disgust*, that affective ambivalence whereby intense aversion to an object coexists with intense attraction to it.[71] Turn disgust over, with a tentatively extended digit, and

---

70. As has long been recognized. Among critical commentators on John, none wrestled more diligently with this paradox than Rudolf Bultmann. He wrote: "This is the paradox which runs through the whole [Fourth G]ospel: the δόξα [glory] is not to be seen *alongside* the σάρξ [flesh], nor *through* the σάρξ as through a window; it is to be seen in the σάρξ and nowhere else" (*The Gospel of John: A Commentary*, trans. G. R. Beasley-Murray, R. W. N. Hoare, and J. K. Riches [Eugene, OR: Wipf & Stock, 2014], 63, emphasis original). To this paradox Bultmann returns again and again in his commentary. The most incisive recent engagement with the issue of flesh in the Fourth Gospel comes from outside the field of New Testament studies: theologian Mayra Rivera's *Poetics of the Flesh* (Durham, NC: Duke University Press, 2015), 19–28. She writes: "I remain intrigued by the peculiar vitality of flesh in this ancient text—even when the subtle movements of this flesh are often swept away by gusts of metaphysical pronouncements. I note the places where those gusts directly impact the verses I read. But I do not follow their path" (19).

71. See Kolnai, *On Disgust*, 42–43; Brinkema, *Forms of the Affects*, 164–65. Sara Ahmed also makes much of this paradox; see *Cultural Politics of Emotion*, 84–100.

what is revealed, wriggling away from the light, is, more often than not, an obscene craving: an irrational desire for proximity and intimacy with the abhorrent thing.[72] In the Fourth Gospel, flesh is not only what must be strenuously renounced, flesh is also what must be intimately embraced. It must be pushed outside but it must also be pulled inside. It must be chewed and gulped down; it must be masticated, ingested, and digested (see 6:50–58). No longer is it a case of smelling only, but of smelling and swallowing. Brinkema's reflections on the relations of olfaction and ingestion are apt: "A dangerous intimacy between object and body figures even more in the case of taste than in that of smell, for it requires the ingestion or consumption of its object of sense, a blurring of the object with the flesh, even a disintegrating equivalence in the case of taken-in food that … literally becomes us—indeed, tells others what we *are*." This is the dangerous intimacy, the hyperqueer carnal knowledge, that the Johannine Jesus urges on his hearers and readers. Those who eat his flesh and drink his blood will "abide" (*menō*) in him and he in them (6:56). He will envelop them, enfold them, and refold them. They will ingest and digest him, but he will absorb and assimilate them.

"Does this offend you?" Jesus asks his open-mouthed disciples (6:61), having spread himself out on the table before them.[73] Well he might ask. What renders the paradox of disgust spectacular in the Fourth Gospel is that it is enacted not in a corner, not in a darkened room ("There are many rooms in my Father's house" [14:2]), but out in the open. There is no intimate huddle at a private meal, no patently ritualistic gesture to leech the ghastly act of its horror ("He took a loaf of bread, and after blessing it he broke it, gave it to them, and said, 'Take, this is my body'" [Mark 14:22; cf. Matt 26:26; Luke 22:19; 1 Cor 11:23–24]), but only a raw and shock-

---

72. The entry from Michelet's 1839 journal on the occasion of his wife's exhumation, quoted earlier, provides a particularly arresting instance of the paradox of disgust. As we saw, the entry begins: "I scarcely saw anything but worms. It is said: 'returned to the earth.' It is a figure of speech. The corpse's inanimate substance reanimates a living substance. That aspect is hideous to the eye." But the entry continues: "However, when I observed the gaping grave from above, I powerfully felt, as I have felt on the sea or from the top of a tower, the attraction of death!… Farewell. I must abstain even from writing about this sad and too alluring subject" (*Mother Death*, 89–90).

73. "Think me, Jesus says to his friends while burdening their arms, in advance, with a bloody corpse. Prepare the shrouds, the bandages, the oily substance." Jacques Derrida, *Glas*, trans. John P. Leavey Jr. and Richard Rand (Lincoln: University of Nebraska Press, 1986), 66a.

ing public announcement ("The one who gnaws on my flesh [*ho trōgōn mou tēn sarka*] and drinks my blood has eternal life…; for my flesh is true food and my blood is true drink" [John 6:54–55; cf. 6:51–58]) to a suitably shocked and scandalized audience ("How can this man give us his flesh to eat?" [6:52]).[74] The high Johannine Christology is also a high gastronomy. More precisely, it is *haut goût*, as we are about to see, the *haute cuisine* practice, deliciously risky, of preparing and consuming decomposing food.[75]

"Your ancestors ate the manna in the wilderness, and they died," the Johannine Jesus reminds "the Jews," contrasting "the living bread" that will enable the eater to live forever (6:49–51; cf. 6:31, 58). The ancestors ate the manna and they died and decayed, but the manna itself was also subject to decay: "It bred worms and became foul" (Exod 16:20), like Lazarus in his tomb. Ostensibly, "the living bread that [comes] down from heaven" in the Fourth Gospel, the bread that is actually flesh ("the bread that I will give

---

74. For an analysis of John 6:51–58 that absolutizes its differences from the synoptic and Pauline eucharistic narratives, see Meredith J. C. Warren, *My Flesh Is Meat Indeed: A Nonsacramental Reading of John 6:51–58* (Minneapolis: Fortress Press, 2015). Further on 6:54–55, including the question of how much dental violence is encoded in the verb *trōgō*, see 117–18 below. For a rather different angle than mine on the issue of Johannine cannibalism, see J. Albert Harrill, "Cannibalistic Language in the Fourth Gospel and Greco-Roman Polemics of Factionalism (John 6:52–66)," *JBL* 127 (2008): 133–58. Harrill's study begins: "This essay names the elephant in the room around which scholarly interpreters of John 6:52–66 have long been tiptoeing with their overly circumspect discussions of the eucharistic imagery in the passage. That elephant is cannibalism, of course, and ignoring it leaves fundamental exegetical questions about this famous *crux interpretum* unanswered and even unasked" (133). For yet another angle on the issue, see Tina Pippin, "Feasting with/on Jesus: John 6 in Conversation with Vampire Studies," in *The Recycled Bible: Autobiography, Culture, and the Space Between*, ed. Fiona C. Black, SemeiaSt 51 (Atlanta: Society of Biblical Literature, 2006), 87–100. Pippin previews her project as follows: "I want to make connections between vampire theory and the rhetoric of the Eucharist in John 6. A poster for the film *Interview with the Vampire* spoke with Johannine overtones: 'Drink from me and live forever.' What can the ancient (and modern) myths of the vampire tell us about the ancient (and modern) myths of Christian sacrificial theology?" (87–88).

75. Brinkema has a section on *haut goût* (*Forms of the Affects*, 164–70), which includes theoretical rumination on such matters as "hung carcasses inching toward decay; wormy crawling meat already in the process of enlivening after death" (170). By now Brinkema is savoring Peter Greenaway's film *The Cook, the Thief, His Wife, and Her Lover*.

for the life of the world is my flesh" [6:51]), is incapable of decay; it cannot breed worms, it cannot rot.

The guarantor of this incorruptibility is the risen body of Jesus. Even on the prolonged path to his own tomb, always dimly visible in the distance, the Johannine Jesus is always already risen, as we noted earlier, is always himself "the resurrection and the life," as he announces outside Lazarus's tomb (11:25). But Jesus's risen body in the Fourth Gospel is an uncertain guarantor of incorruptibility. The marks of death, and hence of corruption, persist indelibly on the risen body, and not as faint scars but as horrific puncture wounds capacious enough to enfold a finger or even an entire hand (20:25, 27). These gruesome wounds silently bespeak the unspeakably atrocious indignities to which all flesh is heir, human flesh no less than animal flesh. Indeed, the traumatic marks on the risen body bloodily smudge, even erase altogether, the human animal/nonhuman animal distinction. The risen body is an animal body,[76] and as an animal body the risen body is always dying, is always decaying. As marks of death, and hence of decomposition, the wounds on the risen body are, in effect, gangrenous, and incurably so. Even risen, then, the flesh of the Johannine Jesus bears the marks of corruption. In consequence, death clings to Jesus throughout the Fourth Gospel; necrosis subtly infects his always already risen body.

In the Fourth Gospel, which is also the Flesh Gospel, flesh remains a thing of horror, even when it is Jesus's flesh, which is why it precipitates the paradox of disgust: "the flesh is worthless" (6:63); "eat my flesh" (6:56). The affective logic of the Fourth Gospel enjoins the eating of Jesus precisely because its narrative logic, culminating in a not entirely successful resurrection,[77] has made him an indirect object of revulsion. The scent of

---

76. It is hardly surprising, therefore, that the wounded risen body appears outright in animal form in Rev 5:6: "I saw a lamb standing as though it had been slaughtered [*hōs esphagmenon*]" (cf. John 1:29, 36). Elsewhere I attempt to focus Revelation's heavenly butchered sheep through the lens of posthuman animality studies; see my "Ruminations on Revelation's Ruminant, Quadrupedal Christ; or, the Even-Toed Ungulate That Therefore I Am," in Koosed, *Bible and Posthumanism*, 301–26.

77. Jesus's risen body is less than glorious in the Fourth/Flesh Gospel, and not only because of its gaping wounds. It no longer looks like Jesus, but not because it is gloriously transfigured. It can be mistaken for the body of a gardener ("[Mary] … saw Jesus standing there, and she did not know that it was Jesus.… Thinking he was the gardener, she said …" [John 20:14–15]) or some other ordinary looking stranger ("Jesus stood on the shore, yet the disciples did not know that it was Jesus" [21:4; cf.

death sits lightly on the Johannine Jesus; it is not the stench of Lazarus. But it is a scent that cannot be scrubbed clean. That, more than anything, is why the Johannine Jesus weeps at the tomb of Lazarus.

Luke 24:15–16]). For an extended philosophical meditation on the paradoxical resurrection bodies of John, Luke, and Paul, see John D. Caputo, "Bodies Still Unrisen, Events Still Unsaid: A Hermeneutic of Bodies without Flesh," in *Apophatic Bodies: Negative Theology, Incarnation, and Relationality*, ed. Chris Boesel and Catherine Keller, TTC (New York: Fordham University Press, 2010), 94–116.

3
The Messiah Who Screamed

We must consider the special case of the scream.... It is ... a particularly intense sound.
— Gilles Deleuze, *Francis Bacon*

And at the ninth hour Jesus screamed aloud, *Elōï Elōï lama sabachthani?*
—Mark 15:24

In the climactic moment of the climactic scene in the earliest extant gospel, the protagonist screams. Actually, Jesus screams twice in Mark's crucifixion scene. First he screams or cries out with a "great sound" (*eboēsen ho Iēsous phōnē megalē*)—let's just say, a deafening sound—"My God, my God, why have you abandoned me?" (15:34).[1] Subsequently, he releases another deafening sound and expires (*ho de Iēsous apheis phōnēn megalēn exepneusen* [15:37]).[2] He emits a death scream, in short. The tor-

---

1. Translations of the Gospel of Mark in this chapter are my own; otherwise I employ NRSV.
2. *Boaō*, employed in Mark 15:34, is the first Greek verb listed for "scream" in the standard English-Greek lexicon, S. C. Woodhouse's *English-Greek Dictionary: A Vocabulary of the Attic Language* (New York: Routledge, 1910; repr., 1998). BAGD's definitions of *boaō* include: "to use one's voice at high volume." I render *phōnē* as "sound" in Mark 15:34, 37 rather than the more usual "voice" so as to be able to translate *phōnē megalē* in both verses with the same English expression. "Sound" is also the first meaning listed for *phōnē* in LSJ. Some scholars have argued that the crucified Jesus only cries out once in Mark; see esp. Joel Marcus, who remarks of 15:37: "This phrase, which virtually repeats 15:34..., probably does not denote a second shout but is a back-reference to the cry of dereliction in 15:34" (*Mark 8–16: A New Translation with Introduction and Commentary*, AB 27A [New Haven: Yale University Press, 2009], 1056). Adela Yarbro Collins would seem to agree (*Mark: A Commentary*, Hermeneia [Minneapolis: Fortress, 2007], 753). Raymond E. Brown also leans toward the single

tured man screams, the veil of the temple splits (15:38), and the implied audience shudders.

Innumerable actual audiences, an incalculable multiplicity of hearers, of readers, have continued to shudder, to tremble, to quake, to quiver before this grisly spectacle from the first century down to the present. The violent sensations word-painted in the scene with economic but dramatic strokes have contagiously communicated themselves to hearers and readers and been transmuted into powerful feelings: love, hate, pity, fear, gratitude, awe, worship. These feelings in turn have engendered actions and experiences ranging from the startlingly spectacular to the comfortingly mundane. Francis of Assisi had a vision in which the wounds of the crucified Christ were mystically imprinted on his hands, feet, and side, while uncountable Christians have symbolically joined their own flesh with that of the crucified Christ through the quasi-automatic gestural performance known as the sign of the cross. Catherine of Siena had a vision in which she fastened her lips to the bleeding wounds of the crucified Christ and greedily lapped up his blood, while uncountable Christians have believed that they eat the flesh and drink the blood of the crucified Christ as the climax of their worship services. The Christ volunteer in the annual passion play at Iztapalapa, Mexico, carries a two-hundred-pound cross for three miles up the side of a mountain, while uncountable Christians have carried miniature replicas of the ancient Roman torture implement around their necks. Filipino Ruben Enaje has voluntarily submitted to being nailed to a cross every year since 1985, while uncountable Christians have believed, with Paul, that they have been crucified with Christ so that they themselves no longer live but Christ lives in them (Gal 2:20).

What might Deleuze, who has posthumously become the patron saint of affect theory, have made of the anguished scream of Mark's Messiah and the mass shudder it has elicited through the millennia? What in Deleuzian

---

cry, but notes that Matthew, one of Mark's earliest interpreters, understood Mark to mean that there was a second cry (*The Death of the Messiah: From Gethsemane to the Grave; A Commentary on the Passion Narratives in the Four Gospels*, 2 vols., ABRL [New York: Doubleday, 1994], 2:1079). Mark 15:37 is rendered in Matt 27:50 as: "And Jesus crying out *again* [*palin*]...released his spirit." I myself side with Matthew in what follows, largely because the overwhelming majority of hearers and readers of Mark down through the ages have heard two cries rather than one in Mark 15:34, 37, and I wish to attune myself to that immeasurable multitude.

terms is the Markan crucifixion? Many things, no doubt, but first and foremost, perhaps, an *assemblage*.

The Machine and the Assemblage

Before the assemblage was the machine. Early on, Deleuze borrowed the concept of the machine from Guattari, in the context of literary analysis. The 1970 edition of Deleuze's 1964 book *Proust and Signs* contains a five-chapter addition, a new part 2, titled "The Literary Machine." Introducing that machine, Deleuze states: "To the *logos* ... whose meaning must be discovered in the whole and to which it belongs, is opposed the antilogos, machine and machinery whose meaning (anything you like) depends solely on its functioning."[3] What the literary machine functions to produce are effects—more precisely, "literary effects" that are analogous to "electric effects" or "electromagnetic effects."[4] Deleuze might equally have said that literature is a machine for producing *affects*. For literature or any other art form thus reconceived, there is "no problem of meaning, ... only a problem of use."[5]

From there it is but a short step to the antihermeneutic manifesto with which Deleuze and Guattari's antibook *A Thousand Plateaus* opens. "We will never ask what a book means, as signified or signifier," they announce,

---

3. Gilles Deleuze, *Proust and Signs: The Complete Text*, trans. Richard Howard, TOB 17 (Minneapolis: University of Minnesota Press, 2000), 146.

4. Ibid., 153. Deleuze and Guattari will later insist that literature "is the language of sensations.... The writer uses words, but by creating a syntax that makes them pass into sensation that makes the standard language stammer, tremble, cry, or even sing." That sensation-saturated syntax also causes the standard language to scream, as it happens: "*Elōï Elōï lama sabachthani?*" (Mark 15:24). "This is the style, the 'tone,' the language of sensations, or the foreign language within language that summons forth a people to come." See Gilles Deleuze and Félix Guattari, *What Is Philosophy?*, trans. Hugh Tomlinson and Graham Burchell (New York: Columbia University Press, 1994), 176.

5. Deleuze, *Proust and Signs*, 146. As we have already seen, Deleuze is unsympathetic to any depth hermeneutic predicated upon a concept of interior meaning or the recovery of lost or hidden signification. For him, such a project makes a fetish of the unseen, the opaque, the esoteric, the phantasm, the secret. See Gilles Deleuze and Claire Parnet, *Dialogues*, trans. Hugh Tomlinson and Barbara Habberjam, EP (New York: Columbia University Press, 1987), 47; Deleuze, *Two Regimes of Madness: Texts and Interviews, 1975–1995*, trans. Ames Hodges and Mike Taormina (New York: Semiotext[e], 2007), 15.

we will not look for anything to understand in it. We will ask what it functions with, in connection with what other things it does or does not transmit intensities, in which other multiplicities its own are inserted and metamorphosed.... A book exists only through the outside and on the outside. A book itself is a little machine.... The only question is which other machine the literary machine can be plugged into, must be plugged into in order to work.[6]

This proclamation is not simply a restatement of the theory of intertextuality. The other machines into which the literary machine can be plugged are textual and nontextual, organic and inorganic, discursive and nondiscursive, human and nonhuman. All of which is to say that "literature is an assemblage."[7]

What is an assemblage? It is an open-ended "multiplicity made up of many heterogeneous terms and which establishes liaisons … between them.... The assemblage's only unity is that of co-functioning: it is a symbiosis."[8] As an assemblage, a book "is made of variously formed matters"[9]—innumerable antecedent books, the writer's brain, processed

---

6. Deleuze and Guattari, *A Thousand Plateaus*, 4. The term *intensities*, for Deleuze and Guattari, is intimately bound up with the term *affects*, so much so as frequently to be functionally indistinguishable from it.

7. Ibid. An assemblage, however, is not simply, or even primarily, literary. Literature is merely one kind of assemblage. For the ubiquitous, multiform, ready-to-hand nature of assemblages, see 4 n. 8 above.

8. Deleuze and Parnet, *Dialogues*, 69. The assemblage (*l'agencement*), first developed by Deleuze and Guattari in *A Thousand Plateaus* (see esp. 3–4, 88–90, 323–37, 503–5), has emerged as a prominent theoretical concept. Among the nine catalysts he proposes for the nonhuman turn in contemporary theory, Richard Grusin lists "the *assemblage theory* of Gilles Deleuze, Manuel DeLanda, Latour, and others" ("Introduction," viii, emphasis original). Manuel DeLanda explicates and expands Deleuze and Guattari's version of the theory (*Assemblage Theory*, SR [Edinburgh: Edinburgh University Press, 2016]). Bruno Latour's assemblage theory is less obviously beholden to Deleuze and Guattari's (*Reassembling the Social: An Introduction to Actor-Network Theory*, CLMS [Oxford: Oxford University Press, 2005]). Assemblage theory is also an enabling resource for Jane Bennett's *Vibrant Matter*, an important expression of object-oriented new materialism. Assemblage theory has recently been taken up in biblical studies by Rhiannon Graybill (*Are We Not Men? Unstable Masculinity in the Hebrew Prophets* [Oxford: Oxford University Press, 2016], esp. 37–39, 121–42).

9. Deleuze and Guattari, *A Thousand Plateaus*, 3. As Deleuze says elsewhere in an interview: "In assemblages you find states of things, bodies, various combinations of bodies, hodgepodges; but you also find utterances, modes of expression, and whole

wood pulp, electronic circuits, the laws of genre, discursive conventions, state censors, tenure and promotion committees, publishing houses and editorial boards, the reader's brain, communities of reception, and so on.[10] To attribute a book to an author-creator replete with interiority and resplendent with intentionality "is to overlook this working of matters, and the exteriority of their relations. It is to fabricate a beneficent God to explain geological movements."[11]

A Machine Is Released into the World

It is time to restate the question and answer with which we began: What in Deleuzian or Deleuzoguattarian terms is the Markan crucifixion? Multiple things, no doubt,
   ["Yes, we must always think in terms of packs and multiplicities."[12]]
but above all an assemblage (itself an irreducible multiplicity). This assemblage, like all assemblages, combines human and nonhuman elements: the denuded, impaled man; the wood-and-metal torture device; the divine being peeking improbably from the bowels of the bloody carcass,
   ["And when the centurion standing opposite him saw how he expired, he said, "Truly this man was a Son of God!" (Mark 15:39)]
its numinous face streaked with gore. But we are getting ahead of ourselves in including the unexpected divine visitor in this gruesome assemblage. What is a cross when it does not display a god dripping blood?

At base, a cross is a machine within a machine, a punitive machine within an imperial machine. The imperial machine is also a territorial machine. The latter machine, as Deleuze and Guattari observe as early as *Anti-Oedipus*, is "the machine of primitive inscription, the 'megamachine'

---

regimes of signs. The relations between the two are pretty complex" (*Two Regimes of Madness*, 177).

10. My attempted elaboration of Deleuze and Guattari's "a book is an assemblage" statement and the accompanying aphorism, "There is no difference between what a book talks about and how it is made" (*A Thousand Plateaus*, 4).

11. Ibid., 3. See further Deleuze and Parnet, *Dialogues*, 51–52.

12. Deleuze and Guattari, *A Thousand Plateaus*, 52. The bracketed citations from Deleuze, or Deleuze and Guattari, that punctuate the remainder of this chapter are the statements that originally set me scribbling in the margins of their texts and assembling the ideas that run through the chapter. The Markan insets that punctuate the Deleuzoguattarian insets in turn are the statements those ideas are designed to thread together.

that covers a social field."[13] Within Mark's narrative world and even within Mark's social world, the megamachine that extends to the horizon in every direction is the Roman Empire. As territorial, indeed megaterratorial, this empire is also an assemblage. "The territory is the first assemblage…; the assemblage is fundamentally territorial."[14] Of all the punitive machines this megaterratorial assemblage employed to stabilize and maintain its hegemonic structure, the cross was the machine par excellence,

["**The needles of the machine write the sentence on the body of the condemned ... at the same time as they inflict their torture upon him.**"[15]]

an apparatus of state terror designed to turn enslaved or seditious victims into things of horror.

The central task of Mark's Gospel, itself a machine of another kind,

["**Why a machine? Because the work ... is essentially productive— productive of certain truths.**"[16]]

is to retool the punitive machine, the wood-flesh-metal assemblage, the ultimate instrument of Roman state terrorism. It remains a hideous torture machine even in Mark, but its purpose is no longer that of stabilizing the imperial megamachine by manifesting its apparently irresistible, utterly crushing power. In Mark, the punitive machine is retooled so as to become "a set of cutting edges that insert themselves into the assemblage" that deploys it,[17] namely, the imperial assemblage. The aim is deterritorialization of the assemblage; for every assemblage, even or especially a megaterritorial imperial assemblage, contains the potential for deterritorialization, for lines of escape, for lines of flight.[18] Such lines are "a sort of mutation or creation drawn not only in the imagination but also in the very fabric of social reality."[19] What they create, in particular, are other machines. "Whenever a territorial assemblage is taken up by a movement that deterritorializes it…, we say that a machine is released."[20]

---

13. Deleuze and Guattari, *Anti-Oedipus*, 141.
14. Deleuze and Guattari, *A Thousand Plateaus*, 323.
15. Gilles Deleuze and Félix Guattari, *Kafka: Toward a Minor Literature*, trans. Dana Polan, THL 30 (Minneapolis: University of Minnesota Press, 1986), 43.
16. Deleuze, *Proust and Signs*, 146.
17. Deleuze and Guattari, *A Thousand Plateaus*, 333.
18. Deleuze and Guattari, *Kafka*, 86.
19. Deleuze and Guattari, *A Thousand Plateaus*, 229.
20. Ibid., 333.

3. The Messiah Who Screamed

On Golgotha a machine is released into the world. It is unwittingly constructed by the imperial agents themselves: "And they bring him to the place called Golgotha, which means 'Place of a Skull.' ... And they crucify him" (Mark 15:22, 24). The machine that is constructed is a miniscule machine for now, but destined to become a colossal machine, a megamachine,

> ["There is the 'megamachine' of the State, a functional pyramid that has the despot at its apex, an immobile motor."[21]]

capable of engulfing entire continents (but that is a later act in our saga, which is also Mark's saga). The cross machine is made of wood and flesh that have been fastened together with nails and glued together with blood. Its capacity to become a megamachine inheres in the fact that it is an affective machine, a generator of affects. Arguably, indeed, it is the most powerful affect generator ever assembled. As such it is the quintessential assemblage, for the efficacy of an assemblage inheres in the affects it generates.[22]

This is most of all true of the assemblage that Deleuze and Guattari name *the war machine*. In our case, the war machine is powered by the cross machine, which functions as its engine. Now, the war machine is not necessarily, or not only, a machine for war. In its distinctive Deleuzoguattarian form, it "has as its object not war but the drawing of a creative line of flight, the composition of a smooth space and of the movement of people in that space."[23] In pursuit of that revolutionary goal, "the machine does indeed encounter war, but as its supplementary or synthetic object, now directed against the State and against the worldwide axiomatic expressed by States."[24] In other words, the war machine becomes an instrument for mass mobilization against empire

> ["We have the rigid segmentarity of the Roman Empire, with its center of resonance and periphery, its State, its *pax romana*, its geometry, its camps, its *limes* (boundary lines)."[25]]

and against empires. But how is this mobilization accomplished? "The regime of the war machine is ... that of *affects*," Deleuze and Guattari

---

21. Deleuze and Guattari, *Anti-Oedipus*, 194.
22. See Deleuze and Guattari, *A Thousand Plateaus*, 399–400.
23. Ibid., 422.
24. Ibid., 422.
25. Ibid., 222.

explain. "Affect is the active discharge of emotion, … whereas feeling is an always displaced, retarded, resisting emotion."[26]

Between affect and feeling thus defined, the entire Markan plot circulates.

What Mark's Messiah Is Wearing under His Robe

The divine war machine—still surreally spindly, improbable, even impossible—trundles into Galilee early in Mark's narrative with the crazed peasant Messiah

> ["They said, 'He's out of his mind!'" (Mark 3:21)]

at its controls. "The time is fulfilled and the Empire of God is at hand," he intones (1:14). This unlikely Messiah is already affixed to the cross assemblage, screwed into it by his hands and feet, although secretly for now. But this excruciating assemblage is what makes him more and other than human, a Son of God. The demons, fellow nonhumans, discern the contours of the cross assemblage under his robe. They spontaneously acknowledge him in an *active discharge of emotion*: "Whenever the unclean spirits saw him, they prostrated themselves before him, crying out 'You are the Son of God!'" (3:11; see also 1:23–24; 5:6–8). The common people are "astounded" (*thambeomai*), "astonished" (*existēmi*), and "amazed" (*thaumazō, ekthaumazō*) at what he does, meanwhile (1:27; 2:12; 5:20, 42; cf. 12:17), but without understanding what he is, a transpersonal show of feeling that amounts to *displaced emotion*, as it relates only obliquely to its object. When the secretive Messiah finally lifts his robe, exposing his flesh-and-wood assemblage to his disciples ("And he began to teach them that the Son of Man must suffer many things …" [8:31]), *retarded and resisting displays of emotion* ensue: shocked rejection (8:32), stultified terror (9:6), fearful incomprehension (9:32), terrified amazement (10:32), and naked lust for glory (10:35–37)—all culminating in craven cowardice (14:50–51; 66–72) once the cross-assemblage into which Jesus is locked has frog-marched him all the way to Jerusalem, the timid disciples in trail,

> ["They were on the road…, and Jesus was going ahead of them, and they were astonished, and those who followed were afraid." (Mark 10:32)]

and into the hands of his torturers and executioners.

---

26. Ibid., 400, emphasis original.

3. The Messiah Who Screamed

Meanwhile, an unnamed woman has enacted another active discharge of emotion by wordlessly discharging the contents of an alabaster jar of nard
["**Affect becomes sensation, sentiment, emotion or even impulse.**"[27]]
over Jesus's head (14:3). Jesus performs his own active discharge of emotion by emitting a chilling death scream, as we have seen and heard (15:37). But the narrative ends with a final retarded and resisting display of emotion: Jesus's female followers fleeing his empty tomb in terror and astonishment and being too afraid to say anything to anyone of what they have seen (16:8).

The divine war machine that lumbered all the way from Galilee to Jerusalem now seems to have ground to a halt, its driver unaccountably missing, and the active affects required to fuel it having run out. Or have they? Perhaps this most decrepit and most unlikely of war machines does not fuel up at the tomb but rather at the cross.

How (Not) to Be Nailed Down

"Learning to undo things, and to undo oneself, is proper to the war machine," as Deleuze and Guattari explain.[28] The counterimperial movement of the divine war machine in Mark turns on the undoing of hegemonic structures through a systematic undoing of the self. Proper to the affective life of this paradoxical war machine is the nonrational emulation of such unwarlike role models as the child (*paidion*) and the servant (*diakonos*) or slave (*doulos*) (9:35–37; 10:13–16, 42–45; cf. 13:34), coupled with the nonrational renunciation of all personal authority and power (9:33–37; 10:17–31, 35–44; cf. 12:41–44). At the controls of the war machine, meanwhile, is a no less paradoxical commander, one who demands "not to be served but to serve" (10:45). His own systematic self-voiding culminates on Golgotha
[**"How can we unhook ourselves from the points of subjectification that secure us, nail us down to a dominant reality?"**[29]]
and the climactic public revelation of what he has secretly been ever since his first appearance in the narrative: an assemblage composed of a crude torture instrument brutally joined to a quivering mass of hypersensitized

---

27. Deleuze, *Cinema 1*, 97.
28. Deleuze and Guattari, *A Thousand Plateaus*, 400.
29. Ibid., 160.

flesh. Jesus is divine in Mark, more and other than human, nonhuman, only because of his willingness to be nailed into this inhuman assemblage
> ["**Mistress, ... you may tie me down on the table, ropes drawn tight, for ten to fifteen minutes, time enough to prepare the instruments.**"[30]]

from the moment he assumes his mission. When Jesus emerges from the river Jordan, therefore, in his first scene in Mark and hears the heavenly voice identifying him as Son of God (1:9–11), it is only because the water of the river already runs red with his blood. He has been screwed to the wood to become a human-nonhuman assemblage and a human-divine agent.

The Crucified Body without Organs

Within the wood and flesh assemblage erected on Golgotha, the body of Mark's Messiah publicly assumes its narratively predestined form. The monstrous forces that buffet Mark's narrative universe (more on this below) also form and deform this body. More than a body in extremis, it is Deleuze's Body without Organs (or BwO),
> ["**For the judgment of God weighs upon and is exercised against the BwO; it is the BwO that undergoes it.... The BwO howls.**"[31]]

that hyperkinetic, irreducibly dynamic, affect-imbued body that continually resists coagulation as an organism, as an ordered, hierarchical collection of organs; "for the organism is not life, it is what imprisons life,"[32] even when it hovers on the threshold of death, as here. The crucified Body without Organs in Mark's passion narrative,
> ["**The book has become the body of passion.**"[33]]

altogether undescribed but viscerally implicit, "operates entirely by insufflation, respiration, evaporation, and fluid transmission."[34] It is "occupied, populated only by intensities" that "pass and circulate."[35] It is traversed by waves of sensation, which is the default state of the Body

---

30. Ibid., 151.
31. Ibid., 159.
32. Deleuze, *Francis Bacon*, 40. See also Deleuze, *Two Regimes of Madness*, 130: "If I call it a body-without-organs, it is because it opposes all strata of organization, the organism's organization as well as power organizations."
33. Deleuze and Guattari, *A Thousand Plateaus*, 127 (italics removed).
34. Deleuze, *The Logic of Sense*, 88.
35. Deleuze and Guattari, *A Thousand Plateaus*, 153.

3. The Messiah Who Screamed

without Organs. "Sensation is not qualitative and qualified, but has only an intensive reality.... Sensation is vibration."[36] The crucified Christ vibrates like a tuning fork in response to the unbearable forces that pass through him. His Body without Organs is scoured flesh and exposed nerve; "a wave flows through it and traces levels upon it; a sensation is produced when the wave encounters the forces acting [upon it], an 'affective athleticism,'

> ["Well beyond the apparent sadism, the bones are like a trapeze apparatus (the carcass) upon which the flesh is the acrobat. The athleticism of the body is naturally prolonged in the acrobatics of the flesh."[37]]

a scream-breath."[38]

What Forces a Scream?

What are the forces acting upon the crucified Body without Organs and eliciting its self-shattering scream-breath? There is an ineffability to force, to forces, in Deleuze's construal of them. Force is what engenders sensation, and the confluence of forces engenders bodies, but force, or forces, may not be experienced directly. "How can one make invisible forces visible?" Deleuze inquires on behalf of Francis Bacon,[39] whose torturous paintings of the crucifixion loom so large in Deleuze's book on him. Making invisible forces visible might also be said to be the central problem with which the Gospel of Mark grapples. That grappling comes to a climax in the crucifixion scene, and most of all in the scream with which it concludes. "If we scream," surmises Deleuze, "it is always as victims of invisible and insensible forces," forces that, ultimately, "lie beyond pain and feeling."[40] The scream "is the operation through which the entire body"— let us say the Body without Organs, the hypersensitized body touched by insensible forces—attempts to

> ["Now it is inside the body that something is happening.... The body ... waits to escape from itself in a very precise manner."[41]]

---

36. Deleuze, *Francis Bacon*, 39.
37. Ibid., 21.
38. Ibid., 40.
39. Ibid., 49.
40. Ibid., 51.
41. Ibid., 15.

flee through the mouth, "no longer a particular organ but the hole through which the entire body escapes."[42]

["It is not I who attempts to escape from my body, it is the body that attempts to escape from itself."[43]]

Forces Divine, Demonic, and Roman

Forces produce the scream, then, causing it to erupt from the body upon which the forces have converged. In Mark those forces are both divine and demonic. In Mark the body of the protagonist is the site of a cosmic struggle between invisible warring forces. At the outset of the narrative, that body is violently "thrust forth" (*ekballō*) into the wilderness by the unseen force Mark calls "the Spirit" (*to pneuma*) to be tested by another unseen force he calls "Satan" (*ho Satanas* [1:12–13]). Jesus's first act of power in Mark is the expulsion of an "unclean spirit" (*pneuma akatharton*)

["It escapes from itself through the open mouth, through the anus or the stomach, or through the throat."[44]]

from a possessed man (1:23–27). But in this demon-haunted narrative, this is merely the first of many exorcisms (see also 1:32–34, 39; 5:1–20; 6:7, 13; 7:24–30; 9:14–29; cf. 3:11–12, 14–15; 9:38–40), which Jesus himself styles as a cosmic battle with Satan (3:22–27). In the most spectacular of the exorcisms, Jesus expels a multitude of demons

["What we encounter are the demons, the sign-bearers: powers of the leap, the interval, the intensive."[45]]

from a single howling, tormented body (5:1–20). The self-identification of the demons as "Legion" ("Legion is my name, for we are many" [5:9]) invites their construal as a figure for the Roman military forces occupying the Jewish homeland, the possessed man becoming in turn a figure for the occupied land.[46]

---

42. Ibid., 24.
43. Ibid., 15.
44. Ibid., 43.
45. Gilles Deleuze, *Difference and Repetition*, trans. Paul Patton (New York: Columbia University Press, 1994), 145.
46. Hans Leander has traced the exegetical identification of Legion with the Roman military back to 1830 (*Discourses of Empire: The Gospel of Mark from a Postcolonial Perspective*, SemeiaSt 71 [Atlanta: Society of Biblical Literature, 2013], 107). With the "turn to empire" in recent New Testament studies, the interpretation of Mark 5:1–20 as a national allegory in which Legion symbolizes Rome and the possessed man

3. The Messiah Who Screamed

Invisible divine forces have operated through visible political forces to nail Jesus to a Roman cross ("'Abba, Father, ... not what I desire,
> ["**Desire is wholly a part of the functioning heterogeneous assemblage.... It is an affect, as opposed to a feeling.**"[47]]

but what you desire.' ... And they laid hands on him and arrested him" [14:36, 46]). But the partition between the visible political forces and the invisible demonic forces is equally porous, as the example of Legion makes plain, the demons of possession transmuting into the armies of occupation and Satan's empire (cf. 3:24–26) morphing into Rome's empire. God's empire, Satan's empire, and Rome's empire are a jumble of tangled limbs in Mark's empire-obsessed narrative. In consequence, Satan is as close to the crucified Messiah as God is—or perhaps considerably closer ("My God, my God, why have you abandoned me?" [15:34])—intimately intertwined with him within the cross assemblage, causing him to scream in horror,
> ["**The meat howls under the gaze of a dog-spirit perched on top of the cross.**"[48]]

just as the demon-possessed have screamed throughout the gospel (1:26; 5:5, 7; 9:26; cf. 3:11).[49]

Painting the Scream without Painting the Horror

The crucifixion is the climactic scene in Mark, relative to which its ambiguous empty tomb scene is thoroughly anticlimactic. Why, then, do the physical horrors of the crucifixion go undescribed in Mark?[50] Because the invisible forces that ultimately produce the scream of the crucified are

---

the Jewish homeland has become increasingly common; for a notable recent example, see Warren Carter, "Cross-Gendered Romans and Mark's Jesus: Legion Enters the Pigs (Mark 5:1–20)," *JBL* 134 (2015): 139–55. I first read the Legion episode myself this way in my *Empire and Apocalypse*, 24–32.

47. Deleuze, *Two Regimes of Madness*, 130.
48. Deleuze, *Francis Bacon*, 23.
49. See Frederick W. Danker, "The Demonic Secret in Mark: A Reexamination of the Cry of Dereliction (15.34)," *ZNW* 61 (1970): 48–69; Marcus, *Mark 8–16*, 1063.
50. Mark's description of what ensues when Jesus arrives at the place of execution is restricted to: "And they crucify him [*kai staurousin auton*], and divide his clothes, casting lots for them, to decide who should take what" (15:24). Contrast Seneca: "Yonder I see crosses, not all alike...: some suspend a man so that his head hangs toward the ground, others impale his private parts, still others stretch out his arms on a crossbeam" (*Marc.* 20.3, my translation).

the true theme of the scene, not the crucifixion itself, which is merely the torturous relay.⁵¹ Deleuze cautions: "The forces that produce the scream, that convulse the body until they emerge at the mouth..., must not be confused with the visible spectacle before which one screams, nor even with the perceptible and sensible objects whose action decomposes and recomposes our pain":⁵² the scourge that has scoured our back and buttocks clean of skin,

> **["One hundred lashes at least, a pause of several minutes.... Now you go on to the second phase."⁵³]**

the rough-surfaced wood of the cross that now abrades our hypersensitized flesh, the iron spikes that have been driven through our wrists and insteps and from which our entire weight is now suspended. Paraphrasing Deleuze on Bacon and projecting intentionality onto the impersonal text, the literary machine, we customarily personify as Mark, we might say: Either I word-paint the horror and I do not paint the scream, or I word-paint the scream and I do not paint the horror. But if I settle on the scream, allowing it to resound chillingly in the unnatural darkness with which I have shrouded the landscape,

> **["And when the sixth hour arrived, darkness descended on the entire land until the ninth hour." (Mark 15:33)]**

it is only so that it may signal the contorting, crushing presence of invisible forces converging unbearably on the body that emits the scream.

The War of the Machines

The forces that crush the body also call seductively to the body. The irresistible siren call of the invisible divine/demonic forces lure Jesus to Jerusalem and the cross during the second half of Mark's narrative. But the crucified Jesus seems also to have been seduced in advance by the imperial forces that now ravage

---

51. Neither is the reason for the scream to be located in a deep interior reservoir of emotion within the character, contra R. T. France, who remarks: "The loudness of the cry ... serves to underline the depth of the emotion it expresses" (*The Gospel of Mark: A Commentary on the Greek Text*, NIGTC [Grand Rapids: Eerdmans, 2002], 652). Compare 28–31 above.

52. Deleuze, *Francis Bacon*, 51.

53. Deleuze and Guattari, *A Thousand Plateaus*, 151 (italics removed).

3. The Messiah Who Screamed

> ["And Pilate ... having scourged Jesus, handed him over to be crucified." (Mark 15:15)]

his flesh. Earlier, Jesus has told us what he expects his death torture to effect. It will be but the prelude to his being raised (8:31; 9:31; 10:34; 14:28; cf. 16:6), to his being projected high into the heavens to land "at the right hand of Power" (*ek dexiōn ... tēs dynameōs*) and onto the throne that awaits him there (14:62).[54] Armed with that awful power he will then return to earth—an earth, indeed a cosmos, that will dissolve before him as though in terror: "The sun will be darkened, and the moon will not give its light, and the stars will be falling from heaven" (13:24–25). He will return as an omnipotent emperor ready to exercise absolute rule: "And then they will see the Son of Man coming in clouds with immense power and glory [*meta dynameōs pollēs kai doxēs*]" (13:26; cf. 8:38–9:1). The cross to which he was formerly affixed will have folded and refolded

> ["The fold is Power.... Force itself is an act, an act of the fold."[55]]

to form a throne. The cross-torture victim assemblage will have reconfigured to become a throne-emperor assemblage.

With the new emperor's arrival, what will have become of the divine war machine, with the cross assemblage as its control cabin, that had set out against the Roman imperial machine at the outset of the narrative? As Deleuze and Guattari explain, "the war machine has an extremely variable relation to war itself."[56] As we saw earlier, the war machine can manifest itself in a form antithetical to war as such, devoted instead to "the drawing of a creative line of flight, the composition of a smooth space and of the movement of people in that space."[57] At the other extreme, however, the war machine "takes war for its object and forms a line of destruction prolongable to

> ["The stars will be falling from heaven, and the powers in the heavens will be shaken." (Mark 13:25)]

the limits of the universe."[58]

Two war machines lumber across the surface of Mark's text, then, one controlled by the suffering Messiah encaged in his cross assemblage,

---

54. Invisible in Mark, this throne is made visible in Matthew (see Matt 19:28; 25:31; cf. Luke 1:32).
55. Deleuze, *Fold*, 18.
56. Deleuze and Guattari, *A Thousand Plateaus*, 422 (italics removed).
57. Ibid.
58. Ibid., 422.

the other controlled by the glorified Messiah enthroned in his throne assemblage. These two war machines would appear to be on a collision course, forcing us to choose between them, to decide which of them will roll over us.

Deleuze and Guattari write: "One of the fundamental problems of the State is to appropriate [the] war machine that is foreign to it and make it a piece in its apparatus."[59] Confronted with the two war machines in the Gospel of Mark, and in the Gospels of Matthew and Luke that modeled themselves on Mark, the Christianized Roman state under Constantine and his successors had an easy choice. The war machine controlled by the enthroned emperor-Messiah was driven into the main bay of the war machine controlled by the enthroned Roman emperor and locked inside it,

["**Recaptured in the end, … sealed in, tied up, reknotted, reterritorialized.**"[60]]

the massive door clanging shut with a sound that would resound through the centuries of Christendom whose inauguration that co-opting confinement announced.

The Glorious, Yet Unrisen, Body without Organs

Mark's other war machine, however, was never demolished. And in a denouement worthy of this gospel of improbable endings, that suffering Messiah war machine—rough hewn, crudely constructed from a few wooden beams, held together by a few nails—has been more effective than the glorious Messiah machine, at least if effectiveness is to be measured affectively. "The regime of the war machine is … that of *affects*," as we earlier heard Deleuze and Guattari declaim.[61] It is not the omnipotent imperial Christ on his cloud but the tortured peasant Christ on his cross—not the throne assemblage, then, but the cross assemblage—that has been the hyperaffective megamachine for the ages. Christians do not, after all, wear tiny gold or silver replicas of Christ's throne around their necks; they do not trace the sign of the throne on their bodies even in moments of consummate triumph (scoring a World Cup goal, say, or breaking an Olympic record) when such a sign might seem more apt than the sign of the cross; nor does any volunteer in a reenactment of the events deemed crucial in

---

59. Ibid., 230.
60. Ibid., 229.
61. Ibid., 400, emphasis original.

the life of Christ stagger up a steep hill with a two-hundred-pound throne on his back. The cross assemblage, laden with throbbing, suffering human flesh, is what Christ adorers want to touch,

> ["We can no longer say 'I see, I hear,' but I FEEL, totally physiological sensation."[62]]

not the throne assemblage, resplendent with radiant, glorious human flesh.

But perhaps the suffering/glorious dichotomy is entirely irrelevant if the crucified body of Mark's screaming Messiah is indeed a Body without Organs. The BwO, for Deleuze,

> ["Body without Organs...: subatomic particles, pure intensities, prevital and prephysical singularities."[63]]

is also—and especially—"the glorious body."[64] The glorious body of Jesus is ostensibly missing from the final chapters of Mark,

> ["You never reach the Body without Organs, you can't reach it, you are forever attaining it, it is a limit."[65]]

but only because we have been looking for it in the wrong place. It is found, not outside the rear exit of the tomb, but rather at the threshold of the tomb, which is to say on the cross.

In John's Gospel the glorious body

> ["It is on this body that assemblages are made and come apart, ... this body-without-organs."[66]]

elicits the awed exclamation "My Lord and my God!" only after it has emerged from the grave (20:28), but in Mark's Gospel it elicits the corresponding acknowledgment, "Truly this man was a Son of God!," while it still hangs on the cross (15:39). The Roman centurion who does the exclaiming in Mark has regularly been taken by scholars to be a surrogate for the Markan community that produced the gospel, the centurion's confession being interpreted as giving succinct expression to the crucifixated faith of that community, its counterintuitive construal of Jesus's crucifixion as the consummate manifestation of Jesus's divinity. But crucifixation has been the default orientation of Christians in every age, including our own. The centurion might equally be said, then, to be a surrogate for all Chris-

---

62. Deleuze, *Cinema 2*, 158.
63. Deleuze and Guattari, *A Thousand Plateaus*, 40.
64. Deleuze, *Logic of Sense*, 88, 92–93, 129.
65. Deleuze and Guattari, *A Thousand Plateaus*, 150.
66. Deleuze, *Two Regimes of Madness*, 130.

tians in every time and place who have felt touched by divinity, affected by it, more at the cross than at the tomb or throne.

Messiah and Meat

This affective encounter with divinity, however, is not an encounter with a face, for Jesus is never said to have a face in Mark; much less does he have a face that is described. For Deleuze, "the face is a structured, spatial organization that conceals the head,"[67] and the head is apprehended as bodily, as fleshly, to a degree that the face is not. Mark's Jesus is a body with a head but without a face. The two emblematic reactions that Jesus's body elicits in Mark, reverence and violence, also befall his head in the two instances in which it is mentioned: it is anointed by a woman (14:3), and it is struck by soldiers (15:19).

John the Baptist points the way, as always, gesturing to Jesus's secret identity and destiny—or, rather, John's head does. John's severed head is an important actant in Mark (6:24–28). John, or rather his head, transmutes into a ghastly entrée,

> **["I desire that you present me at once with the head of John the Baptist on a dish!" (Mark 6:25)]**

morphs into the meat that it always, in any case, was. John's execution in Mark is commonly said to presage Jesus's execution, to preenact it in its essential elements. What is not generally said is that John's public display as butchered meat anticipates Jesus's own public display as butchered meat.

The specific body displayed on the Markan cross is iconic of the body in general, for "meat is the state of the body," as Deleuze observes.[68] Meat is also the "zone of indiscernibility or undecidability" between human and animal,[69] their common condition, at once glorious and abject. The climactic sound uttered by the Markan Messiah on his cross is an animal shriek,

> **["What constitutes sensation is the becoming animal or plant, which wells up like a flayed beast or peeled fruit."[70]]**

---

67. Deleuze, *Francis Bacon*, 19.
68. Ibid., 20.
69. Ibid.
70. Deleuze and Guattari, *What Is Philosophy?*, 179.

a bestial roar. On the Markan cross, a howling mouth is "hollow[ed] out … from solid meat."[71]

On the one hand (an outstretched hand with a nail driven through it), there is no incarnation in Mark in the sense that there is no preexistent Christ in Mark who secondarily assumes human flesh, who is remade as meat.[72] On the other hand (also outstretched and also impaled by a nail), there is nothing *but* incarnation in Mark, nothing but a Christ who in his consummate moment of self-revelation is encountered only as sensate flesh, as scoured flesh, as meat. Flesh, meat, sacrificed meat, which is to say butchered meat, is the sacred place in which the human encounters the divine in Mark,

> ["**He goes to the butcher shop as if it were a church, with the meat as the crucified victim.**"[73]]

in which the human shudders before the divine, is affected by the divine, and in ways that theologians have labored unsuccessfully for millennia to explain. For the logic of the crucifixion is the logic of sensation, and the sensational is irreducible to the propositional.

---

71. Deleuze, *Francis Bacon*, 23.

72. In contrast, classically, of course, to John: "In the beginning was the Word…. He was in the beginning with God…. And the Word became flesh [*sarx*] and pitched his tent among us" (1:1–2, 14).

73. Deleuze, *Francis Bacon*, 21–22.

4

The Dog-Woman of Canaan and Other Animal Tales*

So far, my tale has emphasized a litter of critters made up of dogs, humans, and slaughtered animals.
—Donna Haraway, *Staying with the Trouble*

And Jesus went forth from there and withdrew to the regions of Tyre and Sidon. And behold, a Canaanite woman from those parts came forth and cried out, "Have pity on me, Lord, Son of David; my daughter is severely possessed by a demon." But he answered her not a word. And his disciples came and begged him, "Send her away, because she keeps shouting after us." But he answered, "I was sent only to the lost sheep of the house of Israel." And she came and worshiped him saying, "Lord, help me!" But he answered, "It is not fair to take the children's bread and toss it to the dogs." And she said, "Yes, Lord, yet even the dogs eat the crumbs that fall from their masters' table." Then Jesus answered her, "Woman, great is your faith! Let what you desire be done for you." And her daughter was instantly healed.
—Matt 15:21–28

Narrative time distorts severely and queerly in the Canaanite woman episode of Matthew's Gospel. The unnamed woman is a grotesquely distended character, as we shall see, impossibly stretched between a remote past and a distant future. First, her name, which, of course, is not a proper name but rather an archaic designation: "And behold, a Canaanite woman

---

* An earlier version of this chapter appeared in a Festschrift for Fernando Segovia as "The Dog-Woman of Canaan and Other Animal Tales from the Gospel of Matthew," in *Soundings in Cultural Criticism: Perspectives and Methods in Culture, Power, and Identity in New Testament Interpretation*, ed. Francisco Lozada Jr. and Greg Carey (Minneapolis: Fortress, 2013). I rededicate the essay to him with gratitude and admiration.

from those parts came forth" (15:22).[1] Matthew has changed Mark's *gynē ... Hellēnis, Syrophoinikissa tō genei* ("[the] woman ... a Greek, Syrophoenician by birth"), terms already bristling with ethnic valence, to *gynē Chananaia* ("a Canaanite woman"), an epithet more redolent of ethnic violence.[2] It has been suggested, perhaps implausibly, that *Canaanite* was a Phoenician self-designation when this gospel was written.[3] What is more certain is that the term opens vertiginously onto a scriptural temporal trajectory that extends steeply backwards through the conquest narratives and the exodus and wilderness narratives to the patriarchal narratives and the primeval history.

It is impossible in principle to say which of the approximately 170 instances of *Canaan* or *Canaanite* in Jewish Scripture swirled about in our implied author's paper skull as he made his terminological substitution, but it is tempting as always to project into that infinitely capacious space. For instance, the Matthean Jesus encounters the woman in the region not just of Tyre, as in Mark 7:24, but of Tyre and Sidon (Matt 15:21), and according to the postdiluvian genealogy, "Canaan [was] the father of Sidon" (Gen 10:15; cf. 1 Chr 1:13). Consequently, "the territory of the Canaanites extended from Sidon ... as far as Gaza" (Gen 10:19). In the Israelite myth of origins, however, the territory possessed by the Canaanites is always already destined for dispossession: "And I will give to you [Abraham], and to your offspring after you, ... all the land of Canaan, for a perpetual holding" (Gen 17:8; cf. Exod 3:8). How is this dispossession to occur? Deuteronomy 20:17 puts it succinctly: "You shall annihilate them" (cf. Zeph 2:5). Their annihilation must be absolute, moreover, but why? Because their idolatry is a constant temptation for Israel (see Lev 18:3).

---

1. Translations of the Gospel of Matthew in this chapter are my own; otherwise I employ NRSV.

2. See Kwok Pui-lan, *Discovering the Bible in the Non-biblical World*, BL (Maryknoll, NY: Orbis, 1995), 71–83; Leander, *Discourses of Empire*, 109–15; Jin Young Choi, *Postcolonial Discipleship of Embodiment: An Asian and Asian American Feminist Reading of the Gospel of Mark*, PR (New York: Palgrave Macmillan, 2015), 85–108; Leticia A. Guardiola-Sáenz, "Borderless Women and Borderless Texts: A Cultural Reading of Matthew 15:21–28," *Semeia* 78 (1997): 69–81; Musa W. Dube, *Postcolonial Feminist Interpretation of the Bible* (St. Louis, MO: Chalice, 2000), 147–53; Surekha Nelavala, *Liberation beyond Borders: Dalit Feminist Hermeneutics and Four Gospel Women* (Saarbrücken: Lambert, 2009), 61–95.

3. See, for example, Ulrich Luz, *Matthew 8–20*, Hermeneia (Minneapolis: Fortress, 2001), 338.

But does Israel enact the genocide with which it is divinely charged? No, it does not, insists the tradition accusingly (see esp. Ps 106:34–42).

Matthew's Canaanite woman is a representative figure, then, and what she represents is an unerased remnant, a polluted people (cf. 1 Esd 8:69: "The people of Israel ... have not put away from themselves the alien peoples of the land and their pollutions") whose name connotes idolatry and hence abomination (more on this below). Yet the pericope of the Canaanite woman also symbolically enacts the completion of Yahweh's genocidal commission, although by means other than the sword. This completion is accomplished through temporal distortion—or *queer temporality*, to invoke a more theoretically potent term.

Queering Canaan

Coupling the term *queer* with the term *temporality* entails a temporary decoupling of queer theory from sex and sexuality. A scant three years after the term *queer theory* was coined, Sedgwick was already able to report: "Recent work around 'queer' spins the term outward along dimensions that can't be subsumed under gender and sexuality at all: the ways that race, ethnicity, postcolonial nationality criss-cross with these and other identity-constituting, identity-fracturing discourses, for example."[4] One such dimension is that of *time*—or, more precisely, time as socially constructed, periodized, politicized, regulated, subordinated to heteronormativity, capitalist productivity, and so on.[5] Rebecca Fine Romanow is

---

4. Eve Kosofsky Sedgwick, *Tendencies* (Durham, NC: Duke University Press, 1993), 9. See also Michael Warner, "Introduction," in *Fear of a Queer Planet: Queer Politics and Social Theory*, ed. Warner, CP 6 (Minneapolis: University of Minnesota Press, 1993), x–xi; Judith Butler, "Against Proper Objects," *differences* 6 (1994): 21. See 85–86 below on the heterogeneous origins of queer theory.

5. As Elizabeth Freeman observes on the contemporary instrumentalization of time: "In the United States, for instance, states now license, register, or certify birth (and thus citizenship, eventually encrypted in a Social Security ID for taxpaying purposes), marriage or domestic partnership (which privatizes caretaking and regulates the distribution of private property), and death (which terminates the identities linked to state benefits, redistributing these benefits through familial channels).... In the eyes of the state, this sequence of socioeconomically 'productive' moments is what it means to have a life at all" (*Time Binds: Queer Temporalities, Queer Histories*, PM [Durham, NC: Duke University Press, 2010], 4–5). *Time Binds* is a catalytic text for the concept of queer temporality, as are Carolyn Dinshaw, *Getting Medieval: Sexualities*

among those who have given the notion of queer temporality an explicit postcolonial spin, arguing that the (post)colonial arena is a cultural and political pressure cooker productive of all manner of fractures and aberrations, temporal as well as geographical.[6]

So how does queer temporality play out in the ethnically and colonially charged space conjured up in Matt 15:21–28? To state it summarily, polytheism self-deconstructs spontaneously in this scene in the face of a Christian mission from the future that invades the woman's present and rewrites the mythic past. Midway through the episode, the polytheistic woman is already on her knees before the numinous figure who, other than Matthew's God, is the sole sanctioned object of worship in Matthew's symbolic universe: "And she came and worshiped him [*prosekynei autō*] saying, 'Lord, help me!'" (15:25). She has previously hailed the stranger with a messianic title: "Have pity on me, Lord, Son of David" (15:22; cf. 1:1; 21:9).[7] The new Joshua is accomplishing what the old Joshua could not: "Now Joshua was old and advanced in years; and the Lord said to him, 'You are old and advanced in years, and very much of the land still remains to be possessed'" (Josh 13:1). In consequence, even the impersonal name from the distant past, applied to the woman at the outset ("a Canaanite woman from those parts"), is drained of its primary (polytheistic) con-

---

and Communities, Pre- and Postmodern, SerQ (Durham, NC: Duke University Press, 1999); Lee Edelman, *No Future: Queer Theory and the Death Drive*, SerQ (Durham, NC: Duke University Press, 2004); J. Jack Halberstam, *In a Queer Time and Place: Transgender Bodies, Subcultural Lives*, Sexual Cultures (New York: New York University Press, 2004); Jonathan Goldberg and Madhavi Menon, "Queering History," *PMLA* 120 (2005): 1608–17; Carla Freccero, *Queer/Early/Modern*, SerQ (Durham, NC: Duke University Press, 2006); Dinshaw et al., "Theorizing Queer Temporalities," *GLQ* 13 (2007): 177–95; and José Esteban Muñoz, *Cruising Utopia: The Then and There of Queer Futurity*, Sexual Cultures (New York: New York University Press, 2009). For biblical-critical engagements with queer temporality, see Joseph A. Marchal, "'Making History' Queerly: Touches across Time through a Biblical Behind," *BibInt* 19 (2011): 373–95; the biblical essays in Kent L. Brintnall, Joseph A. Marchal, and Stephen D. Moore, eds., *Sexual Disorientations: Queer Temporalities, Affects, Theologies*, TTC (New York: Fordham University Press, 2017); Denise Kimber Buell and Stephen D. Moore, eds., *Queer Times: Futurity, Hauntology, and Utopia in and after Biblical Texts*, *BibInt* (forthcoming).

6. Rebecca Fine Romanow, *The Postcolonial Body in Queer Space and Time* (Newcastle, UK: Cambridge Scholars, 2008), esp. 3–4.

7. The term *kyrios* flickers ambiguously in this scene (15:22, 25, 27), meaning both "sir" in the profane sense and "Lord" in the christological sense.

notations as the episode unfolds and as she is possessed by a Christology from the future—that of the Matthean community, retrojected back into the present of the historical Jesus as it compulsively tells, retells, and reconfigures his tale.

Past and future are thus accessed in this episode. All that is inaccessible is the woman's present. Can the subaltern speak in this scene?[8] Not in the present tense, it would seem, except when articulating the plight of her daughter, that other possessed character in the narrative: "My daughter is severely possessed by a demon" (Matt 15:22). Even here, however, the woman is subsumed in an ethnic stereotype with roots in the archaic past. Canaanites and demons go hand in hand, after all. The idols that Canaanites worship are nothing other than demons, the tradition contemptuously claims (Deut 32:15–17; Ps 106:36–37; Bar 4:7; 1 Cor 10:20; Rev 9:20).[9] In accordance with the implacable logic of the narrative, therefore, as soon as the woman engages in sanctioned worship, thereby relinquishing her Canaanite identity, the switch that causes the demon to depart from her daughter is automatically triggered: "'Woman, great is your faith! Let what you desire be done for you.' And her daughter was instantly healed" (Matt 15:28).

By what narrative logic, however, is Canaan represented as a woman in this scene? The scriptural echo chamber activated by the term "Canaanite" again suggests possible answers.[10] Canaan is styled a slave from the outset

---

8. See Gayatri Chakravorty Spivak, "Can the Subaltern Speak?," in *Marxism and the Interpretation of Culture*, ed. Cary Nelson and Larry Grossberg (Urbana: University of Illinois Press, 1988), 271–313.

9. See Louise J. Lawrence, "Crumb Trails and Puppy-Dog Tales: Reading Afterlives of a Canaanite Woman," in *From the Margins 2: Women of the New Testament and Their Afterlives*, ed. Christine E. Joynes and Christopher C. Rowland, BMW 27 (Sheffield: Sheffield Phoenix, 2009), 264: "[Epiphanius the Latin], like Hilary of Poitiers, imagines the woman as 'a mother of demon-possessed Gentiles' who suffer terribly from demon-possession having been 'led astray by idolatry and sin' and thus are nothing more than 'dogs who worship idols' and 'bark at God' (*Interpretation of the Gospels* 58)." For differently focused explorations of the significance of demon possession in the Canaanite woman and Syrophoenician woman pericopae respectively, see Elaine M. Wainwright, "Not Without My Daughter: Gender and Demon Possession in Matthew 15.21–28," in *A Feminist Companion to Matthew*, ed. Amy-Jill Levine with Marianne Blickenstaff (Sheffield: Sheffield Academic, 2001), 126–37; Laura E. Donaldson, "Gospel Hauntings: The Postcolonial Demons of New Testament Criticism," in Moore and Segovia, *Postcolonial Biblical Criticism*, 97–114.

10. The reflections that follow build on those of Musa Dube, who writes: "To

in the primeval history: "Lowest of slaves shall he be to his brothers" (Gen 9:25; cf. 9:26–27). In the dominant gender ideology of the ancient Mediterranean world, slave and female occupied contiguous positions on the gender gradient, both parties consigned to the will and the whim of a free elite male, to do with as he pleased (cf. Neh 9.24 LXX, where the Canaanites are delivered to Israel "to do with them as it pleased" [*poiēsai autois hōs areston enōpion autōn*]). Confronted with a paragon of hegemonic masculinity, the only appropriate response from a social or ethnic inferior was fawning obeisance. In our pericope, slavish Canaan, represented as a woman, debases herself before Israel, represented by the Son of David, submissively picking up with her mouth the humiliating dog epithet he hurls at her (15:26–27).[11] The scene is thus intensely racialized and eroticized—and, again, is temporally out of joint. The obeisance luridly on display here represents a national allegory, or nationalistic fantasy, less oriented to the actual conditions of the Rome-dominated present (Yahweh's elect again squirming impotently under the heel of an idol-worshiping conqueror) than the mythic conditions of the archaic past—although a necessarily revised and reimagined past in which Israel subjugates Canaan finally and decisively, Canaan being feminized in the transaction and Israel being hypermasculinized. The colonial cauldron, seething with intolerable pressures and unattainable desires, has once again produced displacement and distortion in the temporal plane—"a 'queer,' nonnormative … temporality," as Romanow might phrase it.[12]

---

intertextually characterize a foreign woman as a 'Canaanite' is to mark her as one who must be invaded, conquered, annihilated; or, if she is to survive, then … she must parrot the superiority of her subjugators and betray her own people and land. Basically, she must survive only as a colonized mind, a subjugated and domesticated subject" (*Postcolonial Feminist Interpretation*, 147).

11. Augustine aptly paraphrased 15:27 as follows: "Yes, Lord, I am a dog, I desire crumbs" (*Serm.* 77.12 [*NPNF*]). What of the fact that the term *kynaria* in 15:26–27, ordinarily translated "dogs," is a diminutive form, and, if it is not to be regarded as a "faded diminutive," might instead be translated "little dogs," even "puppies," connoting affection, even cuteness, to the modern ear? Warren Carter cuts deftly through any such attempt to soften the affront: "To refer to her as a dog or bitch, even a 'little bitch' or puppy, since a diminutive form is used, is offensive and insulting (Josephus, *Con Ap* 2.85)" (*Matthew and the Margins: A Sociopolitical and Religious Reading*, BL [Maryknoll, NY: Orbis, 2000], 324).

12. Romanow, *Postcolonial Body in Queer Space and Time*, 3.

An important question remains, however, perhaps the most pressing question of all: Why is the Canaanite woman represented as a dog in this scene?

The Dog-Woman and the Inhuman One

"Do not give what is holy to dogs," the Matthean Jesus earlier enjoined his audience (7:6), anticipating his initial refusal of miraculous aid to the Canaanite dog-woman. But why are dogs not worthy of what is holy? Ancient Near Eastern and ancient Mediterranean cultures provide a harmonious chorus of answers. Sextus Empiricus, a philosopher and physician active in the late second and early third centuries CE, voices an already ancient prejudice when he declaims: "The dog, ... which is held to be the most worthless of animals" (*Pyrrh.* 1.63 [LCL]). Neither is ancient Israelite or early Jewish tradition kind to dogs (1 Sam 17:43; 24:14; 2 Sam 9:8; 16:9; 2 Kgs 8:13; Ps 22:16, 20; Prov 26:11; cf. Phil 3:2; 2 Pet 2:22; Rev 22:15). These and other such ancient sources have long been adduced to make sense of Matt 15:26–27.[13] What other kind of sense might the dog epithet yield? As we shall see, Jesus's exchange with the animalized woman participates in a more extensive Matthean discourse on human-animal relations. The Matthean Jesus is himself fully enmeshed in that discourse and partially constructed by it. Let us turn the animal question from the woman, then, to the man. What kind of creature is the Matthean Jesus? Oceans of ink have been spilled on his relationship to divinity. What of his relationship to animality?

The "Son of Man" title provides the most illuminating answer to that question. Already a towering title for Jesus in Mark, *ho huios tou anthrōpou* occurs about twice as often in Matthew, as it also features prominently in

---

13. Although Greco-Roman literature and material culture also yield more positive appraisals of dogs, as Elaine M. Wainwright has shown. These positive appraisals enable her own ecological reappraisal of the Matthean Jesus's exchange with the Canaanite woman. See Wainwright, "Of Dogs and Women: Ethology and Gender in Ancient Healing; The Canaanite Woman's Story—Matt 15:21–28," in *Miracles Revisited: New Testament Miracle Stories and Their Concepts of Reality*, ed. Stefan Alkier and Annette Weissenrieder, SBR 2 (Berlin: de Gruyter, 2013), esp. 66–69; see also Wainwright, "Of Borders, Bread, Dogs and Demons: Reading Matthew 15.21–28 Ecologically," in *Where the Wild Ox Roams: Biblical Essays in Honor of Norman C. Habel*, ed. Alan H. Cadwallader and Peter Trudinger, HBM 59 (Sheffield: Sheffield Phoenix, 2013), 114–26.

Matthew's Q source. Daniel 7 is widely viewed as the primary source for the Son of Man title in the synoptic tradition. The nonhuman animal is the constitutive other of the Danielic "Son of Man" (*bar ĕnāš*).[14] Indeed, the animal, or, rather, the animals, are the reason for the formulation "one like a son of man/one like a human being."[15] Daniel's vision initially is of "four great beasts," the first like a lion with eagles' wings, the second like a bear, the third like a leopard with four wings and four heads, and the fourth a "terrifying and dreadful and exceedingly strong" beast with "great iron teeth" and multiple horns (7:3-8). The throne-room scene ensues and the judgment of the beasts is described, after which Daniel sees "one like a human being coming with the clouds of heaven" (7:13). "One like a human being" apparently means "one not like a beast." Yet the human one may not be altogether human, or even human at all. He is only *like* a human being, after all. Many have argued that that the *bar ĕnāš* of Dan 7 is an angelic figure, since ostensibly human figures seen in the remaining visions of the book regularly turn out to be angels (8:15-16; 9:21; 10:5-6; 12:5-7; cf. 3:25).[16]

Daniel 7 presents us with a cosmology that both anticipates and complicates the absolutized, hierarchical, human/animal dichotomy characteristic of modern Western thought since Descartes.[17] On the one hand, Dan 7 articulates an analogous dualism. If the expression "one like a human being" means "one who is not a beast," then bestiality or animality in turn in Dan 7 is the master metaphor for a humanity out of alignment

---

14. Dan 7 falls within the Aramaic section of the book.

15. As John Collins notes, "There is near universal consensus that the phrase 'one like a son of man' means simply 'one like a human being'" (*Daniel: A Commentary on the Book of Daniel*, Hermeneia [Minneapolis: Fortress, 1993], 304). Or as Jennifer L. Koosed and Robert Paul Seesengood put it, "'One like the son of man' simply means 'one who looks human,' in contrast with the hyperanimal hybrid beasts Daniel first sees" ("Daniel's Animal Apocalypse," in Moore, *Divinanimality*, 188).

16. See, for example, Collins, *Daniel*, 305-6; Matthias Albani, "'The One Like a Son of Man' (Dan. 7.13) and the Royal Ideology," in *Enoch and Qumran Origins: New Light on a Forgotten Connection*, ed. Gabriele Boccaccini (Grand Rapids: Eerdmans, 2005), 47; Lawrence M. Wills, "Daniel," in *The Jewish Study Bible*, ed. Adele Berlin and Marc Zvi Brettler, 2nd ed. (Oxford: Oxford University Press, 2014), 1656-57.

17. Descartes is commonly seen within animality studies as the creator of the animal in the peculiarly modern sense of the term. I have summarized the argument elsewhere ("Introduction: From Animal Theory to Creaturely Theology," in Moore, *Divinanimality*, 203-7).

with the divine order, as emerges from 7:16–27, the interpretation of the vision. On the other hand, the human in Dan 7 is anything but "Cartesian man"—a deep interior repository of essentialized humanity constituted in absolute contradistinction to a roboticized animality. Instead, the human is a flickering, interstitial element in Dan 7, a hyphen between the animal, the angelic, and the divine.[18] It is impossible to say where the animal ends and the human begins in Dan 7 (as in Dan 4). In a surreal, proto-Darwinian twist, the lion of Daniel's vision, which already is also an eagle, has its wings "plucked off" and is "made to stand on two feet like a human being, and a human mind [is] given to it" (7:4), while the "little horn" on the fourth beast has "eyes like human eyes" and "a mouth speaking arrogantly" (7:8). Human-animal hybridity runs rampant in this vision.

The precarious position of the "one like a human being" in Dan 7 invites a radical reconsideration of the *huios tou anthrōpou* title in Matthew's Gospel. Against the Danielic backdrop, one explicitly evoked in certain of the eschatological *huios tou anthrōpou* sayings in Matthew (24:30; 26:64; cf. 16:27–28; 19:28; 24:15, 27; 25:31), the title might be said to parse out fully only in relation to the nonhuman animals from which it acquires its meaning; for what does it mean to say that the Matthean Jesus is "the human being"—or "the human animal," as we might say today—if not that he is *not* a nonhuman animal or beast?

But it is not only the imperial beasts of Daniel's "troubling" and "terrifying" vision (7:15)[19] that the Son of Man is not. The Son of Man is also, and more immediately, not the more mundane beasts that populate his own discourse—metaphoric beasts, like the Danielic beasts, for the most

---

18. Koosed and Seesengood write of Daniel's "complex polyglot, polymorphous zoology that disrupts the interstitial space(s) between God, human, and animal" ("Daniel's Animal Apocalypse," 190). Compare Jacques Derrida, *The Beast and the Sovereign*, trans. Geoffrey Bennington, 2 vols., SJD 1–2 (Chicago: University of Chicago Press, 2009–2011), 1:13: "There are gods and there are beasts, there is, there is only, the theo-zoological, and in the theo-anthropo-zoological, man is caught, evanescent, disappearing, at the most a simple mediation, a hyphen between the sovereign and the beast, between God and cattle." Derrida describes his work on animality as "a summons issued to Descartes" (*The Animal That Therefore I Am*, trans. David Wills, PCP [New York: Fordham University Press, 2008], 75).

19. "As for these four great beasts," Daniel is informed by an angelic interpreter, "four kings shall arise out of the earth" (7:17). These four kings, kingdoms, or empires are most often taken by critical scholars to be Babylon, Media, Persia, and (Seleucid) Greece (see 8:20–21; 10:20).

part, and hence further human entities trotting, flying, or slithering in diverse animal masks. We hear of metaphoric sheep in particular (7:15; 9:36; 10:6, 16; 25:32–33; 26:31; cf. 2:6), including in the Canaanite woman pericope (15:24), but also of metaphoric fish (4:19; 13:47); pigs (7:6); wolves, serpents, and doves (7:15; 10:16); other birds (13:4, 32); goats (25:32–33)—and, of course, dogs (7:6; 15:26–27). In contrast to Daniel's bestiary, the metaphoric beasts of Matthew's bestiary are nonimperial entities. Rome is not a beast in Matthew, in contrast to Revelation, say, or 4 Ezra, and so neither are its primary representatives. The centurion of Capernaum (Matt 8:5–13) is not an animal; neither is the prefect of Judea (27:2, 11–26, 58, 62–65) or the centurion at the foot of the cross (27:54). The textual logic indicates that the centurion of Capernaum is intimately related to the Canaanite woman: both are gentiles who seek out Jesus, hail him as "Lord," beseech him to heal a beloved dependent, elicit a statement from him concerning Israel, are lauded by him for their exceptional faith, and have their loved one healed from afar.[20] But whereas Jesus is able to encounter the centurion as a fellow elite male, he can only encounter the woman as a beast, a dog, a dog-woman. Why is this?

Several of the well-signposted detours through Greco-Roman literature would provide answers of one kind to this question. The particular set of answers I wish to explore, however, emerge only when the beastly woman and the sovereign Human One are approached through the second volume of Derrida's *The Beast and the Sovereign*.[21] Derrida himself is reading *Robinson Crusoe*, customarily hailed as the first English novel, in the lectures that comprise the volume and discovering that what Crusoe thinks of his animal companions is all but indistinguishable from what Descartes, Kant, and their philosophical progeny think of the animal in general.[22] What Derrida analyzes in *Robinson Crusoe* are the conditions

---

20. See W. D. Davies and Dale C. Allison, *A Critical and Exegetical Commentary on the Gospel according to Saint Matthew*, 2 vols., ICC (Edinburgh: T&T Clark, 1991), 2:558.

21. The Common English Bible consistently renders *ho huios tou anthrōpou* as "the Human One." Derrida's ruminations on animality, especially in the "The Animal That Therefore I Am (More to Follow)," reprinted with three related lectures in Derrida, *Animal That Therefore I Am*, and now supplemented by the two volumes of *Beast and the Sovereign*, have been the principal theoretical catalyst for posthuman animality studies.

22. Daniel Defoe, *The Life and Strange Surprizing Adventures of Robinson Crusoe, of York, Mariner* (London: Taylor, 1719); Derrida, *Beast and the Sovereign*, 2:278.

4. The Dog-Woman of Canaan

of a "Cartesian-Robinsonian" existence, but much of what he has to say applies *mutatis mutandis* to the conditions of existence created by the Matthean Jesus through his words and deeds.[23]

Like Crusoe, the Son of Man seems to occupy an island on which, as Derrida remarks, there are "only men and beasts…. And when I say men, I mean men, not only humans but men without women and without sex…. Or, if you prefer, men without sexual difference and without desire, without obvious sexual concern as such."[24] This is so, in any case, until the closing pages of the novel, Crusoe by then having left his island, when two women are finally mentioned; and until the closing pages of the gospel, Jesus by then having departed this life, when Jesus's female followers are finally mentioned (Matt 27:55–56). The (Robin)Son-of-Man state is essentially a first-stage Edenic state, post-Adam but pre-Eve.[25] Sexual difference has not yet intruded forcibly into the Son of Man's world. Like Robinson, the Son of Man—or, more simply, the Man—seems to assume "some secret contract between sovereign euphoria, paradisiacal euphoria, and the absence of women."[26]

---

23. Ibid., 2:53. This should not surprise us unduly, a historian might be imagined to remark, since Descartes's philosophical contribution in the area of human-animal relations was to hone to razor sharpness an already obdurate anthropocentrism whose essential elements had originally been forged by Artistotle and the Stoics and widely disseminated in antiquity (see Gary Steiner, "Descartes, Christianity, and Contemporary Speciesism," in *A Communion of Subjects: Animals in Religion, Science, and Ethics*, ed. Paul Waldau and Kimberley Patton [New York: Columbia University Press, 2006], esp. 120–23). Philo, e.g., in his dialogue *De animalibus* follows the Aristotelian-Stoic line (see Ingvild Saelid Gilhus, *Animals, Gods and Humans: Changing Attitudes to Animals in Greek, Roman and Early Christian Ideas* [New York: Routledge, 2006], 42–44).

24. Derrida, *Beast and the Sovereign*, 2:56. In the case of the Son of Man, the little island has designs on bigger islands: "And when the Son of Man comes in his glory … all the nations will be assembled before him" (Matt 25:31–32). Derrida is much taken with James Joyce's postcolonial take on *Robinson Crusoe*—"the prefiguration of an imperialist, colonialist sovereignty, the first herald of the British empire, the great island setting off to conquer other islands, smaller islands (like Ireland) but above all islands bigger than it, like Africa, New Zealand or Australia" (Derrida, *Beast and the Sovereign*, 2:16; paraphrasing James Joyce, "Daniel Defoe," *BS* 1 [1964]: 1–25).

25. See Derrida, *Beast and the Sovereign*, 2:54. Appropriately enough, the SV translation of the gospels renders *ho huios tou anthrōpou* in Matthew and throughout as "the Son of Adam."

26. Derrida, *Beast and the Sovereign*, 2:54. Adam's Hebrew name, *ha-'ādām*, means just that—"the man."

For sovereignty is indeed the issue here, and sovereignty is a solitary affair. On Crusoe's island "there is a sort of slave [Friday], there are some animals and nobody else."[27] On the Man's island, too, there are slaves of a sort. Disciples stand in the same relation to their teacher as slaves (*douloi*) do to their master, as the Man unequivocally declares in 10:24–25 (cf. 8:9); while in certain of his parables the Man styles himself the master of the house (*ho oikodespotēs*) and those who serve him his slaves (13:24–30; 20:1–16; 24:45–51; cf. 12:29; 21:33–43).[28] When the Man becomes undisputed sovereign of all, arriving "in his glory" to sit on "the throne of his glory," his slaves morph into the docile sheep they always were in any case ("he will set the sheep at his right hand" [25:31–33; cf. 10:16; 26:31]). "That's sovereignty," exclaims Derrida, "that's solitary and exceptional sovereignty: slave, animal, and no woman. No desire to come along and limit sovereignty."[29] For sovereignty begins with self-sovereignty—self-discipline, self-control. Although Derrida is not discoursing on antiquity, no other principle better encapsulates the elite Greco-Roman concept of masculinity.[30] How might such a superior, self-controlled sovereign relate to his inferiors? What Derrida says of Defoe's protagonist applies equally well to Matthew's protagonist: "And the relation to savages as well as to women and beasts was the condescending, descending, vertical relation of a superior master to his slaves, … sovereign to his submissive subjects—submissive or submissible, mastered or to be mastered, by violence if need be—subjected."[31]

Savages, women, beasts. The dog-woman of Canaan embodies all three contiguous categories, always and at once. She was long seen as a savage or heathen, and never more insistently, perhaps, than when the modern, European, Christian empires engulfed the non-Christian peoples of Africa, the Americas, and other regions of the earth in their civilizing, missionizing maw. Typical of learned construals of the Canaanite

---

27. Ibid., 2:55.
28. See further Janice Capel Anderson and Stephen D. Moore, "Matthew and Masculinity," in *New Testament Masculinities*, ed. Moore and Anderson, SemeiaSt 45 (Atlanta: Society of Biblical Literature, 2003), 79–81.
29. Derrida, *Beast and the Sovereign*, 2:55.
30. See Stephen D. Moore and Janice Capel Anderson, "Taking It Like a Man: Masculinity in 4 Maccabees," in Moore, *The Bible in Theory: Critical and Postcritical Essays*, RBS 57 (Atlanta: Society of Biblical Literature, 2010), esp. 176–85.
31. Derrida, *Beast and the Sovereign*, 2:278.

woman pericope from this period and the assumptions that informed them is that of the Oxford don Willoughby C. Allen in his 1907 commentary on Matthew:

> It would seem, therefore, that the editor has rewritten Mk's narrative with a view to explaining how it was that Christ ... should have extended his compassion to a heathen woman. He did not enter into a house on heathen soil. Rather the woman came out to Him. At first He paid no attention to her entreaty.... When she still importuned Him, He told her that the children's bread, *i.e.* privileges intended for the Jews, should not be cast to dogs, *i.e.* to heathen women like herself.... As in the previous case of condescension to a heathen (8^{5-13}), faith forced the barrier of Christ's rule of working only among His own people.... Why does the editor lengthen the dialogue? Partly perhaps to heighten the effect. Not at once, and only because of the woman's earnest importunity, did Christ condescend to her. And partly, to explain the ambiguity of Mk 7^{27} "Let first the children be fed." There is no specific explanation given in Mk. of this "children." The reader is left, as the woman was, to apply it to the Jews as contrasted with the heathen (dogs).[32]

Elsewhere I have argued that the term "heathen" in a nineteenth- or early twentieth-century biblical commentary readily conjured up a contemporary as well as an ancient reality—the "unsaved" dark-skinned mass of polytheistic humanity in need of Christ, in need of civilizing, in need of colonizing.[33] Yet colonial-era commentaries like Allen's throw ordinarily unobserved features of Matthew's Gospel into cartoonish relief. Like a classic colonial master, the Matthean Son of Man—a Man among un-men,

---

32. Willoughby C. Allen, *A Critical and Exegetical Commentary on the Gospel according to S. Matthew*, ICC (Edinburgh: T&T Clark, 1907), 169.

33. Moore, *God's Beauty Parlor*, 158–65. Innumerable examples of the seamless rhetorical transition from the ancient to the modern heathen in biblical scholarship from this era could be cited. Particularly arresting, however, given our topic, is the following assertion from a discussion of Canaanite religion in a history of the world first published in 1894: "The accounts which have been preserved of the ceremonies around the altars of Astarte may well remind the reader of the frenzied violence and contortions of the howling dervishes who, to this day, in the countries of the Eastern Mediterranean, astonish the rational people of the West with their frightful rituals" (John Clark Ridpath, *With the World's People: An Account of the Ethnic Origin, Primitive Estate, Early Migrations, Social Evolution, and Present Conditions and Promise of the Principal Families of Men*, 12 vols. [Cincinnati: Jones Bros., 1912], 8:342).

so much so that men and women alike tend to morph into animals in his discourse, if not his presence—might seem to be the quintessential human being in Matthew, the very measure of the human, the Son of Humanity[34]—and never more conspicuously than when he is confronted by a woman who also happens to be a "heathen."

Yet matters are not quite so simple. The humanity of the Son of Humanity has already been thrown into question in the narrative—and by the Son of Humanity himself. A scribe pledging to follow him wherever he goes is cautioned: "Foxes have holes and birds of the sky have nests, but the Son of Humanity has nowhere to lay his head" (Matt 8:20). In his utter homelessness, his radical itinerancy, the Son of Humanity is more beastly than a fox, more creaturely than a bird. The latter comparison is especially significant, because elsewhere in the narrative the bird is singled out as a creature that is notably inferior to the human: "See the birds of the sky.... Are you not of more value than they?" (6:26); "Fear not, therefore; you are of more value than many sparrows" (10:31). In combination, these sayings place significant strain on the humanness of the Son of Humanity.

Nowhere is the animality of the Son of Humanity more evident, however, than in the manner of his death and the metaphors used of it. "The Son of Humanity is about to be betrayed into human hands," he predicts (17:22); but what will ensue when these hostile hands take hold of him will threaten to undo his masculinity and even his humanity. The atrocious abuses to his person that he must endure (20:18-19; 26:67-68; 27:26-50) will threaten to cause him to slide off the lower end of the ancient Mediterranean honor/shame gradient altogether—to slide even beyond "slavish" femininity and plummet into abject animality. That he will pass into death as an animal is suggested by his own performative interpretation of his death: "And taking a cup and giving thanks he gave it to them saying, 'Drink from it, all of you; for this is my blood of the covenant, which is poured out for many for the forgiveness of sins'" (26:27-28; cf. 20:28). The phrase "blood of the covenant" evokes Exod 24:8, and the blood there is that of sacrificed oxen (see 24:5). Through his words over the cup, the Son of Humanity identifies his impending slaughter as that

---

34. Recent biblical scholarship, Bible translation, and liturgical practice have effected a partial displacement of "the Son of Man," the traditional rendering of the title *ho huios tou anthrōpou* that occurs eighty-eight times in the New Testament, in favor of more inclusive renderings, notably, "the Son of Humanity," "the Human One," or "the Human Being."

of a sacrificial animal, whether the oxen of the Sinai covenant rite, which in Jewish tradition became a rite of expiation (cf. Heb 9:19–22), or the paschal lamb whose substitutionary slaughter is evoked by the Passover seder at which the Son of Humanity is officiating (Matt 26:1–2, 17–19). Either way, it is not on two legs but on four that the Son of Humanity will be led to the soteriological slaughterhouse. In a reversal of the regular sacrificial sequence, the Son of Humanity is first eaten as an animal and only afterwards is slaughtered as an animal. As such, he is eaten while still alive. Even the metaphor he earlier used to describe his internment in the grave bespeaks his ingestion—his abject, animalizing descent into the belly of the other: "For just as Jonah was in the belly of the sea monster [*en tē koilia tou kētous*] for three days and three nights, so will the Son of Humanity be in the heart of the earth for three days and three nights" (12:40).

In the performative words uttered over the wine, then, and also over the bread ("Take, eat; this is my body" [26:26]), the Son of Humanity enacts an endlessly domesticated abomination that thoroughly contaminates any clean line between humanity and animality. In effect, Derrida parses out the logic of this abomination in *Robinson Crusoe*, a novel obsessed with cannibalism.[35] To be swallowed by the sea through drowning, or the earth through earthquake, is a terrible thing. To be devoured by a fellow living creature is more terrible still—but not because the creature is more other, more alien, than the earth or the sea. The wild beast or sea monster that devours me is less different from me than the earth or the sea. Still closer to me, however, is the cannibal who eats my flesh and drinks my blood: only a fellow anthropoid can be anthropophagic. But the cannibal's "alterity is the more marked for being less marked," as Derrida remarks.[36] The cannibal is more similar to the person being devoured than is the wild beast, but paradoxically the cannibal is also less similar, because the cannibal "eats his fellow, and thus becomes inhuman."[37] One would not say

---

35. The vexed historical question of whether or to what extent cannibalism was, or is, a product of the European colonial imagination is beyond the scope of this chapter. For explorations of the role(s) of cannibalism in colonial discourse, see Francis Barker, Peter Hulme, and Margaret Iversen, eds., *Cannibalism and the Colonial World* (Cambridge: Cambridge University Press, 1998); Barbara Creed and Jeanette Hoorn, eds., *Body Trade: Captivity, Cannibalism and Colonialism in the Pacific* (New York: Routledge, 2001); Graham Huggan and Helen Tiffin, *Postcolonial Ecocriticism: Literature, Animals, Environment* (New York: Routledge, 2010), 168–75.

36. Derrida, *Beast and the Sovereign*, 2:139.

37. Ibid., 2:142.

of the wild beast that it is "inhuman, inhumanly cruel."[38] "To have lost human dignity by being inhuman is reserved for humans alone, and in no way for the sea, the earth, or the beast. Or the gods. One does not say of beasts or of God that they are inhuman. Only humans are said to be inhuman,"[39] and never more so than when they are devouring dismembered members of their own species.

How might all or any of this apply to Matthew's Last Supper?[40] The inhuman abomination that is the execution by torture of the Son of Humanity—his savage scourging, his cruel crucifixion—is preceded by a still more inhuman abomination: his being eaten alive by those who are closest to him—indeed, as close as family ("And stretching forth his hand toward his disciples he said, 'Behold my mother and my brothers!'" [12:49; cf. 10:35–37; 12:50; 19:29; 25:40]). At the Last Supper, through the performative magic of the "words of institution," the Son of Humanity surrounds himself with flesh-eating, bloodthirsty cannibals, who, however, are also his most intimate kin, who devour his about-to-be-shredded body and drink his about-to-be-spilled blood. In that moment, they are no longer human but inhuman. But because they are acting on the orders of the Son of Humanity himself—the Human One—he becomes the Inhuman One in this scene. The profoundly unstable distinction between humanity and animality evident throughout this gospel here collapses altogether. This disintegration is anticipated in certain of the narrative's earlier scenes, most obviously the two miraculous feeding episodes, with their routinely remarked eucharistic elements, their hungry, impatient anticipations of the Last Supper (see esp. 14:19–20; 15:35–36)—but also in the Canaanite woman episode.

"Even the dogs eat the crumbs that fall from their masters' table," mumbles the woman, groveling in the dust (15:27). "It may even be that the bread should be considered a symbol of salvation (cf. the feeding stories)," muse W. D. Davies and Dale C. Allison. "That the table too is symbolic, intended to allude to the Lord's table (cf. 1 Cor 10.21), is, however, too

---

38. Ibid., 2:140.
39. Ibid., 2:141.
40. "Eating is, after all, the great mystery of Christianity," as Derrida elsewhere observes ("An Interview with Jacques Derrida on the Limits of Digestion," conducted by Daniel Birnbaum and Anders Olsson, *e-flux* 2 [2009], https://tinyurl.com/SBL0691b).

much," they add.[41] Yet they have led us to that table by raising the possibility that the bread is "a symbol of salvation": what can that mean other than that the torn bread may be taken to symbolize the torn, sacrificial body of the (In)human One offered to his hungry disciples as the main course of his Last Supper with them? Davies and Allison also usher us to this gory table—actually a stone table, an altar, crimson with blood and littered with cuts of meat—by their suggestion that the *kyriōn* ("masters"/"lords") of 15:27, usually taken to refer to the Jewish people, might "[stand] in effect only for Jesus," the plural being required by the anterior context, that is, by 15:26: "The one plural, 'dogs,' demands the other plural, 'masters.'"[42] The dog-woman's response to the (In)human One might then be paraphrased as: "Yes, Lord, yet even us gentile dogs are permitted to gorge on the gobbets of flesh that fall from your sacrificial table."[43]

---

41. Davies and Allison, *Critical and Exegetical Commentary*, 2:553. Although they do not say so explicitly, Davies and Allison may be recoiling from earlier, more extravagant, precritical ascriptions of a eucharistic subtext to the Canaanite woman pericope. Particularly notable is Thomas Cranmer's 1548 addition to the Anglican communion liturgy: "We do not presume to come to this thy table, O Merciful Lord, trusting in our own righteousness, but in thy manifold and great mercies: *we be not worthy so much as to gather up the crumbs under thy table*: but thou art the same Lord, whose property is always to have mercy: Grant us therefore, gracious Lord, so to eat the flesh of thy dear Son Jesus Christ, and to drink his blood in these holy Mysteries, that we may continually dwell in him, and he in us, that our sinful bodies may be made clean by his body, and our souls washed through his most precious blood. Amen" (quoted in Nancy Klancher, *The Taming of the Canaanite Woman: Constructions of Christian Identity in the Afterlife of Matthew 15:21–28*, SBR 1 [Berlin: de Gruyter, 2013], 263, emphasis added).

42. Davies and Allison, *Critical and Exegetical Commentary*, 2:555–56; so also Stephenson Humphries-Brooks, "The Canaanite Women in Matthew," in Levine and Blickenstaff, *Feminist Companion to Matthew*, 143–44.

43. Jin Young Choi makes a compelling case for a eucharistic reading of the Syrophoenician woman's parallel utterance in Mark 7:28, first noting how its feeding theme is bracketed by Jesus's feeding of the five thousand (6:30–44) and of the four thousand (8:1–10), both feeding miracles employing phrases that anticipate the Last Supper. When due weight is accorded to this encompassing context, the woman may be said to apprehend and anticipate "Jesus' body as being broken and shared with the *ochlos* [crowd] and thereby giving life to it, regardless of gender, ethnicity, and religion," while the healing of the woman's daughter is brought about when she metaphorically "eats the crumbs of bread" that are "the body of Jesus" (Choi, *Postcolonial Discipleship of Embodiment*, 97, 99, 100).

This eucharistic construal of the woman's response would complete the narrative's construction of her as uncannily cognizant of Jesus's identity and mission ("Lord, Son of David.... She worshiped him"). But what else can she be said to know? She seems to know that the distinction between sheep and dogs to which her interlocutor appeals ("I was sent only to the lost sheep of the house of Israel.... It is not fair to take the children's bread and toss it to the dogs") is a treacherously unstable one. The dog-woman's problem, Jesus would seem to be saying, is that she is not a sheep-woman. The more basic problem, she would seem to be replying, is that the sheep Jesus has culled from the flock to follow him must soon metamorphose into dogs so as to be able to heed their master's command to devour his flesh and drink his blood, while he himself must morph into a sheep or some other sacrificial animal so that the ghastly feast may occur.

Yet it is not the meal but the woman who has most often been an object of disgust. For many Christian readers through the ages, the term "Canaanite" in Matt 15:22 has elicited automatic revulsion for an ethnic other whose most abominable association was the ultimate "crime against nature": child sacrifice (Lev 18:21; 20:2–4; 2 Kgs 16:3; 23:10; 2 Chr 28:3; 33:6; Jer 7:31; 32:35; Ezek 16:36).[44] This iconic crime is surely the primary reason why John Chrysostom long ago declared that the Canaanite woman calls to mind "those wicked nations, who overturned from their foundations the very laws of nature" (*Hom. Matt.* 52.1 [*NPNF*]). Paradoxically, however, concern for her child is the overriding trait of the Canaanite woman in our episode, while the Human One's initial response to the child's plight is so uncaring, so callous, as to invite the terms "inhuman" or "unnatural."

---

44. For a recent devotional example, see Mitch Woodard, *What If God? A Personal Devotion/Bible Study* (Bloomington, IN: WestBow, 2016), which thrusts the entire, imagined, demonized Canaanite religion into the arms of this female character: "What if God would use the illustration of a Gentile woman with a heritage of child sacrifice to show us He loves the entire world and desires that all would be saved? This particular woman was of the Canaanite people and their principal deity was Baal with a secondary deity named Asherah. The Canaanites believed Asherah was Baal's mother as well as his mistress. This belief led to immorality, religious prostitution and other wicked practices such as child sacrifice. The Canaanites were actually worshiping demons and these practices were detestable. God instructed His people to completely destroy every living being in the land of Canaan, which God had given His people as an inheritance. But, God in His mercy being the One that created and owns all souls knew the heart of this Canaanite woman who made her living as a prostitute" (106).

Much that is coded in the term "Canaanite," indeed, is more readily applicable to the Human One and his followers than to the dog-woman. The text anathemizes her by projecting abomination onto her, "abominable" being a virtual synonym for "Canaanite" (see especially Ezra 9:1, 11, 14; also Lev 18:21–30; 1 Kgs 14:23–24; 21:26; 2 Kgs 21:2; Jer 16:18; Ezek 8:9–10). The real locus of abomination in Matthew's narrative, however, is the detestable death torture of its protagonist, coupled with the still more abominable preenactment of that punitive execution: the anthropophagic devouring of his atrociously abused, altogether animalized body by those whom he earlier designated his true family (12:49). At the heart of this symbolic abomination, then, is a savaging of conventional familial bonds, the mother and the brothers wolfing down the living flesh and warm blood of the "beloved son" (3:17; 12:18; 17:5).

Queering the Last Supper

All of this returns us to the intricate operations of queer temporality in Matthew's narrative. A prominent facet of queer temporality passed over in our earlier discussion of it is elucidated by J. Jack Halberstam: "Queer subcultures produce alternative temporalities by allowing their participants to believe that their futures can be imagined according to logics that lie outside of those paradigmatic markers of life experience—namely, birth, marriage, reproduction, and death." Again: "Queer time … is … about the potentiality of a life unscripted by the conventions of family, inheritance, and child rearing."[45] By this definition, the Matthean Jesus would be an ancient exemplar of an alternative temporality that invites the label "queer." His life, offered as a model to his disciples (Matt 4:18–22; 10:1, 24–25a; 11:29; 16:24; 19:10–12, 27–29; 20:22–23; 21:20–21; 23:8, 10; 28:19–20), is unscripted by the ancient Mediterranean institutions of

---

45. Halberstam, *In a Queer Time and Place*, 2. In effect, Elizabeth Freeman's musings on time take up where Halberstam's leave off. In the introduction to *Time Binds*, Freeman writes: "Throughout this book, I try to think against the dominant arrangement of time and history" (xi). Freeman coins the term *chrononormativity* to name the process whereby "naked flesh is bound into socially meaningful embodiment through temporal regulation," the goal being "maximum productivity" (3). For Freeman, temporal regulation and economic regulation are inextricably intertwined and reproduction is subordinated to production.

marriage, biological progeny, conventional labor, or material inheritance.[46] His conception and birth take place outside the institutional structures of marriage (1:18–25),[47] yet not so far outside as to fail to trouble those structures, to fissure the supports that buttress them. As an adult, he himself eschews marriage and even sex, and hence biological sons and heirs. He seduces his male disciples into abandoning their own marriages (4:18–22; 8:14; 19:27–29; cf. 10:35–37) and holds eunuchhood up to them as an ultimate model: "For there are eunuchs [*eunouchoi*] who were born thus from the womb of their mother, and there are eunuchs who were made eunuchs by human beings, and there are eunuchs who made themselves eunuchs on account of the kingdom of heaven. Let anyone accept this who can" (19:12).[48] The movement inaugurated by the Matthean Jesus, then, can be reconceived as a queer subculture productive of an alternative temporality that is implicitly anti-imperial, entailing as it does a present and a future imagined according to logics that lie outside the paradigmatic markers of ancient Mediterranean life experience. The Matthean Jesus and his disciples do not run on Roman time.[49]

---

46. For an in-depth study of the gospel Jesuses and the historical Jesus in their relationships to ancient household structures, see Halvor Moxnes, *Putting Jesus in His Place: A Radical Vision of Household and Kingdom* (Louisville: Westminster John Knox, 2003), esp. 22–71.

47. See Thomas Bohache, "Matthew," in *The Queer Bible Commentary*, ed. Deryn Guest et al. (London: SCM, 2006), 496.

48. Further on this remarkable pronouncement, unique to Matthew, see Anderson and Moore, "Matthew and Masculinity," 87–91; Moxnes, *Putting Jesus in His Place*, 72–90; J. David Hester, "Eunuchs and the Postgender Jesus: Matthew 19.12 and Transgressive Sexualities," *JSNT* 28 (2005): 13–40; Bohache, "Matthew," 507–11; Rick Franklin Talbott, "Imagining the Matthean Eunuch Community: Kyriarchy on the Chopping Block," *JFSR* 22 (2006): 21–43; Stephen R. Llewelyn, Gareth J. Wearne, and Bianca L. Sanderson, "Guarding Entry to the Kingdom: The Place of Eunuchs in Mt. 19.12," *JSHJ* 10 (2012): 228–46.

49. Neither does Paul seem to run on Roman time, least of all in 1 Cor 7, proclaiming "it is well for a man not to touch a woman" (7:1); "to the unmarried and the widows I say that it is well for them to remain unmarried as I am" (7:8); "concerning virgins … I think that, in view of the impending crisis, it is well for you to remain as you are" (7:25–26), and other antinormative injunctions—not that Paul can blithely be assimilated with the queer in its most radical forms, nor can the Matthean Jesus or any other ancient Jesus. But it is interesting to note that queer time is not entirely out of joint with the charter documents of Christian culture.

4. The Dog-Woman of Canaan

Not unexpectedly, then, the scene that represents the most spectacular symbolic assault on the institution of the family in this narrative—the Last Supper, that most unsettling of family meals—also evinces the narrative's most spectacular example of queer temporality. The sacrificial meal is bloodless (which, of course, is why Christian theology and piety have been able to digest it so painlessly), but the torturous death from which the meal derives its efficacy is not. Although narratively anterior to the atrocious death, the meal so presupposes the animalizing slaughter that the slaughter can be said to precede the meal, as with any regular sacrificial rite. Time bends and warps once again in the Matthean narrative, as it already did in the Canaanite woman episode that anticipated this ghoulish feast, and once again it twists around themes that make that bending queer, those themes being the natural and the normal interlaced with the familial bonds and biological ties designed to hold them in place. Jesus's disciples, it will be recalled, are his true family, his closest relatives, the fictive kin who earlier displaced his biological kin ("Someone said to him, 'Look, your mother and brothers are standing outside, seeking to speak to you.' But he answered..., 'Who is my mother, and who are my brothers?' And stretching forth his hand toward his disciples he said, 'Behold my mother and my brothers!'" [12:47–49]). Prior to the Last Supper, then, Jesus is already the head of a queer family, a homosocial household (see also 10:35–37; 19:29). It is only at the Last Supper, however, that this already aberrant family bursts every residual natural or normal human bond. And just as in the Canaanite woman episode, the colonial cauldron is what causes time and causality in the Last Supper episode to warp and species distinctions to queer and dissolve. For it is on a colonial cross that the Human One must be subjected to sacrificial animal slaughter, and it is in the long shadow of that looming cross that his fictive kin must themselves mutate into dogs to devour his flesh and lap up his blood, just as the dog-woman foretold.

The Colonial Bestiary

Why are human/animal distinctions so fraught, so tension-laden in Matthew's Gospel? What is in play, arguably, is an internalized discourse of animalization. The anathematized ethnic other, the idolatrous and abominable "Canaanite," is animalized in this Jewish text. "Canaan" is animalized and also feminized, made to grovel abjectly at the feet of "Israel" in the person of the Son of David (Matt 15:22, 25).[50] But because the Jewish community out of which the narrative has come is itself part of a conquered people, is itself dependent on the crumbs that fall from its Roman master's table, it is already soiled by the animalizing discourse with which it daubs the Canaanite woman. "When the colonist speaks of the colonized he uses zoological terms," Frantz Fanon flatly states. "Allusion is made to the slithery movements of the yellow race, the odors from the 'native' quarter, to the hordes, the stink, the swarming, the seething, and the gesticulations."[51] And, no doubt, to every perceived filthy habit or craven disposition that elicits the contemptuous epithet "dog." Colonists of every age have had ready recourse to the colonial bestiary, not least those of the ancient Mediterranean world.[52]

Fanon adds spiritedly: "The colonized … roar with laughter every time they hear themselves called an animal by the other. For they know they are not animals."[53] But the colonizer's laughter is even louder when the colonized attempts to turn the animalizing barbs back on him, so con-

---

50. The abject elements of the scene are those the Christian artistic tradition has most often picked up on through the ages. As Nancy Klancher notes, "The Canaanite woman most often appears on her knees, desperate, submissive, and pleading" (*Taming of the Canaanite Woman*, 287).

51. Frantz Fanon, *The Wretched of the Earth*, trans. Richard Philcox (New York: Grove, 2004), 7.

52. In the ancient world, animalizing language was commonly applied to slaves, and at the highest levels of discourse, ranging from Aristotle's assimilation of slaves to domestic animals to the Roman Lex Aquilia's judicial equation of slaves with such animals. See Keith Bradley, "Animalizing the Slave: The Truth of Fiction," *JRS* 90 (2000): 110–25; Catherine Hezser, *Jewish Slavery in Antiquity* (Oxford: Oxford University Press, 2005), 55–68. Myles Lavan has shown how the Roman conquest of ethnic others "is often described in terms of breaking animals to harness," and "since slaves are often assimilated to domesticated animals, these animalizing metaphors resonate with the broader language of enslavement" (*Slaves to Rome: Paradigms of Empire in Roman Culture*, CCS [Cambridge: Cambridge University Press, 2013], 83; see further 83–88). Cicero identified Jews, along with Syrians, to be "peoples born to be slaves" (*nationibus natis servituti* [*Prov. cons.* 5.10]) and also declared: "[The Jewish] nation has shown by armed resistance what it thinks of our rule; how dear it was to the immortal gods is shown by its having been conquered, subjected to taxes, made a slave" (*Flac.* 28.69 [my trans.]). Animalizing epithets are implicitly entailed in such pronouncements, given Roman ethnic logics, and it is hardly a stretch to imagine such epithets being hurled explicitly at Jews in many ancient contexts (see Hezser, *Jewish Slavery in Antiquity*, 61).

53. Fanon, *Wretched of the Earth*, 8.

fident is he that he is the absolute antithesis of the animal. The Matthean Pilate inwardly laughs this complacent laugh of the colonizer as he condemns the "King of the Jews" (27:11, 29, 37; cf. 2:2; 21:5) to a dehumanizing, animalizing slaughter. In reducing Jesus to meat, Pilate relinquishes his own humanity. Yet the only character in Matthew's narrative explicitly consigned to the colonial bestiary is the first woman who dares to address Jesus directly and is doubly labeled a Canaanite and a dog. Small wonder that Pilate laughs silently, unheard even by the implied audience, as the self-proclaimed Human One, the Not-a-Beast, is dragged away to be butchered.

5
The Inhuman Acts of the Holy Ghost

> Ghosts are the paradigmatic figure for ... historical limit-cases, often appearing ... as tactile experiences not only of dead people but also repressed events and social formations.
> —Elizabeth Freeman, *Time Binds*

> The Holy Ghost attests to me in every city that bonds and afflictions await me.
> —Acts 20:23

Queer theory has never been content to limit its analytic appetites to sexual queerness, or even to sex of any stripe, queer or straight. Even before the moniker *queer theory* had been coined, queer theory *avant la lettre* had turned its attention to race and ethnicity and other forces that intersect with sex and sexuality.[1] In time, queer theory turned *to* time. Just as the inaugural works of queer theory sought to show that sex and gender, together with race and ethnicity, are neither natural nor innate but constructed, conventional, and political, the time-interrogating works of

---

1. The term *queer theory* was coined by Teresa de Lauretis (so the oft-recited saga goes), who organized a conference entitled "Queer Theory: Lesbian and Gay Sexualities" at the University of California, Santa Cruz in 1990, the proceedings of which were published as Teresa de Lauretis, ed., *Queer Theory: Lesbian and Gay Sexualities, differences* 3.2 (1991), and prefaced by a programmatic introduction by de Lauretis (iii–xviii). For the earlier, intersectional studies, see, most conspicuously, Audre Lorde, *Sister Outsider: Essays and Speeches* (Berkeley: Crossing, 1984); but see also Barbara Smith, *Toward a Black Feminist Criticism* (New York: Out & Out, 1977); Cherríe Moraga, *Loving in the War Years: Lo Que Nunca Pasó por Sus Labios* (Boston: South End, 1983); Gloria Anzaldúa, *Borderlands/La Frontera: The New Mestiza* (San Francisco: Aunt Lute, 1987); Hortense Spillers, "Mama's Baby, Papa's Maybe: An American Grammar Book," *Diacritics* 17.2 (1987): 65–81.

queer theory that later followed sought to show that seemingly unassailably commonsensical categories like past, present, and future, together with history, chronology, and periodicity, are no less culturally constructed, no less politically contingent, no less intimately informed by the (il)logics of power and desire. Queer theories of time are associated with such names as Carolyn Dinshaw, Lee Edelman, J. Jack Halberstam, José Muñoz, and Elizabeth Freeman,[2] as we saw earlier, and all these theories offer defamiliarizing and disorienting lenses through which to refocus biblical studies, a discipline founded on certain seemingly solid assumptions about the relationship of past and present and about history and historiography. Two further theorists of queer temporality, however, Carla Freccero and Madhavi Menon, prove even more useful for the present chapter, a critical reflection on ancient and modern historiography centered on the Gospel of Luke and the Acts of the Apostles. Later in the chapter, the related but differently focused work of Grace M. Cho becomes crucial for picking up where Menon and Freccero leave off and steering the discussion deeper into nonhuman territory.

Unhistorical Criticism

Freccero and Menon each provide vignettes of certain enabling assumptions in the field of early modern literature in which they work that mirror corresponding assumptions in the field of biblical studies. Freccero names "a version of historicism" centered on "periodization," "the past's differences from the present," and "anti-anachronism," such historicism being "what most resist[s] queering in [her] field."[3] Menon, meanwhile (and

---

2. Dinshaw, *Getting Medieval*; Dinshaw, *How Soon Is Now? Medieval Texts, Amateur Readers, and the Queerness of Time* (Durham, NC: Duke University Press, 2012); Edelman, *No Future*; Halberstam, *In A Queer Time and Place*; Muñoz, *Cruising Utopia*; Freeman, *Time Binds*.

3. Carla Freccero, "Queer Times," in *After Sex? On Writing since Queer Theory*, ed. Janet Halley and Andrew Parker, SerQ (Durham, NC: Duke University Press, 2011), 17–18. Significantly, Freccero associates these assumptions not with traditionalists in her field (although they would surely share them) but with queer historians such as David Halperin and Valerie Traub. Freccero and Menon have both formulated their best-known historiographical arguments in relation to the history of sexuality, although both of them also see those arguments as applicable to history and historiography more broadly. In this chapter, I focus on that broader applicability so as to maximize the relevance of their arguments to Luke-Acts, scholarship on Luke-Acts,

I engage with her work first), sets up the foil of a traditionally minded Shakespearean scholar who assumes that "any understanding of what Shakespeare means in our time must begin with an acknowledgment of his distance from us, for only then can we be sure that what we find in his work are his concerns rather than our own projections."[4] An unremarkable assumption, to be sure, and one that, *mutatis mutandis*, has been and continues to be foundational for historical critics of the Bible. More remarkable is Menon's construal of that commonplace notion. "[This] embrace of difference as the template for relating past and present produces a compulsory heterotemporality," she argues in her monograph *Unhistorical Shakespeare*, building on a manifesto-like article titled "Queering History" she had earlier published together with Jonathan Goldberg.[5] "Anything other than heterohistoricism," avers Menon, is assumed to be "a projection of the present onto the past"; implicitly, at least, it amounts to a "dismissal of a narcissism that veers too close to a love of the 'same.'"[6] The "same," the "homo," is "actively abject[ed] … in order to assert the triumph of the hetero that historicism has deemed its fit and proper subject."[7] Refocused through Menon's lens, then, the biblical historical critic becomes a heterohistorical critic, and the heterohistory that is his or her professional obsession is, on Menon's account, a "homophobic heterohistory."[8]

What is the other of heterohistory? What, indeed, but *homohistory*? Menon colludes with historicism's abject, homo-tainted narcissism to craft

---

and biblical scholarship in general. In Freccero's terms, I engage in an exploration of queer temporality that further dislodges queerness "from its gossamer attachment to sexuality by thinking 'queer' as a critique of (temporal) normativity *tout court* rather than sexual normativity specifically" ("Queer Times," 21).

4. Madhavi Menon, *Unhistorical Shakespeare: Queer Theory in Shakespearean Literature and Film* (New York: Palgrave Macmillan, 2008), 2; quoting David Scott Kastan, *Shakespeare after Theory* (New York: Routledge, 1999), 17.

5. Menon, *Unhistorical Shakespeare*, 1; Goldberg and Menon, "Queering History," 1608–17. Also relevant are Menon, "Period Cramps," in *Queer Renaissance Historiography: Backward Gaze*, ed. Vin Nardizzi, Stephen Guy-Bray, and Will Stockton (Farnham, UK: Ashgate, 2009), 229–35; Menon, "Introduction: Queer Shakes," in *Shakesqueer: A Queer Companion to the Complete Works of William Shakespeare*, ed. Menon (Durham, NC: Duke University Press, 2011), 1–27; and Goldberg's early but programmatic article, "The History That Will Be," *GLQ* 1 (1995): 385–403.

6. Menon, *Unhistorical Shakespeare*, 2.

7. Ibid., 14.

8. Ibid., 2.

the concept of a homohistory whose other name would be *unhistoricism*.⁹ Unhistoricism, for Menon, is not, however, ahistorical or antihistorical.¹⁰ Unhistoricism and homohistory rather name a queered mode of historiography that is attracted to homo sameness—similarity, proximity, anachronism¹¹—over hetero difference—sociocultural dissimilarity, chronological distance, aversion to anachronism. Menon cites Michel de Certeau's assertion that modern Western historiography begins with the systematic differentiation of the past from the present.¹² Rethinking heterohistory as homohistory, therefore, would necessitate rethinking and reinventing the most intractable assumptions of modern Western historiography— including those of biblical historical criticism.

As such, a work like Luke-Acts, deemed a history of Jesus and the early church by innumerable non-scholars and not a few scholars, becomes a potential model for a queered biblical historical criticism, for a biblical homohistorical criticism or a biblical unhistorical criticism. For Luke-Acts is itself a homohistory, an unhistory, of Jesus and earliest Christianity. What Menon terms "the homotemporal effect," a time-flattening effect that folds the present into the past and the past into the present, is everywhere evident in Luke-Acts.¹³ In particular, the Lukan Jesus is not "the historical Jesus," as we are wont to say, the heterohistorical Jesus who is different from, and other to, any and every gospel Jesus. The Lukan Jesus is rather the homohistorical Jesus who embodies a flattening and folding of difference and otherness into sameness, who is the Jesus of Luke's present, festooned with the christological titles of that present: Christ, Lord, Son of God, Son of Man, Savior. That present Jesus is retrojected into the past as Luke narrates his unhistory, and that past

---

9. "Unhistoricism's investment in homohistory echoes the 'homo' of a homosexuality deemed narcissistic" (ibid., 3). See further Valerie Traub, "The New Unhistoricism in Queer Studies," *PMLA* 128 (2013): 21–39. The unhistoricism that Traub critiques is mainly located in the fields of early modern French and English literature and its main exemplars are Freccero, Goldberg, and Menon.

10. Menon, *Unhistorical Shakespeare*, 3.

11. Terms taken from Goldberg and Menon, "Queering History," 1609.

12. Menon, *Unhistorical Shakespeare*, 3–4; citing Michel de Certeau, *The Writing of History*, trans. Tom Conley, EP (New York: Columbia University Press, 1988), 2.

13. Menon, *Unhistorical Shakespeare*, 6. I am setting aside for the moment all the well-documented ways in which Luke has done due diligence as an (ancient) historian. My assumption is that he has not done so in order to produce heterohistory, as Menon defines the term.

Jesus's future titles become his present property. Luke's homohistorical and unhistorical Jesus is the present become past and the past become future present.

Of course, the homohistoricity of Luke's Jesus is not merely a matter of titles but also of words and deeds. Thoroughly homo, for example, is the mesmerizing reading from the scroll of the prophet Isaiah performed by an illiterate peasant[14] in the Nazareth synagogue (Luke 4:16–20)—a peasant who, however, has been rendered literate by the homotemporal effect so that the literate Luke can present him to the literate Theophilus (1:3; Acts 1:1) for the latter's admiration and edification. The point is not that the homohistorical Jesus is incapable of uttering hetero truth; the point is rather that the homohistorical Jesus tirelessly smudges the line between pastness and presentness and between history and unhistory, thereby constantly causing the hetero to fold into the homo in his words and deeds. The homotemporal effect is yet more evident and insistent, moreover, in Luke's unhistory of the early church. Most obviously, heterotemporality appears to be all but absent from the speeches of Acts. They are all Luke's own speeches, apparently, homohistorical drag king performances in a Peter costume (2:14–36; 3:12–26; 10:34–43), a Stephen costume (7:2–53), and several Paul costumes (13:16–41; 17:22–31; 22:1–21; 24:10–21; 26:2–23).

All of this is a source of pained perplexity and perverse pleasure for the heterohistorical critic. This critic longs to hear the voice of the author of Luke-Acts, yet is constitutionally incapable of hearing it directly, of allowing himself or herself to be enveloped in the work's homotemporal embrace. The critic can hear the author's voice only as coming from a vast distance and through complex cultural relays. To hear this maddeningly elusive voice, to decipher its faint echo, the critic must engage in an immense and elaborate project of paraphrastic translation. Craig Keener, to cite the most prodigious exemplar to date of this project, tells us that the purpose of his four-volume commentary on Acts is to "reconstruct … how this text would have been heard by the audience for which its author(s) constructed it,"[15] and Keener proceeds to devote 4,459 pages to that auditory task. Keener's Luke speaks, but in a language far more arcane than

---

14. Which is what I take the heterohistorical, prechristological Jesus to have been.

15. Craig S. Keener, *Acts: An Exegetical Commentary*, 4 vols. (Grand Rapids: Baker Academic, 2012–2015), 1:17.

Koine Greek. As Menon remarks of comparable historical scholarship in her own field:

> The burden placed on the past is thus not only to speak, but also to speak incoherently to contrast the coherence of the present.... Even as the past is encouraged to speak for itself and to us, it is we who must speak for the past and to the present. Our language must be clear and self-identical so we can translate the incoherent gobbledygook of past ages. In such a hetero framework, the "present" becomes a monad against which all difference is measured, temporally and teleologically. Rather than being understood as perpetually intertwined with sameness, difference is here relegated to a different place and a hetero time.[16]

Keener performs to perfection this suppression of present difference, its subsumption into sameness, and the simultaneous relegation of difference to the remote past, which has become a hyperhetero time. Keener's full sentence from which I quoted earlier reads:

> Although I highly value and in my other work regularly emphasize learning from the perspectives of readers in a variety of [contemporary] cultures, our common basis for discussion across cultures is the text and (as best we can reconstruct it) how this text would have been heard by the audience for which its author(s) constructed it with ancient vocabulary, idioms, and cultural assumptions.[17]

But the heterohistorical critic's preoccupation with difference is only half the story—the pained perplexity portion, not the perverse pleasure portion. Why write four-and-a-half thousand pages on a work, on an author, from which and from whom one feels only distant and detached, removed and remote? What if the historical critic's love of difference, of the hetero, were secretly infected with a desire for sameness, for the homo? What if heterohistory were homohistory all along?

---

16. Menon, *Unhistorical Shakespeare*, 12. Menon is here adapting Eve Kosofsky Sedgwick's *Epistemology of the Closet* (Berkeley: University of California Press, 1990), 44–48. Sedgwick cautions against "counterposing against the alterity of the past a relatively unified homosexuality that 'we' *do* 'know today.' ... 'Homosexuality as we conceive of it today' itself comprises ... a space of overlapping, contradictory, and conflictual definitional forces" (45, emphasis original).

17. Keener, *Acts*, 1:17.

5. The Inhuman Acts of the Holy Ghost   91

Touching the Past

Historian Emily Robinson begins an article on affective historiography by quoting a fellow historian of an earlier generation on his numinous initial encounter with the historical archive:

> I saw ... bundles ... of documents, tied in dirty grey parcels, and ... an indescribable litter of parchments and papers ... [and a] floor ... powdered fine with the dust of broken seals.... Here was the actual past.... I could touch it and peer into it and savour its musty, faint but vivid perfume.... I could ... hear the whispering voices of men and women who, after the silence of centuries, had found a listener and were trying to speak. And gradually I learnt to attune my unaccustomed ears.[18]

As Robinson remarks, such touching, such savoring, such acute listening "is a powerful affective experience."[19] Classically it is conducted in the archive, which, as Achille Mbembe has observed, is a quasi-mystical space, a place where "fragments of lives and pieces of time are interred."[20] For New Testament scholars, the Nestle-Aland *Novum Testamentum Graece* is a moveable archive, a portable shrine. Within the paper vault that is its apparatus, the many moldering manuscripts to which it bears witness sit in orderly rows. We clutch the tome reverently like a totem or fetish. Its apparatus, dense with arcane symbols, conjures up ancient fragmentary documents in scarcely legible scripts, tokens of immense pastness, of unbridgeable temporal distance. Yet it is the expectation, the illusion,

---

18. Arthur Bryant, *The Lion and the Unicorn: A Historian's Testament* (London: Collins, 1969), 36; quoted in Emily Robinson, "Touching the Void: Affective History and the Impossible," *RH* 14 (2010): 503.

19. Robinson, "Touching the Void," 504. For further, differently oriented discussions of affective historiography, see Vanessa Agnew, "History's Affective Turn: Historical Reenactment and Its Work in the Present," *RH* 11 (2007): 299–312; Athena Athanasiou, "Towards a New Epistemology: The 'Affective Turn,'" *Historein* 8 (2012): 5–16; Alicia Marchant, ed., *Historicizing Heritage and Emotions: The Affective Histories of Blood, Stone, and Land from Medieval Britain to Colonial Australia* (New York: Routledge, 2017).

20. Achille Mbembe, "The Power of the Archive and Its Limits," in *Refiguring the Archive*, ed. Carolyn Hamilton et al. (Dordrecht: Kluwer Academic, 2002), 20–21; quoted in Robinson, "Touching the Void," 507. Simon Gikandi, too, reminds us that libraries are haunted by ghosts ("The Fantasy of the Library," *PMLA* 128 [2013]: 12).

of somehow "overcoming that difference, of bridging that distance" that confers an irresistible affective intensity on "the archival encounter."[21]

Why do historians feel a visceral urge to bury themselves in the past? There is an addictive affective dimension to historical work that is rarely admitted in the austere publications it yields but that lures historians into musty archives and archaeological digs and sends them down obstacle-bestrewn paper trails.[22] Even historians bold or rash enough to claim objectivity, disinterestedness, and dispassion for their work do not float free of affect. The passion for objectivity can itself be an intense emotion, "a ferocious devotion."[23] But why do even postpositivist historians "continue to pursue a past they know to be unreachable and unrepresentable?"[24] "The abstractions of theory cannot intrude upon the physical experience of holding a piece of the past," muses Robinson. "But what is the role of touching and feeling in the pursuit of knowing?" she wonders.[25] At issue is a reciprocity of touch.[26] The historian is touched by her sources as she touches them, reaching out blindly toward them through the temporal gloom.

Conjuring the Ghost

Carolyn Dinshaw's *Getting Medieval*, a catalytic work of affective historiography, is very much a book about touch, as she explains, most of all

---

21. Robinson, "Touching the Void," 513.
22. For an illuminating analysis of the affective stakes of the Nag Hammadi find, see Kotrosits, "Romance and Danger," 39–52. Among other things, Kotrosits argues that "the language of 'mystery' or 'intrigue' so often used to describe Nag Hammadi resonates with orientalist discourse of estrangement, of frustrated knowledge and frustrated representation.... The most common trope for selling books on these texts tends to be one of 'uncovering' secrets of the supposed Gnostics or 'revealing' the hidden history of Christianity, an echo of both the voyeurism and sexualized aggression in images of the Orient.... In the wake of orientalist epistemologies, the apparently opaque, esoteric, or mystical (might we say 'veiled'?) qualities of [these] texts ... are impossible to distinguish from those affective projections of the distanced and frustrated colonial gaze" (41).
23. Paul White, "Darwin's Emotions: The Scientific Self and the Sentiment of Objectivity," *Isis* 100 (2009): 825; quoted in Robinson, "Touching the Void," 511.
24. Robinson, "Touching the Void," 504.
25. Ibid., 508.
26. Ibid., 513.

a queer "touch across time" that "intentional[ly] collapse[s] … conventional historical time," thereby enabling identifications and relations with long dead persons and communities, relations that have "an affective or erotic component."[27] Dinshaw's time-folding, affect-infused reconception of historiography prompts certain programmatic questions—how best to conjure up the dead? how best to communicate with ghosts while doing history and being undone by it?—questions especially apropos of a historical or parahistorical work such as Luke-Acts for which death, resurrection, and ghostly persistence are insistent themes. This brings us back to Freccero, who, more even than Dinshaw, models arresting answers to such questions.

Like Menon, Freccero privileges the homo over the hetero in her historiographical practice, which is to say sameness and identification over difference and dissociation. Unlike Menon, however, and like Dinshaw—only more so—Freccero attends to the affective entanglements of the historiographic task, one she sees as an ethically fraught communion with ghosts. *Queer spectrality* is Freccero's term for a mode of historiography intimately attuned to affective investments in, and attachments to, those who are dead, even long dead, who refuse to die but live on as ghosts and, from beyond the grave, make ethical demands on the present and the future.[28]

If *touching* is Dinshaw's metaphor of choice for how past and present queerly connect, *haunting* is Freccero's, her name for how history impacts as affect in social and psychic life.[29] The past inhabits the present as a form

---

27. Dinshaw, *Getting Medieval*, 3, 12, 21, 39, 50; Dinshaw, "Got Medieval?," *Journal of the History of Sexuality* 10 (2001): 203. This article is Dinshaw's response to seven other articles on her *Getting Medieval*, most of them by scholars of religion, in this issue of the *Journal of the History of Sexuality*. For further engagement with Dinshaw's queer haptic historiography, see Marchal, "'Making History' Queerly."

28. "Queer Spectrality" is the long final chapter of Freccero's *Queer/Early/Modern*. A compressed version of the chapter appears as "Queer Spectrality: Haunting the Past," in *A Companion to Lesbian, Gay, Bisexual, Transgender, and Queer Studies*, ed. George E. Haggerty and Molly McGarry, BCCC (Oxford: Blackwell, 2007), 194–214.

29. Freccero, *Queer/Early/Modern*, 78. Freccero is channeling Derrida's concept of *hauntology*, a neologistic play on "ontology," the uncanny figure of the specter being, for Derrida, a ghost in the ontological machine, one that is neither fully present nor fully absent, neither fully dead nor fully alive. See Jacques Derrida, *Specters of Marx: The State of the Debt, the Work of Mourning and the New International*, trans. Peggy Kamuf (New York: Routledge, 1994). Hauntological reflections on early

of haunting; doing historiography in a mode acutely attuned to the lingering spectral presence of the past, therefore, entails openness to the possibility, indeed the necessity, "of being haunted, even inhabited, by ghosts."[30] The haunted historian has unsettling spectral visions and hears the whispering voices of long-deceased others echoing in her sources; these visions and voices are "hallucinatorily superimposed upon" the present, insisting and persisting within it.[31] Such historiography is a conscious exercise of fantasy and hence a source of intense pleasure to the practitioner.[32] But this pleasure is indissociable from pain, since spectral historiography also attempts to "describe and do justice to the historical and affective legacies"

Christian literature have included Denise Kimber Buell, "God's Own People: Specters of Race, Ethnicity, and Gender in Early Christian Studies," in *Prejudice and Christian Beginnings: Investigating Race, Gender, and Ethnicity in Early Christian Studies*, ed. Elisabeth Schüssler Fiorenza and Laura Nasrallah (Minneapolis: Fortress, 2009), 159–90; Buell, "Hauntology Meets Posthumanism: Some Payoffs for Biblical Studies," in Koosed, *Bible and Posthumanism*, 29–56; Benjamin H. Dunning, *Specters of Paul: Sexual Difference in Early Christian Thought*, Divinations (Philadelphia: University of Pennsylvania Press, 2011); Cavan W. Concannon, *When You Were Gentiles: Specters of Ethnicity in Roman Corinth and Paul's Corinthian Correspondence*, Synkrisis (New Haven: Yale University Press, 2014); Matthew James Ketchum, "Specters of Jesus: Ghosts, Gospels, and Resurrection in Early Christianity" (Ph.D. diss., Drew University, 2015); Peter N. McLellan, "Specters of Mark: The Second Gospel's Ending and Derrida's Messianicity," *Bibint* 24 (2016): 357–81. Buell and Ketchum both employ Avery Gordon's *Ghostly Matters: Haunting and the Sociological Imagination*, 2nd ed. (Minneapolis: University of Minnesota Press, 2008) in tandem with Derrida's *Specters of Marx*. Kotrosits, meanwhile, has recourse in her *Rethinking Early Christian Identity* to a concept of haunting that is influenced by Freccero as well as Gordon. She remarks: "Haunting turns out to be a recurring theme in this book, and one might very well consider this book something like a haunted history, since I repeatedly seek out lingering effects and wisps of the inconspicuous—things which are 'sensed' but perhaps not readily seen" (17). Also highly relevant are Donaldson, "Gospel Hauntings"; Choi, *Postcolonial Discipleship of Embodiment*, 63–84.

30. Freccero, *Queer/Early/Modern*, 80. As Gayatri Chakravorty Spivak earlier put it, herself channeling Derrida's hauntology: "You crave to let history haunt you as a ghost or ghosts, with the ungraspable incorporation of a ghostly body, and the uncontrollable, sporadic, and unanticipatable periodicity of haunting, in the impossible frame of the absolute chance of the gift of time, if there is any" ("Ghostwriting," *Diacritics* 25.2 [1995]: 70).

31. Freccero, *Queer/Early/Modern*, 9.

32. See Louise Fradenburg and Carla Freccero, "Introduction: Caxton, Foucault, and the Pleasures of History," in *Premodern Sexualities*, ed. Fradenburg and Freccero (New York: Routledge, 1996), xvii.

of past traumas,[33] whether the recent past or the remote past. For Freccero, queer spectrality conjures up "a mode of historical attentiveness" to the ways in which the past, but also the future, those no longer living and those not yet living, press upon us in the present with ethical insistence, thereby rendering the present "porous" and "permeable" in relation to the past and the future so that the present becomes "suffused with affect," compelling us to mourn as we look back but also enabling us to hope as we look forward.[34]

What might all or any of this mean for biblical studies? Freccero's challenge to the hegemonic historicisms in her own field of Renaissance studies[35] is, by extension, a challenge to the hegemonic historicisms in biblical studies. She calls us to acknowledge that our own historiographic investments are intimately infused with intense affective attachments and identifications, desires and fantasies; and rather than imagine that such "anachronistic" elements can be exorcised from our critical practices and communities of discourse, to allow ourselves instead to be openly haunted by them and by the long-dead subjects who continue to make spectral and ethical claims on us from beyond the grave.[36]

One long-dead subject who continues conspicuously to make spectral and ethical demands on many of us from beyond the grave is Jesus of Nazareth, and the Gospel of Luke and the Acts of the Apostles are two of the ventriloquistic textual vehicles through which he does so. Rather than take on, in what remains of this chapter, the improbably ambitious project of limning out the contours of an affective spectral homohistory of earliest Christianity, I content myself with reading Luke-Acts as a protohistory of such a project. Luke-Acts is a consummate exercise in homohistory, as we have already seen, but it is also a spectacular instance of queer spectrality. Luke's is the gospel that accords the most prominent role to the Holy Spirit, as is well known, a prominence that further increases in Acts, which once prompted John Chrysostom to style Acts as, in effect, the Acts of the Holy

---

33. Freccero, *Queer/Early/Modern*, 8–9, 79.
34. Ibid., 69–70.
35. A challenge she articulates in "Queer Times," 20–24.
36. For an attempt to approach the women prophets of 1 Cor 11:2–16 in much this way, in dialogue with Dinshaw, Freeman, Freccero and other time-attuned queer theorists, see Joseph A. Marchal, "How Soon Is (This Apocalypse) Now? Queer Velocities after a Corinthian Already and a Pauline Not Yet," in Brintnall, Marchal, and Moore, *Sexual Disorientations*.

Spirit (*Hom. Act.* 1.5). Acts, though, has also been dubbed the Gospel of the Holy Spirit, as has the actual gospel that is its prequel, and that gospel might equally be labeled the Acts of the Holy Spirit, since the Holy Spirit begets Jesus in it (Luke 1:35), descends upon him and possesses him as an adult (3:22), and thrusts him from place to place (4:1, 14) and action to action (4:18; 5:17b; 8:46; 10:21), Jesus himself all the while appearing to propel the plot.

But why not the Gospel and Acts of the Holy *Ghost*? Ghost was good enough, after all, for Wycliffe ("holy goost"—1380), Luther (*Heiliger Geist*—1522), Tyndale ("holy goost"—1534), GNV ("holy goost"—1557), DRB ("Holy Ghost"—1582), KJV ("Holy Ghost"—1611), RV ("Holy Ghost"—1881), and even NKJV ("Holy Ghost"—1979). Granted, ghost, in the contemporary sense of the term, frequently fails as a formal-equivalence rendering of ancient Greek *pneuma*[37]—although not in Luke 24:37, 39 ("They were spooked and terrified, thinking they saw a *pneuma*. And he said to them, … 'A *pneuma* does not have flesh and bones as you see I do' "),[38] where ghost seems to be precisely what *pneuma* means. Technicalities aside, however, ghost has certain advantages over the now more familiar *spirit* as a translation of *pneuma*. It dedomesticates the third of the three founding horrors of Christian theology, the hyperactive ghost taking its rightful place alongside the crucified man and the reanimated corpse. More importantly, ghost captures better than spirit the unsettling uncanniness, the disorienting queerness of *to pneuma to hagion* in Luke-Acts.[39]

---

37. In general, *ghost* seems better suited for the literal rendering of other ancient Greek words, such as *phasma*, *phantasma*, or *skia*.

38. Translations of the Gospel of Luke and the Acts of the Apostles in this chapter are my own. Otherwise I employ NRSV.

39. Just about every scholarly study of the Holy Spirit in Luke-Acts I have consulted assumes that the reader already knows what this spectral entity is—knows it as well as any old friend from Sunday school. The Holy Spirit is human, all too human, in too many of these studies, it seems to me, most of all those that emerge out of a Pentecostal context. Typical of such work is Odette Mainville's *The Spirit in Luke-Acts* (Woodstock, GA: The Foundation for Pentecostal Scholarship, 2016), in which the gender-neutral *to pneuma to hagion* is already an unequivocal "he" in the book's opening sentence: "The church of our century has given the Holy Spirit the place of honor he deserves" (1). Mainville's summary statement on the Spirit's role in Acts reads: "The Spirit intervenes abundantly in Acts: he speaks, inspires, decides, orders, directs, etc. He is really a personified force that carries out God's intentions or has them carried

5. The Inhuman Acts of the Holy Ghost

What is a ghost?[40] For Freccero, a ghost is a product of the "afterlife of trauma"; it returns "suffused with affective materiality" and registers on "subjectivity and history" with "demands that confound the temporalities we call past, present, and future."[41] Told in the afterlife of the twin traumas of the Roman crucifixion of Israel's Messiah and the Roman destruction of Israel's holy city and temple,[42] Luke-Acts is a ghost story. Telling a ghost story entails a desire to cause others to feel haunted and a willingness to feel haunted oneself.[43] But who or what is the entity that haunts the Acts of the Holy Ghost, and how does he, she, or it relate to the ostensible protagonist of the Gospel of the Holy Ghost, the Jesus whom s/he or it possesses and haunts?

"Among the contrasting models of history against which spectrality may be said to work," writes Freccero, "is a necrological model, which foregrounds the idea of burial," of the pastness of the past and the deadness of the dead.[44] Luke-Acts is not a necrology. Luke-Acts is indeed the tale of a dead man, but of a dead man who refuses to remain dead, which is why Luke-Acts is a ghost story. But the ghost who haunts Acts is not simply the ghost of Jesus, which is what makes this ghost story unusual. The Holy Ghost both is and is not the ghost of Jesus. The Holy Ghost *is* Jesus's ghost most obviously in Acts 16:7: "When [Paul and Timothy] had come opposite Mysia, they attempted to enter Bithynia, but the *pneuma* of Jesus did not allow them."[45] As this same Jesus was seen to expire or give

---

out" (2). As I argue in this chapter, the Spirit in Acts, as in Luke, is more and other than that.

40. Derrida poses this question early in *Specters of Marx* (10), and I could contentedly curl up in Derrida's text at this point and not emerge from it until the end of the chapter. But other scholarly ghost hunters have already tracked specters through early Christian literature in the company of Derrida and Gordon, as I noted earlier, and so I seek out other company and other paths in what remains.

41. Freccero, "Queer Times," 22.

42. Synecdoches, to be sure, of other more diffuse traumas. Kotrosits writes of "the thoroughly difficult to document phenomena of trauma and its associated affects" (*Rethinking Early Christian Identity*, 17).

43. See Freccero, *Queer/Early/Modern*, 75; also Halberstam, *In a Queer Time and Place*, 60: "Haunting is a mode within which the ghost demands something like accountability: to tell a ghost story means being willing to be haunted."

44. Freccero, *Queer/Early/Modern*, 70.

45. Presumably the border-guarding *pneuma* of Acts 16:7 is the same entity as the sermon-prohibiting *pneuma* of the preceding verse: "And they went through the region of Phrygia and Galatia, having been prevented by the holy *pneuma* from

up the ghost (*exepneusen*) in Luke 23:46, this is a further Lukan instance[46] of *pneuma* functionally meaning "ghost." Yet the Holy Ghost is also *not* the ghost of Jesus, even in Acts. For instance, it is not the Holy Ghost whose dread words, augmented by a blinding light, drive a terrified Saul to the ground on the road to Damascus (9:3–4; 22:6–7; 26:12–14). By any ordinary reckoning this is Jesus's ghost, but it is not identified as the Holy Ghost. There are at least two ghosts in Acts, then, even if the two are sometimes one.

Again, what is a ghost? Or as Clough puts it, "What is the ontological status of a ghosted body, of a haunted materiality?"[47] Again, too, Freccero's insistence that a ghost is a product of the "afterlife of trauma" is apposite. But Cho, who shares significant theoretical terrain with Clough, propels the ghost-trauma connection in a different if related direction in her searing monograph, *Haunting the Korean Diaspora*.[48] The capacity of trauma to move intergenerationally through time and space confers an uncanny agency on the ghost that is independent of both the human subjects who first experience the ghost-generating trauma and the human subjects who then inherit the trauma and hence the ghost. This is a deindividualized concept of haunting that makes the ghost at once subindividual and transindividual.[49] Cho writes: "When an unspeakable or uncertain his-

---

speaking the word in Asia" (16:6). As is often noted, the Holy Ghost and Jesus also play functionally interchangeable roles in Luke 12:11–12 ("for the holy *pneuma* will teach you in that very hour what you must say") and 21:12–15 ("for I [Jesus] will give you a mouth and wisdom that none of your opponents will be able to withstand or contradict").

46. In addition to Luke 24:37, 39, to which I alluded earlier.

47. Clough, "Introduction," in Clough and Halley, *Affective Turn*, 7.

48. Grace M. Cho, *Haunting the Korean Diaspora: Shame, Secrecy, and the Forgotten War* (Minneapolis: University of Minnesota Press, 2008), a portion of which appears as "Voices from the Teum: Synesthetic Trauma and the Ghosts of the Korean Diaspora," in Clough and Halley, *Affective Turn*, 151–69. Kotrosits employs "Voices from the Teum" to reflect upon the Gospel of John (*Rethinking Early Christian Identity*, 165–68).

49. Paraphrasing Cho, *Haunting the Korean Diaspora*, 40. The notion of transgenerational haunting is especially associated with Nicolas Abraham and Maria Torok; see Abraham and Torok, *The Shell and the Kernel: Renewals of Psychoanalysis*, trans. Nicholas T. Rand, vol. 1 (Chicago: University of Chicago Press, 1994), 165–205. Independently of Cho or Abraham and Torok, Jin Young Choi has argued that the Markan disciples' "experience of Jesus as *phantasma*" (Mark 6:45–52) is best understood "as a haunting that reflects the collective memory of colonized subjects," one that "functions

tory, both personal and collective, takes the form of a 'ghost,' it searches for bodies through which to speak. In this way, the ghost is distributed across the time-space of diaspora."[50] Against "unacknowledged histories of trauma," the ghost summons into existence "listening and speaking bodies that [it] requires as witnesses"; more precisely, what is summoned is "a constellation of affective bodies transmitting and receiving trauma," bodies seeing and speaking the trauma that could not originally be seen and spoken.[51] Yet a ghost, for Cho, channeling and adapting Deleuze and Guattari, is never simply reducible to the human. A ghost is an assemblage composed of "disparate elements in an environment," not all of which are human.[52] A ghost is "a spectral agency made up of different material and immaterial forces."[53] Cho might well have had recourse to Deleuze's own definition of an assemblage as a heterogeneity whose only unity resides in a "cofunctioning," a "symbiosis," and which is never a matter of "filiations" but only of "alliances," not "lines of descent, but contagions, epidemics, the wind."[54] Wind, breath, spirit, *pneuma*.[55] The ghost, holy or not, is all of these.

The Holy Ghost of Luke and Acts readily lends itself to redescription in Cho's evocative terms. The Holy Ghost is indeed "a spectral agency" assembled from "different material and immaterial forces," from assorted human and nonhuman elements. Preeminent among the human elements is the dead Jesus, and preeminent among the nonhuman elements is "the living God" (Acts 14:15); for the Holy Ghost is also God's ghost, as when Jesus announces in the Nazareth synagogue, "God's ghost has possessed me" (*pneuma kyriou ep' eme* [Luke 4:18; cf. 3:22a; 4:1–2a; Acts 10:38]). But the nonhuman components of the Holy Ghost assemblage are not only divine. Let us consider the human and nonhuman constituents in turn.

---

to disrupt the imperial presence and power" (*Postcolonial Discipleship of Embodiment*, 63; see further 78–84).

50. Cho, *Haunting the Korean Diaspora*, 40.

51. Ibid., 41.

52. Ibid., 40. Deleuze and Guattari's assemblage, as will be recalled, is a temporary configuration of radically heterogeneous elements (see 4 n. 8, 44–45 above).

53. Cho, *Haunting the Korean Diaspora*, 40.

54. Gilles Deleuze and Claire Parnet, *Dialogues II*, trans. Hugh Tomlinson and Barbara Habberjam, rev. ed., EP (New York: Columbia University Press, 2007), 69.

55. As is well known, lexical meanings of Greek *pneuma*, as of Hebrew *ruaḥ*, include "wind" and "breath" as well as "spirit."

First of all, the Holy Ghost, although hardly human, is eminently capable of mimicking human speech: "Then the Ghost [*pneuma*] said to Philip ..."; "While Peter was still pondering the vision, the Ghost [*pneuma*] said to him ..."; "While they were worshiping the Lord and fasting, the Holy Ghost [*to pneuma to hagion*] said ..."; "The Holy Ghost [*to pneuma to hagion*] attests to me ... that bonds and afflictions await me"; "Thus says the Holy Ghost [*to pneuma to hagion*] ..." (Acts 8:29; 10:19; 13:2; 20:23; 21:11; cf. 1:2, 16; 2:4; 4:25; 11:12; 16:6; 21:4; 28:25). At other anthropomorphic moments, the Holy Ghost seems to stand solidly shoulder-to-shoulder with human actors: "We are witnesses to these things, and so is the Holy Ghost [*to pneuma to hagion*] ..."; "For it has seemed good to the Holy Ghost [*to pneuma to hagion*] and to us to lay upon you no further burden ..." (5:32; 15:28). The Holy Ghost can be lied to (5:3), put to the test (5:9), and opposed (7:51). All in all, this spectral agent is a more developed character than most of the humans in Luke-Acts;[56] certainly, it has more lines than most of the female characters.

But although the Holy Ghost contains human elements within its assemblage, these human elements do not define this ghost, especially since it is not, or not only, the ghost of a once living human being. In its entirety, the Holy Ghost is a ghost without an individual human antecedent. Symptomatic of the nonhumanity of the Holy Ghost is the fact that in the first scene in Luke-Acts in which it explicitly appears in material form,[57] its body is not human: "The Holy Ghost descended upon [Jesus] in bodily form as a dove [*sōmatikō eidei hōs peristeran*]" (Luke 3:22). When the Holy Ghost later alights on Jesus's disciples, it manifests itself as a "violent wind" (*pnoēs biaias*) and "tongues as of fire" (*glōssai hōsei pyros* [Acts 2:2–3]).[58]

---

56. Lending itself to at least two book-length narrative-critical studies; see William H. Shepherd Jr., *The Narrative Function of the Holy Spirit as a Character in Luke-Acts*, SBLDS 147 (Atlanta: Scholars Press, 1994); Ju Hur, *A Dynamic Reading of the Holy Spirit in Luke-Acts*, JSNTSup 211 (Sheffield: Sheffield Academic, 2001).

57. The extent to which the Lukan *pneuma* is *implicitly* material has tended in scholarly discourse to hinge on the extent to which Stoic influence may plausibly be attributed to it, the classic Stoic conception of *pneuma* being irreducibly materialist, "an impersonal cosmic substance," "the finest form of matter" that "interpenetrate[s] all other matter" (Keener, *Acts*, 1:530–31).

58. Heidrun Gunkel, Rainer Hirsch-Luipold, and John R. Levison argue that "*pneuma* is material" in the Pentecost scene, noting in particular how the constitutive events of the scene are "rich with materiality: actual sound, actual vision" and

The Holy Ghost is like air and fire but also like liquid: it is "poured out" (*ekcheō*) on human subjects (2:17–18, 33; 10:45). The Holy Ghost evokes an entire environment, a transhuman habitat, a "psychic landscape."[59] These more-and-other-than-human dimensions of the Holy Ghost signal the extent to which this specter floats free of individual, or even collective, human agency. At Pentecost, the disciples are collectively incorporated into the human-nonhuman assemblage that is the Holy Ghost, but in terms that do not privilege the human or even the divine—at least the divine construed as the obverse of the material. The relations symbolically encoded in the Holy Ghost assemblage are not premised upon innate human supremacy or matter's mere utility.[60] It is through fluttering, gusting, flickering, flowing life forms, both "animate" and "inanimate," that the Holy Ghost affects human psychic and social life. The things, the matter, that the Holy Ghost is matter.

The polymorphic Holy Ghost also assumes more intangible forms. The Holy Ghost is also an impersonal and imperious force that overflows even Jesus's conscious subjectivity and agency: in response to a hemorrhaging woman's touch it issues forth from him as "power" (*dynamis*), circumventing his volition (Luke 8:46; cf. 5:17; 6:19). At once personal and impersonal, intimate and external, the Holy Ghost in its nonhuman manifestations is akin to affect in the Deleuzian register. The Holy Ghost is a force, an intensity, that impacts bodies, that infiltrates bodies and circulates between them, impelling movement, emotion, and cognition. It flows

---

ascribing that materiality, in effect, to a Stoic philosophical lingua franca ("Plutarch and Pentecost: An Exploration in Interdisciplinary Collaboration," in *The Holy Spirit, Inspiration, and the Cultures of Antiquity: Multidisciplinary Perspectives*, ed. Jörg Frey and John R. Levison, Ekstasis 5 [Berlin: de Gruyter, 2014], 90–91). For a rather differently focused study of the materiality of ancient *pneuma*, see Denise Kimber Buell, "The Microbes and Pneuma That Therefore I Am," in Moore, *Divinanimality*, 63–87. "Microbes, as well as other organic and inorganic compounds that may invisibly make up the air we breathe," suggests Buell, "are provocatively comparable to pneuma in ancient texts where it appears as breath but is also distinguishable as a special material agency that may travel through the air or by other means (through the waters of baptism, the spoken word figured as flesh, the eucharistic elements figured as flesh and blood). Ancient and modern texts abound with assertions of the power of invisible agencies that exceed, enable, and often threaten humans" (67).

59. Cho's term, used in a different context (*Haunting the Korean Diaspora*, 40).

60. Reflections prompted by Cohen, "Introduction," esp. 7. For more on thing theory, see 111–12 below.

incessantly but it does not seem to feel or think. Rather, *it acts*, most of all in the Acts of the Holy Ghost.[61]

Intimately if obscurely related to the intergenerational transmission of trauma, the Holy Ghost passes through and among bodies rather than being locatably contained in an individual traumatized body or even a community of such bodies.[62] Unspeakable atrocity, colossal catastrophe. Luke apparently has the hardest time of any of the four evangelists telling the tale of his Messiah's death torture, omitting altogether the shameful spectacle of Jesus's flogging—he alludes to it (18:33; 23:16) but cannot quite bring himself to display it—and compulsively bathing Mark's harsh, bleak, cruel crucifixion scene in a soft golden light (23:28, 34, 40–43, 46, 48). Luke's Jesus is also the only New Testament Jesus who weeps over the impending destruction of Jerusalem and its temple (19:41–44; cf. 13:33–35). Luke's own tears stream from the eyes of his character, soaking the latter's papery cheeks and causing the ink to run like mascara.

As Cho has seen, when an unspeakable history necessitates the emergence of a ghost, that specter then "searches for bodies through which to speak."[63] More than that, the ghost summons "witnesses" into existence.[64] Luke-Acts is immensely preoccupied with the assembling of witnesses. The disciples are first informed of their witness status in Luke 24:48 ("You are witnesses [*martyres*]"), right after they are told that "repentance ... is to be proclaimed ... to all the nations, beginning from Jerusalem" (24:47; see also Acts 1:8), and right before they are ordered to remain "in the city until [they] have been clothed with [Ghostly] power from on high" (Luke 24:49; see also Acts 1:4–5). Cho's words are uncannily apt here: "In this way, the ghost is distributed across the time-space of diaspora."[65] The disciples, or, more precisely, the apostles are the appointed witnesses, Acts insists again and again (1:8, 22; 2:32; 3:15; 5:32; 10:39, 41; cf. Luke 1:2). In time, Paul is added to their ranks, a "witness [*martys*] to all the world of what [he] has seen and heard" (Acts 22:15; see also 23:11). They are all "witnesses [*martyres*] to these things, and so is the Holy Ghost" (5:32).

---

61. Reflections impelled by Seigworth and Gregg, "Inventory of Shimmers," esp. 1–2. Seigworth and Gregg's conception of affect is thoroughly Deleuzian, as noted earlier.
62. See Cho, *Haunting the Korean Diaspora*, 41.
63. Ibid., 40.
64. Ibid., 41.
65. Ibid., 40.

But the Holy Ghost is more than a witness; the Holy Ghost is *the* witness. Possession, intimate appropriation, by this nonhuman spectral witness is what make the witness of the human witnesses possible: "Do not worry about … what you are to say; for the Holy Ghost will teach you at that very hour what you must say" (Luke 12:11–12).

More than anything else, the witness of the witnesses is an attempt to transmit trauma to the hearers. In the first Ghost-written speech of Acts, that of Peter to the people of Jerusalem and Judea, Luke represents this attempt as resulting in spectacular success. "[This] man attested to you by God with powerful deeds, wonders, and signs," declaims Peter, "handed over to you according to the preestablished plan and foreknowledge of God, you crucified and killed by the hands of lawless men" (2:22–23). The speech ends: "Let the entire house of Israel know with certainty, therefore, that God has made him both Lord and Messiah, this Jesus whom you crucified" (2:36). The result? The opening up of a wound, the transmission of trauma: "And when they heard this, they were cut to the heart [*katenygēsan tēn kardian*] and said to Peter and the rest of the apostles, 'Men, brothers, what should we do?'" (2:37). What, indeed? What else but receive their own uncanny influx of Holy Ghost possession ("Repent, and be baptized …; and you will receive … the Holy Ghost" [2:38]), so that they in turn may become "a constellation of affective bodies transmitting … trauma,"[66] witnesses incessantly speaking the primal trauma that could not previously be spoken because it could not previously be seen.

The Holy Ghost in Luke-Acts also warps time, reverses chronology, queers temporality. The Holy Ghost story that is Luke-Acts is told in the afterlife of the twin traumas of the crucifixion of the Messiah and the destruction of the holy city and its temple, but those twin traumas are so causally interbound, so temporally intertwined for the teller of the ghost story as to constitute one trauma rather than two. Luke's Deuteronomistic theodicy[67] compels him to see the Roman siege and destruction of Jerusalem, the obliteration of its temple, and the massacre and enslavement of its inhabitants as punishment for the refusal of those inhabitants to accept their Messiah (19:41–44; see also 11:45–51; 13:31–35; 20:13–19; 21:5–6, 20–24; 23:27–31; cf. Josephus, *J. W.* 5.362–419; 6.93–110); "these are the

---

66. Ibid., 41.
67. See Thomas Römer and Jean-Daniel Macchi, "Luke, Disciple of the Deuteronomistic School," in *Luke's Literary Achievement: Collected Essays*, ed. C. M. Tuckett, JSNTSup 116 (Sheffield: Sheffield Academic, 1995), 178–87.

days of vengeance," as his Jesus grimly puts it (Luke 21:22). Israel's Messiah is crucified, therefore Israel's holy city and temple are destroyed. With the latter catastrophe, however, the most colossal trauma of all is triggered—"anguish among nations ..., people ... faint[ing] from fear and foreboding of what is coming upon the world, ... the powers of the heavens ... shaken" (21:25–26; see also 17:22–37; 21:34–36). An indefinite, open-ended period separates the arrival of the Lukan Son of Humanity (21:27) from the destruction of Jerusalem that impels his advent, but that period is also described in traumatic terms: "Jerusalem will be trampled underfoot by the gentiles [read: Romans] until the times of the gentiles are fulfilled" (21:24). In terms of the unfolding of Luke's plot, the dreadful coming of the transhuman Son of Humanity (17:22–37) precedes the catastrophic destruction of Jerusalem and its temple and the atrocious slaughter and enslavement of its population (19:41–44; 21:5–6, 20–24), which in turn precedes the horrific execution of the Messiah (23:33–46). Time is already beginning to flow backwards in Luke-Acts.

And if an unspeakable, traumatic, time-unraveling history necessitates the emergence of a ghost, or even a Ghost, then that Ghost is also not going to be bound by linear time. The afterlife of trauma that generates the Ghost retrojects the Ghost, propels it back into the past. The epic ghost story that is the Gospel and Acts of the Holy Ghost has the haunting, trauma-generated specter descend not only upon the followers of the dead Messiah (Luke 24:49; Acts 1:4–5; 2:1–4) but on the still-living Messiah himself (Luke 3:21–22), long before his traumatic execution. The Ghost violently overflows all temporal boundaries, spilling backwards to engulf every aspect of the Messiah's existence, even to the point of instigating his conception in the womb of a Jewish peasant girl: "The Holy Ghost will come upon you," Mary is told by "the angel Gabriel" (Luke 1:35; cf. 1:26), a spectral entity of another kind. Once the Ghost has come upon the adult Messiah in turn (3:21–22), the Ghost suffuses his body with affective materiality, turns it into a conduit for an uncanny power that exceeds it (4:14; 5:17; 6:19; 8:46; Acts 2:22; 10:38), and thoroughly confounds the temporalities we conventionally call past, present, and future.[68] The time-queering activity of the Holy Ghost in the Gospel and Acts of the Holy Ghost scrambles the four ostensibly sequential timelines that traverse the work—Roman time, messianic time, ecclesial time, and apocalyptic

---

68. See Freccero, "Queer Times," 22.

time—and makes Luke's two-volume ghost story a spectacular instance of what Dinshaw has dubbed *asynchrony*: "different time frames or temporal systems colliding in a single moment of *now*."[69]

Haunted Homosociality, Affective Historiography

What, finally, are we to make of this comfortably familiar ancient work that, however, once we allow ourselves to be haunted by it, turns out to be singularly strange, unsettlingly spooky? It is, as we have seen, a ghost story, a tale of an always already dead man (Luke 1:34–35; 18:31; 24:25–27, 44–46) who both accepts and refuses his death, who, from beyond the grave, insists that he is not a ghost (24:39) and yet, also from beyond the grave and hence the realm of ghosts, establishes uncanny homosocial[70] spectral bonds with other men, possessing them intimately and using them utterly to transform the social world by saturating it with unprecedented affects. These affects are effected by another ghost, a Holy Ghost, who and which is at once a personal entity and an impersonal force and who and which is, and yet is not, the specter of the dead Messiah. This Holy Ghost is intimately interconnected with the primal trauma that was the Messiah's death torture since it constantly calls forth witnesses to speak to and for that dislocating event. As they tell and retell their ghost story of a haunting, undead Messiah, these witnesses continually collapse present and past and fold an imagined future eschaton into an asynchronous now.

Acts has long been read as the normative history of early Christianity, emerging organically out of the gospel that is its prequel. This chapter has sought to show that Luke-Acts may be counterread as an altogether queerer, less confirming, more unsettling enterprise.[71] The Gospel and Acts of the Holy Ghost are an emblematic exercise in queer spectrality and hence in queer temporality. Luke-Acts is a homohistory, an unhistory, whose time-flattening effects and affects continually fold the past and the future into the present. As such, its homohistorical and unhistori-

---

69. Dinshaw, *How Soon Is Now?*, 5, emphasis original.

70. In gender studies, the term homosocial is primarily associated with Eve Kosofsky Sedgwick (see her *Between Men: English Literature and Male Homosocial Desire*, 30th anniversary ed., GC [New York: Columbia University Press, 2016]), although I am giving it my own spin here.

71. As Maia Kotrosits has also shown on other grounds; see her *Rethinking Early Christian Identity*, 85–115.

cal Jesus invites affective engagement, a queer touch across time ("Touch me and see" [Luke 24:39]). Simultaneously, its principal representation of the divine, the heterogeneous assemblage we have been calling the Holy Ghost, invites acute attention to human-nonhuman relations in that affective exchange. Thus reimagined, Luke-Acts provides an immensely suggestive precritical model for a postcritical history of proto-Christianity.

6

What a (Sometimes Inanimate) Divine Animal and Plant Has to Teach Us about Being Human

> A human being, an animal, … a bacterium, a virus, a molecule, a microorganism. Or [a] truffle, a tree, a fly, and a pig. These combinations are neither genetic nor structural; they are interkingdoms, unnatural participations.
>
> —Gilles Deleuze and Félix Guattari, *A Thousand Plateaus*

> My interkingdom is not of this world.
>
> —John 18:36, paraphrased

The Johannine Jesus is not, or is not solely, a human being, but not only for the reasons ordinarily adduced. The god-man is also *a nonhuman animal* ("Behold the lamb" [1:36; cf. 1:29; also 3:14]);[1] *a vegetable* ("I am the vine" [15:5; cf. 15:1]);[2] *a vegetable byproduct* ("I am the bread" [6:35; cf. 6:41, 48, 51]; "I am the door [*hē thyra*]" [10:9; cf. 10:7]);[3] *inorganic matter*, namely,

---

1. Translations of the Gospel of John in this chapter are my own; otherwise I employ NRSV.

2. Using *vegetable* here and throughout in its Linnaean sense—that is, as denoting plants in general as opposed to animals or minerals.

3. Taking *thyra* to denote a wooden door in John 10:9, as it does in 18:16 and 20:19, 26. Whether or not the audience is to envision a wooden door in a walled enclosure or an open entrance to an enclosure across which the (good) shepherd (Jesus; see 10:11, 14) lies, he himself thereby becoming the door, does not affect the anchoring image. The wooden door anchors the *paroimia* ("cryptic figure" [10:6; cf. 16:25, 29]) in either instance, and in the *paroimia*, the Johannine Jesus equates himself with a wooden door. In reading 10:7 as "I am the door of the sheep," I am preferring the *lectio difficilior*. As Francis J. Moloney succinctly puts it: "There is ancient textual evidence (P^{75}, Sahidic, Coptic) for the reading 'I am the shepherd of the sheep.' This reading would make excellent sense and for that reason must be rejected" (*The Gospel of John*,

water ("Let anyone who is thirsty come to me, and let the one who believes in me drink" [7:37–38; cf. 4:10, 14]); and *inorganic energy,* namely, electromagnetic radiation ("I am the light" [8:12; cf. 9:5])—all epithets no more or no less metaphoric than the epithet "Son of God."[4] The epistemological equivalence of son language, lamb language, vine language, bread language, door language, and light language is the enabling assumption of the analytic exercise that follows. Of course, it is Son Christology—Son of God, Son of Man, Son of God-in-the-Image-of-Man—that has commanded center stage since at least the fourth century.[5] Throughout Christian history, the Fourth Gospel has been a prop for dominant Western ontologies of the human no less than of the divine—paradoxically so, as this chapter argues. The current posthumanist challenge—or, better, the current challenge emanating from nonhuman theory in its manifold guises and catalyzed in no small part by the global ecological crisis—impels a shift of theological and theoretical attention from Son Christology to animal Christology, vegetal Christology, and inorganic Christology.

After the Animal

What is called for, then, is more than another exercise in animality studies, vital though that work undoubtedly is. The task is not simply that

---

SP 4 [Collegeville, MN: Liturgical Press, 1998], 309). For a study of the Johannine shepherd discourse that accords adequate attention to the door (most do not), see Karoline M. Lewis, *Rereading the "Shepherd Discourse": Restoring the Integrity of John 9:39–10:21,* StBibLit 113 (New York: Lang, 2008).

4. On the metaphoricity of "Son talk," see esp. John Hick, *The Metaphor of God Incarnate: Christology in a Pluralistic Age,* 2nd ed. (Louisville: Westminster John Knox, 2006), 42–45. Feminist reflection on the gendered metaphoricity of Son talk preceded Hicks's classic study; see esp. Mary Daly, *Beyond God the Father: Toward a Philosophy of Women's Liberation* (Boston: Beacon, 1973). Daly writes: "As marginal beings who have no stake in a sexist world, women—if we have the courage to keep our eyes open—have access to the knowledge that neither the Father, nor the Son, nor the Mother *is* God, the Verb who transcends anthropomorphic symbolization" (97, emphasis original).

5. As Daly famously put it, "If God is male, then the male is God" (*Beyond God the Father,* 19). For Hick, the process whereby "a metaphorical son of God" became "the metaphysical God the Son" was inextricably bound up with the formulation of Trinitarian doctrine in the fourth and fifth centuries (*Metaphor of God Incarnate,* 44–45). Hick and Daly are convenient stand-ins for two large subgroups of the throng of theologians, philosophers of religion, and New Testament scholars who have critically pondered the Son language(s) of the Christian testament and the Christian creeds.

of insisting on the situatedness of the Johannine Son of Humanity (*ho huios tou anthrōpou* [1:51; 3:13–14; 5:27; 6:27, 53, 62; 8:28; 9:35; 12:23, 34; 13:31]) on the animal continuum, which is to say his simultaneous status as Son of Animality ("Behold the Lamb [*amnos*] of God!" [1:36; cf. 1:29]; "And as Moses lifted up the snake [*ophis*] in the desert, so must the Son of Humanity be lifted up" [3:14; cf. Num 21:6–9]).[6] That task is complicated by the Son of Humanimality's further identity as Son of Vegetality ("I am the vine [*hē ampelos*]" [15:5; cf. 15:1–6]). The Fourth Gospel apparently knows what we also now know, or something uncannily like it: no absolute attributes separate the plant from the animal. There are no properties of vegetal life that are not also found in the animal world. There are no properties of animal life that are not also found in the vegetal world. As such, the "animal continuum" might equally be termed the "plant continuum," as Massumi notes in his affect theory-inflected experiment in animality studies.[7] To think the human is to think the animal, and to think the animal is to think the vegetal.[8] Analogously, to think the human

---

6. The snake is an interestingly different instance of animality from the lamb. Derrida twice reports that Levinas, when asked at a colloquium whether the animal has a face (in the special Levinasian sense of face—that is, as expressive of the absolute ethical demand "Do not kill me"), declared the question essentially unanswerable, remarking "I don't know if a snake has a face" (Derrida, *Animal That Therefore I Am*, 107–8; see also Derrida, *Beast and the Sovereign*, 1:237). Levinas's example of the snake "is not chosen by chance," as Derrida notes: "In choosing the serpent Levinas ... avoids ... having to answer the question concerning so many other animals ... who it would be difficult to refuse a face and a gaze" and hence "the 'Thou shalt not kill' that Levinas reserves for the face" (*Animal That Therefore I Am*, 110). Derrida's examples of those "many other animals" are "the cat, the dog, the horse, the monkey, the orangutan, the chimpanzee" (110). But he might well have included the sheep or the lamb in this cluster. If nonhuman subjects admit of degrees of nonhumanness (a common but contestable assumption), then Jesus the Snake is more nonhuman than Jesus the Lamb. But their fate is identical in the Fourth Gospel: the Snake no less than the Lamb is destined to be cruelly pinioned to a cross and run through with a lance. Neither the Snake nor the Lamb elude their hunters or butchers. Neither of them qualify for the "Thou shalt not kill" exemption and so neither of them possess a face in the Levinasian sense. When Jesus assumes animal form in John, it is only in order to qualify for slaughter and thereby be treated as most animals have always been treated by humans.

7. Brian Massumi, *What Animals Teach Us about Politics* (Durham, NC: Duke University Press, 2014), 53. Massumi draws this conclusion from Henri Bergson, *Creative Evolution*, trans. Arthur Miller (Mineola, NY: Dover, 1998), 105–6.

8. See Massumi, *What Animals Teach Us*, 54.

Johannine Jesus is to think the animal Johannine Jesus, and to think the animal Johannine Jesus is to think the vegetal Johannine Jesus.

In this chapter, impelled in part by the emerging ecofield known as critical plant studies or plant theory,[9] I make a (mainly vegetarian) meal out of the leftovers from the millennia-long feast of Johannine Christology as conducted in the traditional anthropocentric style. As Michael Marder observes: "If animals have suffered marginalization throughout the history of Western thought, then non-human, non-animal living beings, such as plants, have populated the margin of the margin, the zone of absolute obscurity undetectable on the radars of our conceptualities."[10] Again: "Plants are the weeds of metaphysics: devalued, unwanted in its carefully cultivated garden."[11] Jeffrey Nealon adds: "Saint Thomas Aquinas, that *bête noir* of animal studies, concisely sums up the philosophical [and theological] prejudice: 'Even brute animals are more noble than plants.'"[12]

---

9. Representative work includes Michael Marder, *Plant-Thinking: A Philosophy of Vegetal Life* (New York: Columbia University Press, 2013), widely regarded as the groundbreaking text in this field (two apt vegetal metaphors); Marder, *The Philosopher's Plant: An Intellectual Herbarium* (New York: Columbia University Press, 2014); Eduardo Kohn, *How Forests Think: Toward an Anthropology beyond the Human* (Berkeley: University of California Press, 2013); Randy Laist, ed., *Plants and Literature: Essays in Critical Plant Studies*, CPS 1 (Amsterdam: Rodopi, 2013); Luce Irigaray and Michael Marder, *Through Vegetal Being: Two Philosophical Perspectives*, CLS (New York: Columbia University Press, 2016); Jeffrey T. Nealon, *Plant Theory: Biopower and Vegetable Life* (Stanford, CA: Stanford University Press, 2016); Patrícia Vieira, Monica Gagliano, and John Ryan, eds., *The Green Thread: Dialogues with the Vegetal World*, ETP (Lanham, MD: Lexington, 2016). The philosophy of Deleuze frequently figures prominently in this emerging field, whether as influence, foil, or both (see, for example, the work of Marder and Nealon). After all, "follow the plants" is one of the prime directives of *A Thousand Plateaus* (11). Also worth consulting, then, is Hannah Stark, "Deleuze and Critical Plant Studies," in Roffe and Stark, *Deleuze and the Non/Human*, 180–96.

10. Marder, *Plant-Thinking*, 2. Laist argues relatedly: "Animal studies is essentially an extension of human studies; it is relatively easy to imagine the subjectivity of animals.... When it comes to plants, however, we encounter a much more significant barrier to our imagination" ("Introduction," in Laist, *Plants and Literature*, 12).

11. Marder, *Plant-Thinking*, 90.

12. Nealon, *Plant Theory*, xii, quoting Thomas Aquinas, *Sum. theol.* 3.44.4.1. Aquinas's views on plants have their roots in Aristotle's *De anima*. For Aristotle, as Nealon notes, plants constitute "the lowest limit of the living": they live, they reproduce, they die, but that is all they do. Animals, in contrast, exhibit some "higher" (more human-like) functions "such as sensation, movement, awareness of their sur-

The Jesus Thing

If definitively disentangling the animal from the vegetal is a fruitless enterprise, so too is categorically separating the organic from the inorganic. On this the Fourth Gospel is as insistent as particle physics.[13] The man and the lamb cannot be strictly separated from the vine, the bread, the door, the water, or the light. Yet these elements do not all dissolve into one another so as to become a "goo of undifferentiation."[14] Rather, they "interpenetrate without blurring,"[15] preserving their distinctive contours, in pairs, in trios, in quartets, in quintets. The Johannine god-*man* is also and always a god-man-*animal*, and the god-man-animal is also and always a god-man-animal-*plant*, and the god-man-animal-plant is also and always a god-man-animal-plant-*thing*.

The thing, too, has entered theory. Things, objects, stuff, matter have never mattered more for theorists and philosophers than they do at present. Things loom large in speculative realism, in object-oriented ontology, in agential realism, in vital materialism, in thing theory—or—to paint the object-populated still life with broader and cruder strokes—in new materialism and the nonhuman turn in theory.[16] This chapter locates the

---

roundings, and appetite." But the lead role in the Aristotelian biodrama is, of course, played by "man," sole possessor of speech and reason (*logos*) and as such is closer to the divine (Nealon, *Plant Theory*, 32–33; see further Marder, *Plant-Thinking*, 15–90 passim). Aristotle writes: "Man alone partakes of the divine, or at any rate partakes of it in a fuller measure than the rest" (*Part. An.* 656a1–10). Even though the Fourth Gospel introduces its protagonist as the *logos* (1:1, 14), it also implicitly unsettles Aristotle's tripartite hierarchy of the forms of life. In declaring "I am the true vine," for example, the Johannine Jesus simultaneously announces his divinity (the Johannine "I am" is a theophanic formula, as has long been recognized) and his vegetality.

13. Channeling particle physics, Massumi sternly warns: "Do not hold out hope that the category of inorganic matter will save the categorical day by providing an empirical dividing line enabling you to parse out where animality, consciousness, and life begin and end" (*What Animals Teach Us*, 94; see also 52). Mel Y. Chen describes "the 'facts' by which humans are not animals are not things (or by which humans cannot be animals cannot be things)" as "the real uncanny permeating the world we know" (*Animacies: Biopolitics, Racial Mattering, and Queer Affect*, PM [Durham, NC: Duke University Press, 2012], 236).

14. Massumi's phrase (*What Animals Teach Us*, 51).

15. Ibid.

16. For introductions to speculative realism, see Peter Gratton, *Speculative Realism: Problems and Prospects* (New York: Bloomsbury, 2014); Steven Shaviro, *The Uni-*

Fourth Gospel within this object-strewn critical landscape. For the stuff of Johannine Christology is not just human stuff, animal stuff, and vegetal stuff; it is also inanimate stuff (as conventionally defined): a door, bread, light, water, a corpse.

The Fourth Gospel elides three distinctions commonly thought to be constitutive of human beings: that they are not animals, that they are not plants, that they are not things. The Johannine Son of Humanity, or Human One, is also an animal, a vegetable, and an object and as such is also a Not-Altogether-Human One, a Son of More-Than-Humanity. The Johannine Jesus is incarnated *as human* ("And the Word became flesh" [1:14]) to die *as animal* ("Behold the lamb of God who takes away the sin of the world!"; "None of his bones shall be broken" [1:29; 19:36]) and to live on *as vegetable* ("I am the vine, you are the branches" [15:5]) and *as vegetable byproducts* ("I am the bread of life" [6:35]; "I am the door for the sheep" [10:7])[17]—not least as a papyrus book, as we shall see. The

---

verse of Things: On Speculative Realism, Posthumanities 30 (Minneapolis: University of Minnesota Press, 2014). For introductions to object-oriented ontology (which overlaps substantially with speculative realism), see Timothy Morton, *Realist Magic: Objects, Ontology, Causality*, NM (London: Open Humanities, 2013); Peter Wolfendale, *Object-Oriented Philosophy: The Noumenon's New Clothes* (Falmouth, UK: Urbanomic Media, 2014); Katherine Behar, ed., *Object-Oriented Feminism* (Minneapolis: University of Minnesota Press, 2016). For agential realism, see Karen Barad, *Meeting the Universe Halfway: Quantum Physics and the Entanglement of Matter and Meaning* (Durham, NC: Duke University Press, 2007). For vital materialism, see Bennett, *Vibrant Matter*. For thing theory, see Bill Brown, ed., *Things*, CIB (Chicago: University of Chicago Press, 2004). The theorists commonly considered exemplars of new materialism, meanwhile, notably Barad and Bennett, reject the term, predictably enough. But that has not prevented volumes on new materialism from appearing anyway: see esp. Diana Coole and Samantha Frost, eds., *New Materialisms: Ontology, Agency, and Politics* (Durham, NC: Duke University Press, 2010); Rick Dolphijn and Iris van der Tuin, *New Materialism: Interviews and Cartographies*, NM (Falmouth, UK: Open Humanities, 2012). For the intersection of new materialism(s) and religion, see most recently Catherine Keller and Mary-Jane Rubenstein, eds., *Entangled Worlds: Religion, Science, and New Materialisms*, TTC (New York: Fordham University Press, 2017).

17. The Johannine narrator intones "None of his bones shall be broken," words lifted from the instructions for the preparation of the Passover lamb (Exod 12:46; Num 9:12; cf. Ps 34:19–20), over the dead Jesus, having earlier emphasized that Jesus's sentencing by Pilate occurred around noon on the day of preparation for the Passover (John 19:13–16; cf. 18:28), the day when the mass slaughter of (four-legged) Passover lambs would have been underway in the temple precincts (Josephus, *J. W.* 6.423; Philo, *Spec.* 2.145). For elaboration of these interpretations (which are part of the stock-in-

characters in the surreal tale that is the Fourth Gospel include a heavenly man, a slaughtered sheep, a crucified snake, a bottomless body of water, a flesh-flavored loaf of bread, a star-sized source of light, a wooden door, a vast vine. What is remarkable is that all these unlikely characters are ostensibly one composite character. He, or better it, is an ambulatory allegory of the divine in the human, the animal in the human, the vegetal in the human and the animal, and the thinghood of everything (and not just every thing). The ontological economy of the Fourth Gospel is at once vertical and horizontal. It is a vertical hierarchy of being but also a horizontal plane of being. The Father is above the Son (5:19, 36; 8:28; 14:28), and the Son is above the world even when in the world (8:23; 16:28, 33; 18:36). But the world is also in the Son since the Son is the things of the world, including the things that make the world possible: light, water, plants, animals.[18] Attending to matter—making it matter—"draws human attention sideways," as Jane Bennett notes, "away from an ontologically ranked Great Chain of Being and toward ... the complex entanglements of humans and nonhumans"[19]—a horizontal entanglement vividly displayed, tattooed in spiraling patterns, on the narrative skin of the Fourth Gospel, notwithstanding its hierarchical skeleton.

The Jesus Assemblage

That the Johannine Jesus is a consummate hybrid has long been recognized. But his hybridity has been diminished through being conceived as divine-human hybridity only. The current challenge, occasioned by the escalating planetary ecocrisis, is to reconceive the Johannine Jesus as a divine-human-nonhuman composite. But something more is needed for this task than the now-jaded concept of hybridity, something that nonhuman theory may be able to provide. The agential subject of nonhuman theory is, most often, a human-nonhuman assemblage, and the Johannine Jesus may himself/itself be reconceived as such an assemblage. Associated

---

trade of Johannine commentary), see, for example, Craig S. Keener, *The Gospel of John: A Commentary*, 2nd ed., 2 vols. (Grand Rapids: Baker Academic, 2012), 2:1129–31, 1155–56. Even as Jesus is animal and vegetable in John, so too are his followers: they are sheep (10:1–16, 25–28; 21:15–17), and they are vine branches (15:1–8).

18. "Everything was made through him [*panta di' autou egeneto*]," the Johannine prologue proclaims (1:3); but he, or it, is also made from every thing.

19. Bennett, *Vibrant Matter*, 112.

114　　　Gospel Jesuses and Other Nonhumans

particularly with the para-poststructuralist thought of Deleuze and Guattari, as we saw earlier, an assemblage is a configuration of heterogeneous elements that enter into temporary relations with one another and produce affects, effects, and entire realities. More specifically, the Deleuzoguattarian assemblage is an intricate four-part configuration. For purposes of this chapter I restrict myself to one of the four dimensions, what Deleuze and Guattari call "a *machinic assemblage* of bodies, of actions and passions, an intermingling of bodies reacting to one another."[20] They write: "We think the material or machinic aspect of an assemblage relates … to a precise state of intermingling of bodies in a society, including all the attractions and repulsions, sympathies and antipathies, alterations, amalgamations, penetrations, and expansions that affect bodies of all kinds in their relations to one another."[21] Bennett adds: "Much like Russian *matryoshka* dolls, assemblages contain a sequence of ever smaller ones—functioning groupings of actants in a series of larger, more complex congregations."[22] Within the mega-assemblage that is academia, for instance, biblical scholarship is nested (often uncomfortably). Within the assemblage that is biblical scholarship, the Fourth Gospel, as critically construed, is (more comfortably) nested. Within the Fourth Gospel, the Johannine Jesus is nested.

The Johannine Jesus is an assemblage of heterogeneous materials, some human and some nonhuman. Assemblages are not administered by any central intelligence, by any central agency, by any central intelligence agency. The assemblage that is the Johannine Jesus is not administered either by

---

20. Deleuze and Guattari, *A Thousand Plateaus*, 88, emphasis original. This is all "on the one hand"; "on the other hand, [an assemblage] is a *collective assemblage of enunciation*, of acts and statements, of incorporeal transformations attributed to bodies." All of this makes up the "horizontal axis" of the assemblage. "Then on a vertical axis, the assemblage has both *territorial sides*, or reterritorialized sides, which stabilize it, and *cutting edges of deterritorialization*, which carry it away" (88, emphasis original). I omitted these difficult-to-assemble details from my earlier introduction(s) to the Deleuzoguattarian assemblage. In what follows, I continue to work with a stripped-down version of the assemblage concept, emboldened by the example of certain prominent theorists who have also had recourse to this simplifying strategy: see Bennett, *Vibrant Matter*, 20–38; Puar, *Terrorist Assemblages*; Puar, "'I Would Rather Be a Cyborg Than a Goddess': Becoming-Intersectional in Assemblage Theory," *PhiloSOPHIA* 2 (2012): 49–66.

21. Deleuze and Guattari, *A Thousand Plateaus*, 90. Further on the relationship of the machine to the assemblage, see 43–45 above.

22. Bennett, *Vibrant Matter*, 45.

6. What a Divine Animal and Plant Has to Teach Us about Being Human 115

the brain of that literary character, nested invisibly within its paper skull, or by the still more occluded brain of the no less fabricated figure whom we biblical scholars call "the Fourth Evangelist" and whose mind we purport to read with such confidence. Each member of the assemblage that is the Johannine Jesus possesses a degree of agency, but there is also an agency of the assemblage as such, a combined, conflicted agency that is not reducible to the intentions or actions of anybody, or any body, within it.

Certain of the points at which these bodies cross paths within the Johannine Jesus assemblage are more heavily trafficked than others,[23] and so intensity, affectivity, and power are not distributed equally across the assemblage. Deeply trodden for Johannine scholars is the path that connects the Johannine Jesus to the "Johannine community" (the latter a body that hovers insubstantially above the surface of the text even while seeming to sit solidly behind it).[24] But the most heavily trafficked path, historically speaking, is that which connects the Johannine Jesus to the Johannine God: since the fourth century at least, theologically minded interpreters have never ceased to scurry back and forth, antlike, between these two nodes but without ever exiting the assemblage, without ever transcending it, no matter how stratospherically high their Christologies have floated. For even as preexistent Word ("In the beginning was the Word" [1:1]), the Johannine Jesus is always embedded in a machinic assemblage because language, even divine language, is always mechanically mediated, always culturally enfleshed, always a matter *of* matter. As Chen insists, "Language … is certainly material. For humans and others"—even divine others, gods or a God—spoken or written language necessitates "the tongue, vocal tract, breath, lips, hands, eyes, and shoulders. It is a corporeal, sensual, embodied act."[25] As preexistent Word, then, the Johannine Jesus depends on the divine vocal chords, or else on the divine stylus hovering above the divine papyrus; on countless human speakers of innumerable languages who have yet to come into existence; and on sundry other paradoxes.[26]

---

23. See ibid., 24.

24. The discursive construct that is the Johannine community, now ubiquitous in Johannine studies, was first developed by Raymond E. Brown, as David Lamb reminds us. Lamb traces in detail the emergence and refinement of the construct in Brown's writings (*Text, Context and the Johannine Community: A Sociolinguistic Analysis of the Johannine Writings*, LNTS [New York: Bloomsbury T&T Clark, 2014], 29–55).

25. Chen, *Animacies*, 53.

26. As Donna J. Haraway puts it in a rather different context, "The word is made

The Word presupposes everything it supposedly precedes. The Word that became flesh was always already flesh. In the beginning was the Word; in the beginning too, therefore, was the Tongue, the Vocal Tract, the Breath (which is to say, the *pneuma*), the Lips, the Eyes, the Hands, and everything connected corporeally to them. In the beginning was a corporeal Father speaking or writing a corporeal Word and holding that always newly birthed Word tenderly to his womanly breast. "It is God the only Son, who reclines on the bosom of the Father [*ho ōn eis ton kolpon tou patros*], who has made [God] known," the Johannine prologue concludes (1:18). This Son, who or which is also a Sun ("I am the light of the world"—8:12; 9:5), manifests the divine not only as human flesh but also as animal flesh, vegetable matter, and inorganic matter. His body—its body—is a transspecies body, but also a transmatter body, since not all the bodies that animate it are themselves animate, as we have seen. That is why the kingdom of God in the Fourth Gospel (3:3, 5; 18:36) is an *interkingdom*, a convergence of unnatural participations,[27] a divine-human-nonhuman assemblage. That is also why the Johannine Jesus is an interking.[28]

Jesus through the Large Intestine

What, if anything, regulates the interrelationships of the bodies that make up the Johannine Jesus assemblage? As Deleuze and Guattari explain, "What regulates the obligatory, necessary, or permitted interminglings of bodies is above all an alimentary regime and a sexual regime."[29] The sexual regime regulating the assemblage that is the Johannine Jesus is occluded (although it appears to pass through the Beloved Disciple: "One of his disciples—the one whom Jesus loved—was reclining on Jesus's breast [*en tō kolpō tou Iēsou*]" [13:23; see also 19:26; 20:2; 21:7, 20]), but the alimentary regime regulating it is clearly manifest. Eating, drinking, ingestion, and digestion are everywhere associated with the Johannine Jesus. He must be

---

flesh in mortal naturecultures" (*The Companion Species Manifesto: Dogs, People, and Significant Otherness* [Chicago: Prickly Paradigm, 2003], 100).

27. See the epigraphs to this chapter.
28. "So you're a king?" Pilate asks Jesus at his trial, to which Jesus replies, "You say I'm a king" (John 18:37). He might, however, have answered more precisely, "You say I'm a king, but I'm really an interking."
29. Deleuze and Guattari, *A Thousand Plateaus*, 90.

6. What a Divine Animal and Plant Has to Teach Us about Being Human 117

eaten as the bread of life (6:31–58), as we saw earlier.[30] But he must also be drunk as the living water (4:10–15; 7:37–38). He is the grape-bearing vine (15:1–6). He is the sacrificial lamb who, implicitly, is destined to be devoured (1:29, 36). And he is the light that enables all organic life to exist, the eaters no less than the eaten (1:3b–5, 9; 3:19–21; 8:12; 9:5; 11:9–10; 12:35–36, 46).

The Johannine Jesus, then, is edible matter. He/it exists alongside, but also potentially inside, other organic bodies. As foodstuff, he/it is anything but quiescent stuff, passive matter.[31] He/it is an immensely potent agent, a foodstuff that utterly transforms the human stuff with which it comes into contact.[32] In the nutritheology of the Fourth Gospel, the human believer is what s/he eats: an immortal being, like the one who is eaten. "This is the bread that comes down from heaven," intones the Johannine Jesus, gesturing to his own doughy flesh, "so that one may eat of it and not die" (6:50; cf. 6:58). He is not dead matter (even when dead) but "living flesh" (6:51; cf. 6:58).

The Johannine Jesus craves incorporation into the body of another. He longs to be drunk; he desires to be devoured. To that end, the Johannine Jesus repeatedly transmutes—from lamb to water, from bread to vine, and so on—so as to invite, ever anew, hungry ingestion. The polymorphic body that is the Johannine Jesus is always already destined for violence in the narrative in which it is nested, and not only the violence of the cross. As edible matter the Johannine Jesus invites violent ingestion—explicitly so, indeed. "The one who gnaws, munches, crunches my flesh [*ho trōgōn mou tēn sarka*] … has eternal life," he declares (6:54; cf. 6:56–58). Scholars have long debated whether or not the switch from *esthiō* to *trōgō* in John 6:50–58 connotes a shift to a more graphic, more visceral verb of ingestion.[33] Whether or not the author(s) of the gospel intended to heighten the shock value of the bread of life discourse, however, by substituting *trōgō* for *esthiō*, English verbs such as "gnaw," "munch," and "crunch" merely make explicit the violence always implicit anyway in the consumption of

---

30. See 36–37 above.
31. To adapt Bennett's terminology, the Fourth Gospel is infused with a concept of "vital materiality" in which nonsentient matter is not mere "quiescent stuff" (*Vibrant Matter*, 40).
32. See ibid., 44.
33. For a deft summary of the debate, see Warren, *My Flesh Is Meat Indeed*, 41–44. Warren herself concludes that this verbal shift is not consequential.

animal flesh—and, indeed, of foodstuffs of any kind. Brillat-Savarin ably captures that visceral violence: "Lips stop whatever might try to escape; the teeth bite and break it; saliva drenches it; the tongue mashes and churns it; a breathlike sucking pushes it toward the gullet; the tongue lifts it up to make it slide and slip; … and it is pulled down into the stomach to be submitted to sundry baser transformations."[34] In repeatedly representing himself as edible matter, the Johannine Jesus repeatedly invites his/its own dissolution. As Bennett notes, "food bobs above and below the threshold of a distinct entity."[35] As bread, the Johannine Jesus enters the eater's gnawing, munching, crunching oral cavity with a distinct form, with a discrete identity; once masticated, swallowed, and digested, however, that identity dissipates. Nothing effects a thoroughgoing deconstruction of identity quite like the large intestine.[36]

The issue of disintegration evokes the specter of dehumanization. As bread, as water, as vegetable, as meat, as object, the Son of Humanity, or Human One, risks dehumanization, risks becoming the Son of Subhumanity, the Subhuman One. The machinery of dehumanization, indeed, drives the plot engine of the Fourth Gospel. The Johannine Jesus is an ethnically marked subject ("How is it that you, a Jew [*Ioudaios*], ask a drink of me, a woman of Samaria?" [4:9; cf. 4:22; 18:35; 19:19]) who is animalized through being subjected to bloody slaughter ("Behold the lamb" [1:29, 36; cf. 19:14, 36; Exod 12:46; Num 9:12]).[37] Moreover, the Johannine Jesus on the colonial cross is as much a thing as an animal. Colonial discourse analyst Aimé Césaire long ago equated colonization with "thingification" (*chosification*).[38] The Roman colonial cross was an instrument, a machine, designed to turn the slave body or the rebel body into a thing of horror.

---

34. Jean Anthelme Brillat-Savarin, *The Physiology of Taste, or, Meditations on Transcendental Gastronomy*, trans. M. K. F. Fisher (New York: Vintage, 2009), 54.

35. Bennett, *Vibrant Matter*, 49.

36. As medieval theologians, contemplating the sanitized savagery of the eucharistic rite, well understood: "With concern and anxiety, [they] follow the descent of Christ's body into the *antrum*, the damp and smelly bowels" (Piero Camporesi, "The Consecrated Host: A Wondrous Excess," in *Fragments for a History of the Human Body*, vol. 1, ed. Michel Feher with Ramona Naddaff and Nadia Tazi [New York: Zone, 1989], 228).

37. And is duly devoured (6:50–56), as we have just seen, even if not as lamb.

38. Aimé Césaire, *Discourse on Colonialism*, trans. Joan Pinkham (New York: Monthly Review, 2000), 36. Césaire also equated colonization with animalization (35), as did Fanon, as we saw earlier (p. 82 above).

6. What a Divine Animal and Plant Has to Teach Us about Being Human   119

And ultimately, of course, to turn it into lifeless, thingified flesh, dead meat, a carcass, a corpse.³⁹

Reanimating a Crucified Corpse

New materialism enables a new look at that troublesome *thing* in the Fourth Gospel: the cold, lifeless corpse of its protagonist: "After these things, Joseph of Arimathea … asked Pilate to let him take away the [dead] body/corpse [*to sōma*] of Jesus. Pilate gave him permission; so he came and removed the body. Nicodemus … also came.… They took the body of Jesus and wrapped it.… Because … the tomb was nearby, they laid Jesus there" (19:38–42).

Chen, introducing *Animacies: Biopolitics, Racial Mattering, and Queer Affect*, explains that it analyzes "how matter that is considered insensate, immobile, deathly, or otherwise 'wrong' animates cultural life" in crucial ways.⁴⁰ Extrapolating from Chen, one might ask: what is more insensate, more immobile, more deathly, more "wrong" than a corpse (an example of liminal matter that, surprisingly, Chen does not consider)?⁴¹ What corpse has animated cultural life more profoundly in the history of this planet than that of Jesus of Nazareth?⁴² It has animated it precisely by constituting an exemplary case of what Chen calls "the

---

39. As such, the Roman practice of crucifixion would also qualify as an extreme instance of what Alexander G. Weheliye has terms a "racializing assemblage" (*Habeas Viscus: Racializing Assemblages, Biopolitics, and Black Feminist Theories of the Human* [Durham, NC: Duke University Press, 2014]). Weheliye's version of the Deleuzoguattarian concept of assemblage is less about the intimate interimplication of the human in the nonhuman and vice versa than about the procedures whereby some humans consign other humans to nonhuman status—or, more precisely, and to cite a formulation that runs through the book, enact the hierarchical distinction of full humans from not-quite humans and nonhumans. Weheliye's searing study fuses the assemblage concept with black feminist theories "that tackle notions of the human as it interfaces with gender, coloniality, slavery, racialization, and political violence" (24)

40. Chen, *Animacies*, 2.

41. Contrast Margaret Schwartz, *Dead Matter: The Meaning of Iconic Corpses* (Minneapolis: University of Minnesota Press, 2015).

42. What Schwartz has to say of the corpse in general is supremely true of Jesus's corpse in particular: "The corpse is a material thing freighted with immensely powerful cultural meaning. To [begin to analyze it] is thus to inquire precisely into the relationship between the material and the textual, between the thing itself and the rich variety of representational texts required to make sense of it" (ibid., 1).

fragile division between animate and inanimate,"[43] which brings us to the concept of *animacy*.

With its roots in the field of linguistics, animacy may be defined at its simplest as "a quality of agency, awareness, mobility, and liveness."[44] Chen, however, is preoccupied with the following question: What if nonhuman animals or inanimate objects "enter the calculus of animacy: what happens then?"[45] What if a sheep, say, or a loaf of bread, or a vine, or a body of water, or a ray of light enters the calculus of animacy?[46] What if a corpse enters it? What happens then? The Fourth Gospel may be read as an elaborate literary and theological exploration of that deanthropocentrizing "what if?"

The Johannine Jesus is always already dead because, as we noted earlier, he is always already risen.[47] The live/dead, animate/inanimate binary is the ultimate one that the Fourth Gospel troubles. This troubling finds expression not just in the gospel's resurrection narratives but also in the "inanimate" metaphors used of the gospel's protagonist. The Fourth Gospel might be said to rewrite in advance "the default grammar of agency" to which we moderns, and even postmoderns, tend to have reflexive recourse, one "that assigns activity to people and passivity to things"[48]—things like plants, other foodstuffs, and corpses.

To put it another way, the Fourth Gospel enacts a profound disturbance of what Chen calls *the animacy hierarchy*,[49] that is, the world-

---

43. Chen, *Animacies*, 2.
44. Ibid.
45. Ibid., 3.
46. As Julian Yates puts it: "There exists a history of … the plant, and the animal, of life, that is simultaneously and necessarily also a history of what has been called 'human,' and … telling that story, without the aura of human exceptionalism, will produce an order of archival vertigo at the proliferation of tracks and the leveling of ontological categories" ("Sheep Tracks: A Multi-Species Impression," in Cohen, *Animal, Vegetable, Mineral*, 198). Earlier Yates makes the apophatic confession, "I do not actually know what a sheep, a singular, historical sheep, or a single, historical flock is, exactly" (184)—which, for me, underwrites the uncanny aptness of "lamb" as a metaphor for divinity in the Fourth Gospel.
47. See pp. 35, 38 above.
48. Bennett, *Vibrant Matter*, 119.
49. A concept Chen draws from linguist Michael Silverstein ("Hierarchy of Features and Ergativity," in *Grammatical Categories in Australian Languages*, ed. R. M. W. Dixon [Canberra: Australian Institute of Aboriginal Studies, 1976], 112–71), although Chen presses the concept through a different theoretical grid than any that was available to Silverstein.

6. What a Divine Animal and Plant Has to Teach Us about Being Human 121

structuring human ranking of inorganic matter, plant life, animal life, disabled life, "fully human" life—and, I would add, divine life—in terms of perceived intrinsic worth and hence of ethical and political priority. As Chen argues, the animacy hierarchy has "broad ramifications for issues of ecology and environment, since objects, animals, substances, and spaces are assigned constrained zones of possibility and agency by extant grammars of animacy."[50] Does the Fourth Gospel affirm or disturb the animacy hierarchy that structures and sustains contemporary Western biopolitics? I submit that what Chen has to say of *Animacies* seems yet truer of the Fourth Gospel: "This book seeks to trouble [the] binary of life and nonlife."[51]

The Jesus Plant

The Johannine Jesus enacts animacy in multiple intersecting nonhuman ways that invite less anthropocentric modes of affective engagement than the Christs of classic orthodoxy, Christs supposedly modeled on the Johannine Jesus, Christs equal parts human and divine. Johannine scholars are accustomed to pondering the anomalous body that the risen Johannine Jesus possesses, a body ordinary enough that its owner can be mistaken for a common laborer ("Thinking he was the gardener [*ho kēpouros*], [Mary Magdalene] said to him …" [20:15; cf. 21:4])[52] and extraordinary enough that it can pass through locked doors ("The doors had been shut, but Jesus came and stood among them" [20:26; cf. 20:19]), yet an anthropomorphic body nonetheless. But it is as vegetable that the Johannine Jesus also lives, and lives on. Speaking from beyond the grave while yet to enter the grave he intones: "I am the true vine [*egō eimi hē ampolos hē alēthinē*], and my Father is the vinegrower. He removes every

---

50. Chen, *Animacies*, 13; see also 55: "Animacy is a craft of the senses; it endows our surroundings with life, death, and things in between."
51. Ibid., 11.
52. Margaret Daly-Denton takes her cue from John 21:15 to read Mary Magdalene's assumption that the Johannine Jesus is a gardener not as an inept misidentification but as an entirely apt identification (*John: An Earth Bible Commentary; Supposing Him to Be the Gardener*, EBC [New York: Bloomsbury T&T Clark, 2017]). For Daly-Denton, the verse unlocks a theme of Edenic restoration that, she argues, runs through the Fourth Gospel.

branch in me that bears no fruit. Every branch that bears fruit he prunes to make it bear more fruit" (15:1–2).

The Jesus who styles himself a climbing, creeping, twining, trailing plant of the Vitaceae family is a Jesus who has yet to die but is already dead and risen, who speaks beyond the grave of things yet to come that have already occurred. "Abide [*meinate*] in me as I abide in you," the vine enjoins his followers. "As the branch cannot bear fruit by itself unless it abides in the vine, neither can you unless you abide in me" (15:4). How are they to abide in him? Through the Spirit whom they are destined to receive ("he abides [*menei*] with you, and he will be in you" [14:17]) once Jesus has expired and returned to the Father (7:39; 14:16, 23, 26; 19:30; 20:22).[53] To be the living, nurturing vine, Jesus must already be dead and buried.[54] As vine, Jesus improbably pushes ever-fresh climbing, creeping, twining, trailing tendrils out of the hollowed rock in which he has been entombed. As vine, he (it?) exists in a persistent vegetative state, technically dead but nonetheless alive, permanently disabled but differently abled and enabling ("apart from me you can do nothing" [15:5]).

The Johannine Jesus, then, lives on beyond his few fleeting anthropomorphic resurrection appearances primarily as vegetable and vegetable byproduct (that is, as bread and wine: "Those who eat my flesh and drink my blood abide [*menei*] in me, and I in them" [6:56]). A less transcendent image would be hard to imagine. "What does it mean to exist at the level of the zero," Chen muses in a different context, "moving away from humanness down the animacy hierarchy?"[55] This is a christological keno-

---

53. See Keener, *The Gospel of John*, 2:988: "Jesus has been talking about disciples 'dwelling' in him after his return from the Father to give them the Spirit (14:23); now he expands this 'dwelling' place image by emphasizing how branches must continue to depend on the vine or perish (15:1–7). Branches that remain attached to and dependent on the vine 'dwell' with or 'remain' in it."

54. And to be the bread of life, that other vegetable-derived life form in which he lives on beyond the grave, Jesus must also be dead: "The bread that I will give for the life of the world is my flesh" (John 6:51). And relatedly: "Truly, truly I say to you, unless a grain of wheat falls into the earth and dies, it remains a single grain; but if it dies, it bears much fruit" (12:24).

55. Chen, *Animacies*, 40. As Chen notes, however, "vegetables, believed to be living, are not at the bottom of the animacy hierarchy, as stones seem to be" (40), a notion that may be traced back to Aristotle. As such, 1 Cor 10:4, "For they drank of the spiritual rock [*petras*] that followed them, and the rock was Christ," begs a new-materialist study all of its own. Such a study might well take Jeffrey Jerome Cohen's

sis with which New Testament scholarship or systematic theology has yet to reckon. Arguably more than any other single term, *vegetable* designates the "discredited human subject," as Chen observes.[56] Human beings said to be in "persistent vegetative states" are "deemed to be at, near, or beyond the threshold of death."[57] At that threshold the Johannine Jesus ever hovers, even or especially in his risen form, his eternally nail-holed hands ("Then he said to Thomas, 'Put your finger here, and see my hands'" [20:27]) forever testifying to his vegetal immobility on the woody stem of the cross, yet that persistent vegetality now manifesting his divinity: "Thomas answered him, 'My Lord and my God!'" (20:28).[58]

Even if the Johannine Jesus is a figural vegetable, when all is said and done,[59] the books in which he is enfleshed have almost always been made of literal vegetable matter,[60] from ancient papyrus reeds down to contemporary wood fibers. Animacy as a concept, then, also enables us to apprehend the vegetal materiality of the Fourth Gospel, the vegetable byproduct that is that particular book, as itself the risen body of the Johannine Jesus. The Fourth Gospel is an inanimate subject that speaks incessantly in the absence of an animate author. As such, the Fourth Gospel is a living, if inanimate, body. Although one of the foundational documents of Western culture, the Fourth Gospel, both as material object and as narrative content, may be read as a testament to the ineluctable illogicality of the biopolitical logics of Western culture that distinguish so confidently and consequentially between human and nonhuman, agent and

---

Stone: An Ecology of the Inhuman (Minneapolis: University of Minnesota Press, 2015) as its point of departure. Cohen writes: "Hurl a rock and you'll shatter an ontology" (1). And possibly a Christology as well.

56. Chen, *Animacies*, 41.

57. Ibid., 7.

58. Vegetality always conceals vitality within its apparent immobility, as Marder observes: "The etymology of 'vegetation' ... points back to the Middle Latin *vegetabilis*, meaning 'growing' or 'flourishing,' the verbs *vegetare* ('to animate' or 'to enliven') and *vegere* ('to be alive,' 'to be active'), and the adjectice *vegetus*, denoting the qualities of vigorousness and activity.... While the predominant usage of the verb 'to vegetate' is negative, linked to the passivity or inactivity of animals or human beings who behave as though they were sedentary plants, its subterranean history relates it to the exact opposite of this privileged meaning" (*Plant-Thinking*, 20).

59. But also a figural Son of God, as I noted at the outset of this chapter. In naming metaphoricity as such, I am not attempting to strip it of its world-creating power.

60. When they have not been made of animal matter: parchment or vellum.

object, dynamic and static, abled and disabled, animate and inanimate, living and dead.

The Unhumanity of God in Christ

The Fourth Gospel unsettles the animacy hierarchy and then topples it head over hoof, horn over root. To demonstrate that it does so, one does not have to read the Fourth Gospel against itself, to read into it things that are not in it, things that are only behind it or alongside it; rather, one only has to read those things that are already in it, or, better, on it, trotting or slithering across its surface or rooted in its soil, not least the things its Jesus becomes. As Chen remarks, "animacy tends to hide its own contradictions, the transubstantiations, the transmatterings that go on underneath, through, and across it."[61] The interest of the Fourth Gospel for the topic of animacy is that it parades its transubstantiations, its transmatterings in plain sight.

The implications for Johannine Christology? It is no longer sufficient to say that the Johannine Jesus is "incarnated," if by that we mean that he is the preexistent divine occupant of a discrete human body, the human thereby becoming the consummate revelation of the divine.[62] The Johannine Jesus is better conceived as "an array of bodies"[63]—or, as we saw earlier, an assemblage of bodies—most of them nonhuman. The divine is definitively revealed in both the human and the nonhuman in the Fourth Gospel, and, presumably, more in the nonhuman than in the human, since the divine is itself nonhuman.[64]

The human and the nonhuman are not exclusive categories, however, whether in the Fourth Gospel or in general. As Bennett notes, we

---

61. Chen, *Animacies*, 236.

62. See Massumi, *What Animals Teach Us*, 97: "Do not [be] misled ... into thinking of the body as waiting, with the infinite patience of dumb matter, to incarnate a mind." Or a god, for that matter.

63. Bennett, *Vibrant Matter*, 112.

64. And, at its most apophatic, is plantlike. Marder remarks: "The other who (or that) bestows upon us our humanity need not be—in keeping with Aristotle's preferred points of comparison in *The Politics*—a god or a beast, the magnificently superhuman or the deplorably subhuman. It may well be the most mundane and unobtrusive instance of alterity, to which we do not (already or yet) dare to compare ourselves: the plant" (*Plant-Thinking*, 36).

humans "are made up of its."⁶⁵ She cites as a near-to-hand instance of her own itness the crook of her elbow, which, if biologists are to be believed, is a teeming ecosystem, "a bountiful home to no fewer than six tribes of bacteria."⁶⁶ Donna Haraway remarks analogously: "I love the fact that human genomes can be found in only about 10 percent of all the cells that occupy the mundane space I call my body; the other 90 percent of the cells are filled with the genomes of bacteria, fungi, protists, and such.... I am vastly outnumbered by my tiny companions.... To be one is always to *become with* many."⁶⁷ The *its*, the animal others, proliferate infinitely in all of us, making our own flesh exotically alien to us. "Don't be mistaken into thinking that the more-than-human is outside, surrounding the human, in the environment," Massumi admonishes. "The more-than-human is also in the makeup of the human. For the human body is an animal body, and ... the farther down one goes into the composition of the animal body, the more levels of unhumanness one finds."⁶⁸

None of this, as it happens, is entirely foreign to the Fourth Gospel, a text that systematically exposes the unhumanness of its protagonist, albeit in a different register, revealing a heavenly Son of Humanity (3:13) who is not altogether human, but not only because he is also the Son of God: additionally he is a nonhuman animal, a plant, and still more thingly things, such as a door—an ostensibly "dead" but agentially charged object with the capacity to include and exclude at an elemental level. The more-

---

65. Bennett, *Vibrant Matter*, 113.
66. Ibid., 112.
67. Donna J. Haraway, *When Species Meet*, Posthumanities 3 (Minneapolis: University of Minnesota Press, 2008), 3–4, emphasis original.
68. Massumi, *What Animals Teach Us*, 93. The "external" environment in which the human subsists is also utterly inhuman, on Haraway's account. She calls the invisible inhabitants of that environment "chthonic ones," from Greek *chthonios*, "of the earth." She writes: "I imagine chthonic ones as replete with tentacles, feelers, digits, cords, whiptails, spider legs, and very unruly hair. Chthonic ones romp in multicritter humus but have no truck with sky-gazing Homo. Chthonic ones are monsters in the best sense.... Chthonic ones are not safe; they have no truck with ideologues; they belong to no one; they writhe and luxuriate in manifold forms and manifold names in all the airs, waters, and places of earth. They make and unmake; they are made and unmade. They are who are. No wonder the world's great monotheisms in both religious and secular guises have tried again and again to exterminate the chthonic ones" (*Staying with the Trouble*, 2). The Synoptic Gospels resound with Jesus's repeated exorcisms of demons, close kin to the chthonic ones. Interestingly, however, there are no exorcisms in the Fourth Gospel.

than-human is not only *outside* the Johannine Jesus in nonhuman animals, in plants, in inorganic matter. The more-than-human is also *inside* the Johannine Jesus, for the human body of the Johannine Jesus is also profoundly unhuman. To descend even shallowly into this body is to encounter multiple levels of unhumanness: animal, vegetal, inorganic, and, of course, divine. The human Johannine Jesus cannot be surgically separated from the nonhuman Johannine Jesus: they exist in indissoluble symbiosis. He and it impel us to engage civilly, even ethically, with the multitudinous nonhumans in the innumerable interlocking assemblages in which we, like him and it, are always already embedded and always already active.[69] If the Fourth Gospel has most often been read as proclaiming a new stage in human development, the becoming human of God and as such the becoming divine of humanity,[70] it now needs to be read more often as illustrating the inseparability of the human, the nonhuman, and the divine and as such the divinity of the nonhuman no less than the human, which is to say its absolute value and ethical entitlement. In an age characterized by unprecedented crisis in the human relationship to the nonhuman, above all by climate catastrophe and mass extinction, a materialist theology may be the only theology that matters, and within the New Testament a new materialist theology finds its most conspicuous resource in the Fourth Gospel and its singularly nonhuman protagonist.

---

69. See Bennett, *Vibrant Matter*, 116.
70. As classically expressed by Athanasius: "For the Son of God became man so that we might become God" (*Inc.* 54.3; PG 25.192B).

Bibliography

Abraham, Nicolas, and Maria Torok. *The Shell and the Kernel: Renewals of Psychoanalysis*. Vol. 1. Translated by Nicholas T. Rand. Chicago: University of Chicago Press, 1994.

Agnew, Vanessa. "History's Affective Turn: Historical Reenactment and Its Work in the Present." *RH* 11 (2007): 299–312.

Ahmed, Sara. *The Cultural Politics of Emotion*. 2nd ed. New York: Routledge, 2014.

———. *The Promise of Happiness*. Durham, NC: Duke University Press, 2010.

Aichele, George. *The Play of Signifiers: Poststructuralism and Study of the Bible*. BRP. Leiden: Brill, 2016.

———. *Simulating Jesus: Reality Effects in the Gospels*. BibleWorld. London: Equinox, 2011.

———. *Tales of Posthumanity: The Bible and Contemporary Popular Culture*. BMW 65. Sheffield: Sheffield Phoenix, 2014.

Albani, Matthias. "'The One Like a Son of Man' (Dan 7:13) and the Royal Ideology." Pages 47–53 in *Enoch and Qumran Origins: New Light on a Forgotten Connection*. Edited by Gabriele Boccaccini. Grand Rapids: Eerdmans, 2005.

Alber, Jan, and Monika Fludernik, eds. *Postclassical Narratology: Approaches and Analyses*. TIN. Columbus: Ohio State University Press, 2010.

Allen, Willoughby C. *A Critical and Exegetical Commentary on the Gospel according to S. Matthew*. ICC. Edinburgh: T&T Clark, 1907.

Anderson, Janice Capel, and Stephen D. Moore. "Matthew and Masculinity." Pages 134–48 in *New Testament Masculinities*. Edited by Stephen D. Moore and Janice Capel Anderson. SemeiaSt 45. Atlanta: Society of Biblical Literature, 2003.

Anzaldúa, Gloria. *Borderlands/La Frontera: The New Mestiza*. San Francisco: Aunt Lute, 1987.

Athanasiou, Athena. "Towards a New Epistemology: The 'Affective Turn.'" *Historein* 8 (2012): 5–16.
Barad, Karen. *Meeting the Universe Halfway: Quantum Physics and the Entanglement of Matter and Meaning*. Durham, NC: Duke University Press, 2007.
———. "Posthumanist Performativity: Toward an Understanding of How Matter Comes to Matter." *Signs* 28 (2003): 801–31.
Barker, Francis, Peter Hulme, and Margaret Iversen, eds. *Cannibalism and the Colonial World*. Cambridge: Cambridge University Press, 1998.
Behar, Katherine, ed. *Object-Oriented Feminism*. Minneapolis: University of Minnesota Press, 2016.
Bennett, Jane. "Systems and Things: On Vital Materialism and Object-Oriented Philosophy." Pages 223–40 in *The Nonhuman Turn*. Edited by Richard Grusin. C21. Minneapolis: University of Minnesota Press, 2015.
———. *Vibrant Matter: A Political Ecology of Things*. Durham, NC: Duke University Press, 2010.
Bergson, Henri. *Creative Evolution*. Translated by Arthur Miller. Mineola, NY: Dover, 1998.
Berlant, Lauren. *Cruel Optimism*. Durham, NC: Duke University Press, 2011.
Bohache, Thomas. "Matthew." Pages 487–516 in *The Queer Bible Commentary*. Edited by Deryn Guest, Robert Goss, Mona West, and Thomas Bohache. London: SCM, 2006.
Bradley, Keith. "Animalizing the Slave: The Truth of Fiction." *JRS* 90 (2000): 110–25.
Breed, Brennan W. *Nomadic Text: A Theory of Reception History*. ISBL. Bloomington: Indiana University Press, 2014.
Brennan, Teresa. *The Transmission of Affect*. Ithaca, NY: Cornell University Press, 2004.
Brillat-Savarin, Jean Anthelme. *The Physiology of Taste, or, Meditations on Transcendental Gastronomy*. Translated by M. K. F. Fisher. New York: Vintage, 2009.
Brinkema, Eugenie. *The Forms of the Affects*. Durham, NC: Duke University Press, 2014.
Brintnall, Kent L., Joseph A. Marchal, and Stephen D. Moore, eds. *Sexual Disorientations: Queer Temporalities, Affects, Theologies*. TTC. New York: Fordham University Press, 2017.

Brown, Bill, ed. *Things*. CIB. Chicago: University of Chicago Press, 2004.
Brown, Raymond E. *The Death of the Messiah: From Gethsemane to the Grave; A Commentary on the Passion Narratives in the Four Gospels*. 2 vols. ABRL. New York: Doubleday, 1994.
Bryant, Arthur. *The Lion and the Unicorn: A Historian's Testament*. London: Collins, 1969.
Buell, Denise Kimber. "God's Own People: Specters of Race, Ethnicity, and Gender in Early Christian Studies." Pages 159–90 in *Prejudice and Christian Beginnings: Investigating Race, Gender, and Ethnicity in Early Christian Studies*. Edited by Elisabeth Schüssler Fiorenza and Laura Nasrallah. Minneapolis: Fortress, 2009.
———. "Hauntology Meets Posthumanism: Some Payoffs for Biblical Studies." Pages 29–56 in *The Bible and Posthumanism*. Edited by Jennifer L. Koosed. SemeiaSt 74. Atlanta: Society of Biblical Literature, 2014.
———. "The Microbes and Pneuma That Therefore I Am." Pages 63–87 in *Divinanimality: Animal Theory, Creaturely Theology*. Edited by Stephen D. Moore. TTC. New York: Fordham University Press, 2014.
Buell, Denise Kimber, and Stephen D. Moore, eds. *Queer Times: Futurity, Hauntology, and Utopia in and after Biblical Texts*. BibInt (forthcoming).
Bultmann, Rudolf. *The Gospel of John: A Commentary*. Translated by G. R. Beasley-Murray, R. W. N. Hoare, and J. K. Riches. Eugene, OR: Wipf & Stock, 2014.
Butler, Judith. "Against Proper Objects." *differences* 6 (1994): 1–26.
Camporesi, Piero. "The Consecrated Host: A Wondrous Excess." Pages 220–37 in *Fragments for a History of the Human Body*. Edited by Michel Feher with Ramona Naddaff and Nadia Tazi. Vol. 1. New York: Zone, 1989.
Caputo, John D. "Bodies Still Unrisen, Events Still Unsaid: A Hermeneutic of Bodies without Flesh." Pages 94–116 in *Apophatic Bodies: Negative Theology, Incarnation, and Relationality*. Edited by Chris Boesel and Catherine Keller. TTC. New York: Fordham University Press, 2010.
Carter, Warren. "Cross-Gendered Romans and Mark's Jesus: Legion Enters the Pigs (Mark 5:1–20)." *JBL* 134 (2015): 139–55.
———. *Matthew and the Margins: A Sociopolitical and Religious Reading*. BL. Maryknoll, NY: Orbis, 2000.
Certeau, Michel de. *The Writing of History*. Translated by Tom Conley. EP. New York: Columbia University Press, 1988.

Césaire, Aimé. *Discourse on Colonialism*. Translated by Joan Pinkham. New York: Monthly Review, 2000.

Chen, Mel Y. *Animacies: Biopolitics, Racial Mattering, and Queer Affect*. PM. Durham, NC: Duke University Press, 2012.

Cho, Grace M. *Haunting the Korean Diaspora: Shame, Secrecy, and the Forgotten War*. Minneapolis: University of Minnesota Press, 2008.

———. "Voices from the Teum: Synesthetic Trauma and the Ghosts of the Korean Diaspora." Pages 151–69 in *The Affective Turn: Theorizing the Social*. Edited by Patricia Ticineto Clough with Jean Halley. Durham, NC: Duke University Press, 2007.

Choi, Jin Young. *Postcolonial Discipleship of Embodiment: An Asian and Asian American Feminist Reading of the Gospel of Mark*. PR. New York: Palgrave Macmillan, 2015.

Clough, Patricia Ticineto. "The Affective Turn: Political Economy, Biomedia, and Bodies." Pages 206–27 in *The Affect Theory Reader*. Edited by Melissa Gregg and Gregory J. Seigworth. Durham, NC: Duke University Press, 2010.

Clough, Patricia Ticineto, ed., with Jean Halley. *The Affective Turn: Theorizing the Social*. Durham, NC: Duke University Press, 2007.

Cohen, Jeffrey Jerome. "Introduction: All Things." Pages 1–8 in *Animal, Vegetable, Mineral: Ethics and Objects*. Edited by Jeffrey Jerome Cohen. Washington, DC: Oliphaunt, 2012.

———. *Stone: An Ecology of the Inhuman*. Minneapolis: University of Minnesota Press, 2015.

Colebrook, Claire. *Death of the Posthuman: Essays on Extinction*. Vol. 1. Ann Arbor, MI: Open Humanities, 2014.

Collins, Adela Yarbro. *Mark: A Commentary*. Hermeneia. Minneapolis: Fortress, 2007.

Collins, John J. *Daniel: A Commentary on the Book of Daniel*. Hermeneia. Minneapolis: Fortress, 1993.

Concannon, Cavan W. *When You Were Gentiles: Specters of Ethnicity in Roman Corinth and Paul's Corinthian Correspondence*. Synkrisis. New Haven: Yale University Press, 2014.

Coole, Diana, and Samantha Frost, eds. *New Materialisms: Ontology, Agency, and Politics*. Durham, NC: Duke University Press, 2010.

Creed, Barbara, and Jeanette Hoorn, eds. *Body Trade: Captivity, Cannibalism and Colonialism in the Pacific*. New York: Routledge, 2001.

Currie, Mark. *Postmodern Narrative Theory*. 2nd ed. Transitions. New York: Palgrave, 2010.

Cvetkovich, Ann. *An Archive of Feelings: Trauma, Sexuality, and Lesbian Public Cultures.* SerQ. Durham, NC: Duke University Press, 2003.

———. *Depression: A Public Feeling.* Durham, NC: Duke University Press, 2012.

Daly, Mary. *Beyond God the Father: Toward a Philosophy of Women's Liberation.* Boston: Beacon, 1973.

Daly-Denton, Margaret. *John: An Earth Bible Commentary; Supposing Him to Be the Gardener.* EBC. New York: Bloomsbury T&T Clark, 2017.

Danker, Frederick W. "The Demonic Secret in Mark: A Reexamination of the Cry of Dereliction (15.34)." *ZNW* 61 (1970): 48–69.

Davies, W. D., and Dale C. Allison. *A Critical and Exegetical Commentary on the Gospel according to Saint Matthew.* 2 vols. ICC. Edinburgh: T&T Clark, 1991.

Defoe, Daniel. *The Life and Strange Surprizing Adventures of Robinson Crusoe, of York, Mariner.* London: Taylor, 1719.

DeLanda, Manuel. *Assemblage Theory.* SR. Edinburgh: Edinburgh University Press, 2016.

Deleuze, Gilles. *Cinema 1: The Movement-Image.* Translated by Hugh Tomlinson and Barbara Habberjam. London: Athlone, 1984.

———. *Cinema 2: The Time-Image.* Translated by Hugh Tomlinson and Robert Galeta. Minneapolis: University of Minnesota Press, 1989.

———. *Difference and Repetition.* Translated by Paul Patton. New York: Columbia University Press, 1994.

———. *Expressionism in Philosophy: Spinoza.* Translated by Martin Joughin. New York: Zone, 1990.

———. *The Fold: Leibniz and the Baroque.* Translated by Tom Conley. CI. Minneapolis: University of Minnesota Press, 1993.

———. *Foucault.* Translated by Seán Hand. CI. Minneapolis: University of Minnesota Press, 1988.

———. *Francis Bacon: The Logic of Sensation.* Translated by Daniel W. Smith. CI. Minneapolis: University of Minnesota Press, 2003.

———. *The Logic of Sense.* Translated by Mark Lester. 2nd ed. New York: Columbia University Press, 1990.

———. *Negotiations, 1972–1990.* Translated by Martin Joughin. New York: Columbia University Press, 1995.

———. "Pensée nomade," followed by discussion. Pages 105–21, 159–90 in *Intensités.* Vol. 1 of *Nietzsche aujourd'hui?* Edited by Maurice de Gandillac and Bernard Pautrat. Colloque de Cerisy. Paris: Union Générale d'Éditions, 1973.

———. *Proust and Signs: The Complete Text*. Translated by Richard Howard. TOB 17. Minneapolis: University of Minnesota Press, 2000.

———. *Two Regimes of Madness: Texts and Interviews, 1975–1995*. Translated by Ames Hodges and Mike Taormina. New York: Semiotext(e), 2007.

Deleuze, Gilles, and Claire Parnet. *Dialogues*. Translated by Hugh Tomlinson and Barbara Habberjam. EP. New York: Columbia University Press, 1987.

———. *Dialogues II*. Translated by Hugh Tomlinson and Barbara Habberjam. Rev. ed. EP. New York: Columbia University Press, 2007.

Deleuze, Gilles, and Félix Guattari. *Anti-Oedipus: Capitalism and Schizophrenia*. Translated by Robert Hurley, Mark Seem, and Helen R. Lane. CI. Minneapolis: University of Minnesota Press, 1983.

———. *Kafka: Toward a Minor Literature*. Translated by Dana Polan. THL 30. Minneapolis: University of Minnesota Press, 1986.

———. *A Thousand Plateaus: Capitalism and Schizophrenia*. Translated by Brian Massumi. CI. Minneapolis: University of Minnesota Press, 1987.

———. *What Is Philosophy?* Translated by Hugh Tomlinson and Graham Burchell. New York: Columbia University Press, 1994.

Derrida, Jacques. *The Animal That Therefore I Am*. Translated by David Wills. PCP. New York: Fordham University Press, 2008.

———. "The Animal That Therefore I Am (More to Follow)." Pages 1–51 in Jacques Derrida, *The Animal That Therefore I Am*. Translated by David Wills. PCP. New York: Fordham University Press, 2008.

———. *The Beast and the Sovereign*. 2 vols. Translated by Geoffrey Bennington. SJD 1–2. Chicago: University of Chicago Press, 2009–2011.

———. "'Eating Well,' or the Calculation of the Subject." Pages 255–87 in *Points…: Interviews, 1974–1994*. Edited by Elizabeth Weber. Meridian. Stanford, CA: Stanford University Press, 1995.

———. "Economimesis." Translated by Richard Klein. *Diacritics* 11.2 (1981): 2–25.

———. *Glas*. Translated by John P. Leavey Jr. and Richard Rand. Lincoln: University of Nebraska Press, 1986.

———. "An Interview with Jacques Derrida on the Limits of Digestion." Conducted by Daniel Birnbaum and Anders Olsson. *e-flux* 2 (2009). https://tinyurl.com/SBL0691b.

———. *Specters of Marx: The State of the Debt, the Work of Mourning and the New International*. Translated by Peggy Kamuf. New York: Routledge, 1994.

Dinshaw, Carolyn. *Getting Medieval: Sexualities and Communities, Pre- and Postmodern*. SerQ. Durham, NC: Duke University Press, 1999.

———. "Got Medieval?" *Journal of the History of Sexuality* 10 (2001): 202–12.

———. *How Soon Is Now? Medieval Texts, Amateur Readers, and the Queerness of Time*. Durham, NC: Duke University Press, 2012.

Dinshaw, Carolyn, Lee Edelman, Roderick A. Ferguson, Carla Freccero, Elizabeth Freeman, Judith Halberstam, Annamarie Jagose, Christopher S. Nealon, and Tan Hoang Nguyen. "Theorizing Queer Temporalities: A Roundtable Discussion." *GLQ* 13 (2007): 177–95.

Dolphijn, Rick, and Iris van der Tuin. *New Materialism: Interviews and Cartographies*. NM. Falmouth, UK: Open Humanities, 2012.

Donaldson, Laura E. "Gospel Hauntings: The Postcolonial Demons of New Testament Criticism." Pages 97–113 in *Postcolonial Biblical Criticism: Interdisciplinary Intersections*. Edited by Stephen D. Moore and Fernando F. Segovia. BP 8. New York: T&T Clark International, 2005.

Dube, Musa W. *Postcolonial Feminist Interpretation of the Bible*. St. Louis, MO: Chalice, 2000.

Duncan, Pansy. *The Emotional Life of Postmodern Film: Affect Theory's Other*. RRCMS 81. New York: Routledge, 2015.

———. "Taking the Smooth with the Rough: Texture, Emotion, and the Other Postmodernism." *PMLA* 129 (2014): 204–22.

Dunning, Benjamin H. *Specters of Paul: Sexual Difference in Early Christian Thought*. Divinations. Philadelphia: University of Pennsylvania Press, 2011.

During, Simon. "The Postcolonial Aesthetic." *PMLA* 129 (2014): 498–503.

Edelman, Lee. *No Future: Queer Theory and the Death Drive*. SerQ. Durham, NC: Duke University Press, 2004.

Elliott, Matthew A. *Faithful Feelings: Rethinking Emotion in the New Testament*. Grand Rapids: Kregel, 2006.

Elliott, Scott S. *Reconfiguring Mark's Jesus: Narrative Criticism after Poststructuralism*. BMW 41. Sheffield: Sheffield Phoenix, 2011.

Fanon, Frantz. *The Wretched of the Earth*. Translated by Richard Philcox. New York: Grove, 2004.

Felski, Rita. *The Limits of Critique*. Chicago: University of Chicago Press, 2015.

Foucault, Michel. *The Order of Things: An Archaeology of the Human Sciences*. Trans. anon. RC. New York: Routledge, 2001.

———. "Theatrum Philosophicum." Pages 165–97 in *Language, Counter-Memory, Practice: Selected Essays and Interviews*. Edited by Donald F. Bouchard. Translated by Donald F. Bouchard and Sherry Simon. Ithaca, NY: Cornell University Press, 1977.

Fradenburg, Louise, and Carla Freccero. "Introduction: Caxton, Foucault, and the Pleasures of History." Pages xiii–xxiv in *Premodern Sexualities*. Edited by Louise Fradenburg and Carla Freccero. New York: Routledge, 1996.

France, R. T. *The Gospel of Mark: A Commentary on the Greek Text*. NIGTC. Grand Rapids: Eerdmans, 2002.

Freccero, Carla. *Queer/Early/Modern*. SerQ. Durham, NC: Duke University Press, 2006.

———. "Queer Spectrality: Haunting the Past." Pages 194–214 in *A Companion to Lesbian, Gay, Bisexual, Transgender, and Queer Studies*. Edited by George E. Haggerty and Molly McGarry. BCCC. Oxford: Blackwell, 2007.

———. "Queer Times." Pages 17–26 in *After Sex? On Writing since Queer Theory*. Edited by Janet Halley and Andrew Parker. SerQ. Durham, NC: Duke University Press, 2011.

Freeman, Elizabeth. *Time Binds: Queer Temporalities, Queer Histories*. PM. Durham, NC: Duke University Press, 2010.

Gallop, Jane. "Close Reading in 2009." *ADEBull* 149 (2010): 15–19.

———. "The Historicization of Literary Studies and the Fate of Close Reading." *Profession* (2007): 181–86.

Gemünden, Petra von. "Emotions and Literary Genres in the Testaments of the Twelve Patriarchs and the New Testament: A Contribution to Form History and Historical Psychology." *BibInt* 24 (2016): 514–35.

Gibson, Andrew. *Towards a Postmodern Theory of Narrative*. PT. Edinburgh: University of Edinburgh Press, 1996.

Giffney, Noreen, and Myra J. Hird, eds. *Queering the Non/Human*. QI. Aldershot, UK: Ashgate, 2008.

Gikandi, Simon. "The Fantasy of the Library." *PMLA* 128 (2013): 9–20.

Gilhus, Ingvild Saelid. *Animals, Gods and Humans: Changing Attitudes to Animals in Greek, Roman and Early Christian Ideas*. New York: Routledge, 2006.

Goldberg, Jonathan. "The History That Will Be." *GLQ* 1 (1995): 385–403.

Goldberg, Jonathan, and Madhavi Menon. "Queering History." *PMLA* 120 (2005): 1608–17.

Goldstone, Andrew, and Ted Underwood. "The Quiet Transformations of Literary Studies: What Thirteen Thousand Scholars Could Tell Us." *NLH* 45 (2014): 359–84.

Gordon, Avery. *Ghostly Matters: Haunting and the Sociological Imagination*. 2nd ed. Minneapolis: University of Minnesota Press, 2008.

Gratton, Peter. *Speculative Realism: Problems and Prospects*. New York: Bloomsbury, 2014.

Graybill, Rhiannon. *Are We Not Men? Unstable Masculinity in the Hebrew Prophets*. Oxford: Oxford University Press, 2016.

Grusin, Richard. "Introduction." Pages vii–xxx in *The Nonhuman Turn*. Edited by Richard Grusin. C21. Minneapolis: University of Minnesota Press, 2015.

Guardiola-Sáenz, Leticia A. "Borderless Women and Borderless Texts: A Cultural Reading of Matthew 15:21–28." *Semeia* 78 (1997): 69–81.

Guattari, Félix. *Molecular Revolution: Psychiatry and Politics*. Translated by Rosemary Sheed. Harmondsworth, UK: Peregrine, 1984.

Gunkel, Heidrun, Rainer Hirsch-Luipold, and John R. Levison. "Plutarch and Pentecost: An Exploration in Interdisciplinary Collaboration." Pages 63–94 in *The Holy Spirit, Inspiration, and the Cultures of Antiquity: Multidisciplinary Perspectives*. Edited by Jörg Frey and John R. Levison. Ekstasis 5. Berlin: de Gruyter, 2014.

Halberstam, J. Jack. *In a Queer Time and Place: Transgender Bodies, Subcultural Lives*. Sexual Cultures. New York: New York University Press, 2005.

Haraway, Donna J. *The Companion Species Manifesto: Dogs, People, and Significant Otherness*. Chicago: Prickly Paradigm, 2003.

———. *Staying with the Trouble: Making Kin in the Chthulucene*. Durham, NC. Duke University Press, 2016.

———. *When Species Meet*. Posthumanities 3. Minneapolis: University of Minnesota Press, 2008.

Harrill, J. Albert. "Cannibalistic Language in the Fourth Gospel and Greco-Roman Polemics of Factionalism (John 6:52–66)." *JBL* 127 (2008): 133–58.

Hester, J. David. "Eunuchs and the Postgender Jesus: Matthew 19.12 and Transgressive Sexualities." *JSNT* 28 (2005): 13–40.

Hezser, Catherine. *Jewish Slavery in Antiquity*. Oxford: Oxford University Press, 2005.

Hick, John. *The Metaphor of God Incarnate: Christology in a Pluralistic Age*. 2nd ed. Louisville: Westminster John Knox, 2006.

Huggan, Graham, and Helen Tiffin. *Postcolonial Ecocriticism: Literature, Animals, Environment*. New York: Routledge, 2010.
Humphries-Brooks, Stephenson. "The Canaanite Women in Matthew." Pages 138–56 in *A Feminist Companion to Matthew*. Edited by Amy-Jill Levine with Marianne Blickenstaff. Sheffield: Sheffield Academic, 2001.
Hur, Ju. *A Dynamic Reading of the Holy Spirit in Luke-Acts*. JSNTSup 211. Sheffield: Sheffield Academic, 2001.
Irigaray, Luce, and Michael Marder. *Through Vegetal Being: Two Philosophical Perspectives*. CLS. New York: Columbia University Press, 2016.
Joyce, James. "Daniel Defoe." *BS* 1 (1964): 1–25.
Kastan, David Scott. *Shakespeare after Theory*. New York: Routledge, 1999.
Keener, Craig S. *Acts: An Exegetical Commentary*. 4 vols. Grand Rapids: Baker Academic, 2012–2015.
———. *The Gospel of John: A Commentary*. 2nd ed. 2 vols. Grand Rapids: Baker Academic, 2012.
Keller, Catherine, and Mary-Jane Rubenstein, eds. *Entangled Worlds: Religion, Science, and New Materialisms*. TTC. New York: Fordham University Press, 2017.
Ketchum, Matthew James. "Specters of Jesus: Ghosts, Gospels, and Resurrection in Early Christianity." Ph.D. diss., Drew University, 2015.
Klancher, Nancy. *The Taming of the Canaanite Woman: Constructions of Christian Identity in the Afterlife of Matthew 15:21–28*. SBR 1. Berlin: de Gruyter, 2013.
Knust, Jennifer. "Who's Afraid of Canaan's Curse? Genesis 9:18–29 and the Challenge of Reparative Reading." *BibInt* 22 (2014): 388–413.
Kohn, Eduardo. *How Forests Think: Toward an Anthropology beyond the Human*. Berkeley: University of California Press, 2013.
Kolnai, Aurel. *On Disgust*. Edited by Barry Smith and Carolyn Korsmeyer. Chicago: Open Court, 2004.
Koosed, Jennifer L., ed. *The Bible and Posthumanism*. SemeiaSt 74. Atlanta: Society of Biblical Literature, 2014.
Koosed, Jennifer L., and Robert Paul Seesengood. "Daniel's Animal Apocalypse." Pages 182–95 in *Divinanimality: Animal Theory, Creaturely Theology*. Edited by Stephen D. Moore. TTC. New York: Fordham University Press, 2014.
Koosed, Jennifer L., and Stephen D. Moore, eds. *Affect Theory and the Bible*. *BibInt* 22.4 (2014).

Kotrosits, Maia. *How Things Feel: Biblical Studies, Affect Theory, and the (Im)personal*. BRP. Leiden: Brill, 2016.

———. *Rethinking Early Christian Identity: Affect, Violence, and Belonging*. Minneapolis: Fortress, 2015.

———. "The Rhetoric of Intimate Spaces: Affect and Performance in the Corinthian Correspondence." *USQR* 62 (2011): 134–51.

———. "Romance and Danger at Nag Hammadi." *BCT* 8 (2012): 39–52.

Kotrosits, Maia, and Hal Taussig. *Re-reading the Gospel of Mark amidst Loss and Trauma*. New York: Palgrave Macmillan, 2013.

Kwok Pui-lan. *Discovering the Bible in the Non-biblical World*. BL. Maryknoll, NY: Orbis, 1995.

Laist, Randy, ed. *Plants and Literature: Essays in Critical Plant Studies*. CPS 1. Amsterdam: Rodopi, 2013.

Lamb, David. *Text, Context and the Johannine Community: A Sociolinguistic Analysis of the Johannine Writings*. LNTS. New York: Bloomsbury T&T Clark, 2014.

Latour, Bruno. *Reassembling the Social: An Introduction to Actor-Network Theory*. CLMS. Oxford: Oxford University Press, 2005.

Lauretis, Teresa de, ed. *Queer Theory: Lesbian and Gay Sexualities. differences* 3 (1991).

Lavan, Myles. *Slaves to Rome: Paradigms of Empire in Roman Culture*. CCS. Cambridge: Cambridge University Press, 2013.

Lawrence, Louise J. "Crumb Trails and Puppy-Dog Tales: Reading Afterlives of a Canaanite Woman." Pages 262–78 in *From the Margins 2: Women of the New Testament and Their Afterlives*. Edited by Christine E. Joynes and Christopher C. Rowland. BMW 27. Sheffield: Sheffield Phoenix, 2009.

Leander, Hans. *Discourses of Empire: The Gospel of Mark from a Postcolonial Perspective*. SemeiaSt 71. Atlanta: Society of Biblical Literature, 2013.

Lewis, Karoline M. *Rereading the "Shepherd Discourse": Restoring the Integrity of John 9:39–10:21*. StBibLit 113. New York: Lang, 2008.

Llewelyn, Stephen R., Gareth J. Wearne, and Bianca L. Sanderson. "Guarding Entry to the Kingdom: The Place of Eunuchs in Mt. 19.12." *JSHJ* 10 (2012): 228–46.

Lorde, Audre. *Sister Outsider: Essays and Speeches*. Berkeley: Crossing, 1984.

Luz, Ulrich. *Matthew 8–20*. Hermeneia. Minneapolis: Fortress, 2001.

Mainville, Odette. *The Spirit in Luke-Acts*. Woodstock, GA: The Foundation for Pentecostal Scholarship, 2016.

Marchal, Joseph A. "How Soon Is (This Apocalypse) Now? Queer Velocities after a Corinthian Already and a Pauline Not Yet." In *Sexual Disorientations: Queer Temporalities, Affects, Theologies*. Edited by Kent L. Brintnall, Joseph A. Marchal, and Stephen D. Moore. TTC. New York: Fordham University Press, 2017.

———. "'Making History' Queerly: Touches across Time through a Biblical Behind." *BibInt* 19 (2011): 373–95.

Marchant, Alicia, ed. *Historicizing Heritage and Emotions: The Affective Histories of Blood, Stone, and Land from Medieval Britain to Colonial Australia*. New York: Routledge, 2017.

Marcus, Joel. *Mark 8–16: A New Translation with Introduction and Commentary*. AB 27A. New Haven: Yale University Press, 2009.

Marder, Michael. *The Philosopher's Plant: An Intellectual Herbarium*. New York: Columbia University Press, 2014.

———. *Plant-Thinking: A Philosophy of Vegetal Life*. New York: Columbia University Press, 2013.

Massumi, Brian. "The Autonomy of Affect." *CC* 31 (1995): 83–109.

———. *Parables for the Virtual: Movement, Affect, Sensation*. PCI. Durham, NC: Duke University Press, 2002.

———. *Politics of Affect*. Cambridge, UK: Polity, 2015.

———. *What Animals Teach Us about Politics*. Durham, NC: Duke University Press, 2014.

Mbembe, Achille. "The Power of the Archive and Its Limits." Translated by Judith Inggs. Pages 19–26 in *Refiguring the Archive*. Edited by Carolyn Hamilton, Verne Harris, Jane Taylor, Michele Pickover, Graeme Reid, and Razia Saleh. Dordrecht: Kluwer Academic, 2002.

McLean, B. H. *Biblical Interpretation and Philosophical Hermeneutics*. Cambridge: Cambridge University Press, 2012.

McLellan, Peter N. "Specters of Mark: The Second Gospel's Ending and Derrida's Messianicity." *BibInt* 24 (2016): 357–81.

Menninghaus, Winfried. *Disgust: Theory and History of a Strong Sensation*. Translated by Howard Eiland and Joel Golb. Albany: SUNY Press, 2003.

Menon, Madhavi. "Introduction: Queer Shakes." Pages 1–27 in *Shakesqueer: A Queer Companion to the Complete Works of William Shakespeare*. Edited by Madhavi Menon. Durham, NC: Duke University Press, 2011.

———. "Period Cramps." Pages 229–35 in *Queer Renaissance Historiography: Backward Gaze*. Edited by Vin Nardizzi, Stephen Guy-Bray, and Will Stockton. Farnham, UK: Ashgate, 2009.

———. *Unhistorical Shakespeare: Queer Theory in Shakespearean Literature and Film*. New York: Palgrave Macmillan, 2008.

Michelet, Jules. *Mother Death: The Journals of Jules Michelet, 1815–1850*. Edited and translated by Edward K. Kaplan. Amherst: University of Massachusetts Press, 1984.

Mirguet, Françoise. "What Is an 'Emotion' in the Hebrew Bible? An Experience That Exceeds Most Contemporary Concepts." *BibInt* 24 (2016): 442–65.

Mirguet, Françoise, and Dominika Kurek-Comycz, eds. *Emotions in Ancient Jewish Literature*. BibInt 24.4–5 (2016).

Moloney, Francis J. *The Gospel of John*. SP 4. Collegeville, MN: Liturgical Press, 1998.

Moore, Stephen D. "A Bible That Expresses Everything While Communicating Nothing: Deleuze and Guattari's Cure for Interpretosis." In *Exegesis without Authorial Intentions?* Edited by Clarissa Breu. BibInt. Leiden: Brill, forthcoming.

———. "Biblical Narrative Analysis from the New Criticism to the New Narratology." Pages 27–50 in *The Oxford Handbook of Biblical Narrative*. Edited by Danna Nolan Fewell. Oxford: Oxford University Press, 2016.

———, ed. *Divinanimality: Animal Theory, Creaturely Theology*. TTC. New York: Fordham University Press, 2014.

———. "The Dog-Woman of Canaan and Other Animal Tales from the Gospel of Matthew." Pages 57–71 in *Soundings in Cultural Criticism: Perspectives and Methods in Culture, Power, and Identity in New Testament Interpretation*. Edited by Francisco Lozada Jr. and Greg Carey. Minneapolis: Fortress, 2013.

———. *Empire and Apocalypse: Postcolonialism and the New Testament*. BMW 12. Sheffield: Sheffield Phoenix, 2006.

———. *God's Beauty Parlor: And Other Queer Spaces in and around the Bible*. Contraversions. Stanford, CA: Stanford University Press, 2001.

———. *God's Gym: Divine Male Bodies of the Bible*. New York: Routledge, 1996.

———. "Introduction: From Animal Theory to Creaturely Theology." Pages 203–207 in *Divinanimality: Animal Theory, Creaturely Theology*.

Edited by Stephen D. Moore. TTC. New York: Fordham University Press, 2014.

———. *Mark and Luke in Poststructuralist Perspectives: Jesus Begins to Write*. New Haven: Yale University Press, 1992.

———. "A Modest Manifesto for New Testament Literary Criticism: How to Interface with a Literary Studies Field That Is Post-literary, Post-theoretical, and Post-methodological." *BibInt* 15 (2007): 1–25.

———. *Poststructuralism and the New Testament: Derrida and Foucault at the Foot of the Cross*. Minneapolis: Fortress, 1994.

———. "Retching on Rome: Vomitous Loathing and Visceral Disgust in Affect Theory and the Apocalypse of John." *BibInt* 22 (2014): 503–28.

———. "Ruminations on Revelation's Ruminant, Quadrupedal Christ; or, the Even-Toed Ungulate That Therefore I Am." Pages 301–26 in *The Bible and Posthumanism*. Edited by Jennifer L. Koosed. SemeiaSt 74. Atlanta: Society of Biblical Literature, 2014.

———. "The Slight Rise and Precipitous Decline of Postmodernism in Biblical Studies." Pages 225–45 in *Simulating Aichele: Essays in Bible, Film, Culture and Theory*. Edited by Melissa C. Stewart. BMW 69. Sheffield: Sheffield Phoenix, 2015.

———. "True Confessions and Weird Obsessions: Autobiographical Interventions in Literary and Biblical Studies." *Semeia* 72 (1995): 19–51.

———. *Untold Tales from the Book of Revelation: Sex and Gender, Empire and Ecology*. RBS 79. Atlanta: SBL Press, 2014.

———. "Why the Johannine Jesus Weeps at the Tomb of Lazarus." Pages 287–309 in *Mixed Feelings and Vexed Passions: Exploring Emotions in Biblical Literature*. Edited by F. Scott Spencer. RBS 90. Atlanta: SBL Press, 2017.

———. "Why There Are No Humans or Animals in the Gospel of Mark." Pages 71–94 in *Mark as Story: Retrospect and Prospect*. Edited by Kelly R. Iverson and Christopher W. Skinner. RBS 65. Atlanta: Society of Biblical Literature, 2011.

Moore, Stephen D., and Fernando F. Segovia, eds. *Postcolonial Biblical Criticism: Interdisciplinary Intersections*. BP 8. New York: T&T Clark International, 2005.

Moore, Stephen D., and Janice Capel Anderson. "Taking It Like a Man: Masculinity in 4 Maccabees." Pages 175–200 in Stephen D. Moore, *The Bible in Theory: Critical and Postcritical Essays*. RBS 57. Atlanta: Society of Biblical Literature, 2010.

Moraga, Cherríe. *Loving in the War Years: Lo Que Nunca Pasó por Sus Labios*. Boston: South End, 1983.
Morton, Timothy. *Realist Magic: Objects, Ontology, Causality*. NM. London: Open Humanities, 2013.
Moxnes, Halvor. *Putting Jesus in His Place: A Radical Vision of Household and Kingdom*. Louisville: Westminster John Knox, 2003.
Muñoz, José Esteban. *Cruising Utopia: The Then and There of Queer Futurity*. Sexual Cultures. New York: New York University Press, 2009.
Nealon, Jeffrey T. *Plant Theory: Biopower and Vegetable Life*. Stanford, CA: Stanford University Press, 2016.
———. *Post-Postmodernism, or, the Cultural Logic of Just-in-Time Capitalism*. Stanford, CA: Stanford University Press, 2012.
Nelavala, Surekha. *Liberation beyond Borders: Dalit Feminist Hermeneutics and Four Gospel Women*. Saarbrücken: Lambert, 2009.
Ngai, Sianne. *Ugly Feelings*. Cambridge: Harvard University Press, 2005.
O'Neill, Patrick. *Fictions of Discourse: Reading Narrative Theory*. T/C. Toronto: University of Toronto Press, 1994.
Pellegrini, Ann, and Jasbir Puar. "Affect." *Social Text* 27.3 (2009): 35–38.
Pippin, Tina. "Feasting with/on Jesus: John 6 in Conversation with Vampire Studies." Pages 87–100 in *The Recycled Bible: Autobiography, Culture, and the Space between*. Edited by Fiona C. Black. SemeiaSt 51. Atlanta: Society of Biblical Literature, 2006.
Puar, Jasbir. "'I Would Rather Be a Cyborg Than a Goddess': Becoming-Intersectional in Assemblage Theory." *PhiloSOPHIA* 2 (2012): 49–66.
———. *Terrorist Assemblages: Homonationalism in Queer Times*. Next Wave. Durham, NC: Duke University Press, 2007.
Ridderbos, Herman N. *The Gospel according to John: A Theological Commentary*. Translated by John Vriend. Grand Rapids: Eerdmans, 1997.
Ridpath, John Clark. *With the World's People: An Account of the Ethnic Origin, Primitive Estate, Early Migrations, Social Evolution, and Present Conditions and Promise of the Principal Families of Men Together with a Preliminary Inquiry on the Time, Place and Manner of the Beginning*. 12 vols. Cincinnati: Jones Bros., 1912.
Riley, Denise. *Impersonal Passion: Language as Affect*. Durham, NC: Duke University Press, 2005.
Rivera, Mayra. *Poetics of the Flesh*. Durham, NC: Duke University Press, 2015.
Robinson, Emily. "Touching the Void: Affective History and the Impossible." *RH* 14 (2010): 503–20.

Roffe, Jon, and Hannah Stark, eds. *Deleuze and the Non/Human*. New York: Palgrave Macmillan, 2015.

———. "Deleuze and the Nonhuman Turn: An Interview with Elizabeth Grosz." Pages 17–24 in *Deleuze and the Non/Human*. Edited by Jon Roffe and Hannah Stark. New York: Palgrave Macmillan, 2015.

Romanow, Rebecca Fine. *The Postcolonial Body in Queer Space and Time*. Newcastle, UK: Cambridge Scholars, 2008.

Römer, Thomas, and Jean-Daniel Macchi. "Luke, Disciple of the Deuteronomistic School." Pages 178–87 in *Luke's Literary Achievement: Collected Essays*. Edited by C. M. Tuckett. JSNTSup 116. Sheffield: Sheffield Academic, 1995.

Runions, Erin. "From Disgust to Humor: Rahab's Queer Affect." Pages 45–74 in *Bible Trouble: Queer Reading at the Boundaries of Biblical Scholarship*. Edited by Teresa J. Hornsby and Ken Stone. SemeiaSt 67. Atlanta: Society of Biblical Literature, 2011.

———. "Prophetic Affect and the Promise of Change: A Response." Pages 235–42 in *Jeremiah (Dis)placed: New Directions in Writing/Reading Jeremiah*. Edited by A. R. Pete Diamond and Louis Stulman. LHBOTS 529. New York: T&T Clark International, 2011.

Schwartz, Margaret. *Dead Matter: The Meaning of Iconic Corpses*. Minneapolis: University of Minnesota Press, 2015.

Sedgwick, Eve Kosofsky. *Between Men: English Literature and Male Homosocial Desire*. 30th anniversary ed. GC. New York: Columbia University Press, 2016.

———. *Epistemology of the Closet*. Berkeley: University of California Press, 1990.

———. *Tendencies*. Durham, NC: Duke University Press, 1993.

———. *Touching Feeling: Affect, Pedagogy, Performativity*. Durham, NC: Duke University Press, 2003.

Sedgwick, Eve Kosofsky, and Adam Frank, eds. *Shame and Its Sisters: A Silvan Tomkins Reader*. Durham, NC: Duke University Press, 1995.

———. "Shame in the Cybernetic Fold: Reading Silvan Tomkins." Pages 93–122 in *Touching Feeling: Affect, Pedagogy, Performativity*. Durham, NC: Duke University Press, 2003.

Seigworth, Gregory J. "From Affection to Soul." Pages 181–91 in *Gilles Deleuze: Key Concepts*. Edited by Charles J. Stivale. New York: Routledge, 2005.

Seigworth, Gregory J., and Melissa Gregg. "An Inventory of Shimmers."

Pages 1–25 in *The Affect Theory Reader*. Edited by Melissa Gregg and Gregory J. Seigworth. Durham, NC: Duke University Press, 2010.

Shaviro, Steven. *The Universe of Things: On Speculative Realism*. Posthumanities 30. Minneapolis: University of Minnesota Press, 2014.

Sheldon, Rebekah. "Affect, Epistemology and the Nonhuman Turn." *Thinking C21*, 27 April 27 2012. https://tinyurl.com/SBL0691a.

Shepherd, William H., Jr. *The Narrative Function of the Holy Spirit as a Character in Luke-Acts*. SBLDS 147. Atlanta: Scholars Press, 1994.

Silverstein, Michael. "Hierarchy of Features and Ergativity." Pages 112–71 in *Grammatical Categories in Australian Languages*. Edited by R. M. W. Dixon. Canberra: Australian Institute of Aboriginal Studies, 1976.

Smith, Barbara. *Toward a Black Feminist Criticism*. New York: Out & Out, 1977.

Spillers, Hortense. "Mama's Baby, Papa's Maybe: An American Grammar Book." *Diacritics* 17.2 (1987): 65–81.

Spivak, Gayatri Chakravorty. "Can the Subaltern Speak?" Pages 271–313 in *Marxism and the Interpretation of Culture*. Edited by Cary Nelson and Larry Grossberg. Urbana: University of Illinois Press, 1988.

⸻. "Ghostwriting." *Diacritics* 25.2 (1995): 64–84.

Stark, Hannah. "Deleuze and Critical Plant Studies." Pages 180–96 in *Deleuze and the Non/Human*. Edited by Jon Roffe and Hannah Stark. New York: Palgrave Macmillan, 2015.

Steiner, Gary. "Descartes, Christianity, and Contemporary Speciesism." Pages 117–31 in *A Communion of Subjects: Animals in Religion, Science, and Ethics*. Edited by Paul Waldau and Kimberley Patton. New York: Columbia University Press, 2006.

Stewart, Kathleen. *Ordinary Affects*. Durham, NC: Duke University Press, 2007.

Stone, Ken. "Animating the Bible's Animals." Pages 444–55 in *The Oxford Handbook of Biblical Narrative*. Edited by Danna Nolan Fewell. Oxford: Oxford University Press, 2016.

⸻. *Reading the Hebrew Bible with Animal Studies*. Stanford, CA: Stanford University Press, 2017.

Strømmen, Hannah M. *Every Living Creature: The Question of the Animal in the Bible*. SemeiaSt. Atlanta: SBL Press, forthcoming.

Sylva, Dennis. *Thomas—Love as Strong as Death: Faith and Commitment in the Fourth Gospel*. LNTS. New York: Bloomsbury T&T Clark, 2013.

Talbott, Rick Franklin. "Imagining the Matthean Eunuch Community: Kyriarchy on the Chopping Block." *JFSR* 22 (2006): 21–43.

Thrift, Nigel. *Non-representational Theory: Space, Politics, Affect*. ILS. New York: Routledge, 2008.

Tomkins, Silvan S. *Affect, Imagery, Consciousness*. 4 vols. New York: Springer, 1962–1992.

———. *Exploring Affect: The Selected Writings of Silvan S. Tomkins*. Edited by E. Virginia Demos. SESI. Cambridge: Cambridge University Press, 1995.

Tompkins, Jane P. "Me and My Shadow." Pages 23–40 in *The Intimate Critique: Autobiographical Literary Criticism*. Edited by Diane P. Freeman, Olivia Frey, and Frances Murphy Zauhar. Durham, NC: Duke University Press, 1993.

Traub, Valerie. "The New Unhistoricism in Queer Studies." *PMLA* 128 (2013): 21–39.

Vander Stichele, Caroline. "The Head of John and Its Reception or How to Conceptualize 'Reception History.'" Pages 79–94 in *Reception History and Biblical Studies: Theory and Practice*. Edited by Emma England and William John Lyons. ST 6. New York: Bloomsbury T&T Clark, 2015.

Vieira, Patrícia, Monica Gagliano, and John Ryan, eds. *The Green Thread: Dialogues with the Vegetal World*. ETP. Lanham, MD: Lexington, 2016.

Voorwinde, Stephen. *Jesus' Emotions in the Fourth Gospel: Human or Divine?* JSNTSup 284. New York: T&T Clark International, 2005.

———. *Jesus' Emotions in the Gospels*. New York: T&T Clark International, 2011.

Wainwright, Elaine M. "Not Without My Daughter: Gender and Demon Possession in Matthew 15.21–28." Pages 126–37 in *A Feminist Companion to Matthew*. Edited by Amy-Jill Levine with Marianne Blickenstaff. Sheffield: Sheffield Academic, 2001.

———. "Of Borders, Bread, Dogs and Demons: Reading Matthew 15.21–28 Ecologically." Pages 114–26 in *Where the Wild Ox Roams: Biblical Essays in Honor of Norman C. Habel*. Edited by Alan H. Cadwallader and Peter Trudinger. HBM 59. Sheffield: Sheffield Phoenix, 2013.

———. "Of Dogs and Women: Ethology and Gender in Ancient Healing; The Canaanite Woman's Story—Matt 15:21–28." Pages 55–69 in *Miracles Revisited: New Testament Miracle Stories and Their Concepts of Reality*. Edited by Stefan Alkier and Annette Weissenrieder. SBR 2. Berlin: de Gruyter, 2013.

Waller, Alexis G. "Violent Spectacles and Public Feelings: Trauma and Affect in the Gospel of Mark and *The Thunder, Perfect Mind*." *BibInt* 22 (2014): 450–72.

Warner, Michael. "Introduction." Pages vii–xxxi in *Fear of a Queer Planet: Queer Politics and Social Theory*. Edited by Michael Warner. CP 6. Minneapolis: University of Minnesota Press, 1993.

Warren, Meredith J. C. *My Flesh Is Meat Indeed: A Nonsacramental Reading of John 6:51–58*. Minneapolis: Fortress, 2015.

Weheliye, Alexander G. *Habeas Viscus: Racializing Assemblages, Biopolitics, and Black Feminist Theories of the Human*. Durham, NC: Duke University Press, 2014.

Weil, Kari. *Thinking Animals: Why Animal Studies Now?* New York: Columbia University Press, 2012.

White, Paul. "Darwin's Emotions: The Scientific Self and the Sentiment of Objectivity." *Isis* 100 (2009): 811–26.

Wills, Lawrence M. "Daniel." Pages 1,640–65 in *The Jewish Study Bible*. Edited by Adele Berlin and Marc Zvi Brettler. 2nd ed. Oxford: Oxford University Press, 2014.

Wolfendale, Peter. *Object-Oriented Philosophy: The Noumenon's New Clothes*. Falmouth, UK: Urbanomic Media, 2014.

Woodard, Mitch. *What If God? A Personal Devotion/Bible Study*. Bloomington, IN: WestBow, 2016.

Woodhouse, S. C. *English-Greek Dictionary: A Vocabulary of the Attic Language*. London: Routledge & Sons, 1910. Repr., 1998.

Yates, Julian. "Sheep Tracks: A Multi-Species Impression." Pages 173–210 in *Animal, Vegetable, Mineral: Ethics and Objects*. Edited by Jeffrey Jerome Cohen. Washington, DC: Oliphaunt, 2012.

Index of Modern Authors

Abraham, Nicolas 98 n. 49
Agnew, Vanessa 91 n. 19
Ahmed, Sara 19, 20, 24, 27 n. 40, 35 n. 71
Aichele, George 1 n. 1, 5 n. 9, 8 n. 15
Albani, Matthias 68 n. 16
Alber, Jan 29 n. 43
Alkier, Stefan 67 n. 13
Allen, Willoughby C. 73
Allison, Dale C. 70 n. 20, 76–77
Anderson, Janice Capel 72 n. 28, 72 n. 30
Anzaldúa, Gloria 85 n. 1
Athanasiou, Athena 91 n. 19
Barad, Karen 4 n. 7, 112 n. 16
Barker, Francis 75 n. 35
Barthes, Roland 4 n. 6
Beasley-Murray, G. R. 35 n. 70
Behar, Katherine 112 n. 16
Bennett, Jane 1, 4 n. 8, 6 n. 11, 7 n. 13, 44 n. 8, 112 n. 16, 113, 114, 117 n. 31, 118, 120 n. 48, 124–25, 126 n. 69
Bennington, Geoffrey 69 n. 18
Bergson, Henri 17, 109 n. 7
Berlant, Lauren 19, 23
Berlin, Adele 68 n. 16
Birnbaum, Daniel 76 n. 40
Black, Fiona C. 37 n. 74
Blickenstaff, Marianne 65 n. 9
Boccaccini, Gabriele 68 n. 16
Bohache, Thomas 80 nn. 47–48
Bouchard, Donald F. 7 n. 14
Bradley, Keith 82 n. 52
Breed, Brennan W. 8 n. 15
Brennan, Teresa 23
Brettler, Marc Zvi 68 n. 16
Breu, Clarissa 8 n. 15
Brillat-Savarin, Jean Anthelme 118
Brinkema, Eugenie 7 n. 13, 15, 24–28, 30, 32–34, 35 n. 71, 36, 37 n. 75
Brintnall, Kent L. 64 n. 5
Brown, Bill 112 n. 16
Brown, Raymond E. 41–42 n. 2, 115 n. 24
Bryant, Arthur 91 n. 18
Buell, Denise Kimber 64 n. 5, 94 n. 29, 101 n. 58
Bultmann, Rudolf 35 n. 70
Burchell, Graham 43 n. 4
Butler, Judith 63 n. 4
Cadwallader, Alan H. 67 n. 13
Camporesi, Piero 118 n. 36
Caputo, John D. 39 n. 77
Carter, Warren 53 n. 46, 66 n. 11
Certeau, Michel de 88
Césaire, Aimé 118
Chen, Mel Y. 13, 111 n. 13, 115, 119–24
Cho, Grace M. 86, 98–99, 101 n. 59, 102, 103
Choi, Jin Young 62 n. 2, 77 n. 43, 94 n. 29, 98–99 n. 49
Clough, Patricia Ticineto 7 n. 13, 18, 98
Cohen, Jeffrey Jerome 6 n. 11, 101 n. 60, 120 n. 46, 122–23 n. 55
Colebrook, Claire 5 n. 10
Collins, Adela Yarbro 41 n. 2
Collins, John J. 68 nn. 15–16
Concannon, Cavan W. 94 n. 29
Conley, Tom 27 n. 39, 88 n. 12

-147-

Coole, Diana	112 n. 16
Cottrill, Amy C.	21
Cranmer, Thomas	77 n. 41
Creed, Barbara	75 n. 35
Currie, Mark	29 n. 43
Cvetkovich, Ann	10 n. 20, 19–20, 23–24
Daly, Mary	108 nn. 4–5
Daly-Denton, Margaret	121 n. 52
Danker, Frederick W.	53 n. 49
Davies, W. D.	70 n. 20, 76–77
Defoe, Daniel	70–72, 75
DeLanda, Manuel	44 n. 8
Deleuze, Gilles	7–10, 11, 13, 17–20, 21 n. 20, 24–25, 27–28, 30, 32 n. 60, 33 n. 67, 41–59, 99, 107, 110 n. 9, 114, 116
Demos, E. Virginia	16 n. 1
Derrida, Jacques	4 nn. 6–7, 7, 33 n. 64, 36 n. 73, 69 n. 18, 70–72, 75–76, 93–94 nn. 29–30, 97 n. 40, 109 n. 6
Descartes, René	28, 68, 69 n. 18, 70–71
Diamond, A. R. Pete	21 n. 20
Dinshaw, Carolyn	63–64 n. 5, 86, 92–93, 95 n. 36, 105
Dixon, R. M. W.	120 n. 49
Dolphijn, Rick	112 n. 16
Donaldson, Laura E.	65 n. 9, 94 n. 29
Dube, Musa W.	62 n. 2, 65–66 n. 10
Duncan, Pansy	20
Dunning, Benjamin H.	94 n. 29
During, Simon	22 n. 22
Edelman, Lee	64 n. 5, 86
Eiland, Howard	33 n. 68
Elliott, Matthew A.	32 n. 59
Elliott, Scott S.	29 n. 44
England, Emma	8 n. 15
Fanon, Frantz	82, 118 n. 38
Feher, Michel	118 n. 36
Felski, Rita	22 n. 22
Fewell, Danna Nolan	6 n. 12
Fisher, M. K. F.	118 n. 34
Fludernik, Monika	29 n. 43
Foucault, Michel	3–4 n. 6, 7, 27 n. 39
Fradenburg, Louise	94 n. 32
France, R. T.	54 n. 51
Frank, Adam	16–17, 18
Freccero, Carla	64 n. 5, 86–87, 88 n. 9, 93–95, 97–98, 104 n. 68
Freeman, Diane P.	9 n. 18
Freeman, Elizabeth	63 n. 5, 79 n. 45, 85, 86, 95 n. 36
Frey, Jörg	101 n. 58
Frey, Olivia	9 n. 18
Frost, Samantha	112 n. 16
Gagliano, Monica	110 n. 9
Galeta, Robert	26 n. 35
Gallop, Jane	23 n. 23
Gandillac, Maurice de	8 n. 17
Gibson, Andrew	28–29 n. 43
Giffney, Noreen	12 n. 21
Gikandi, Simon	91 n. 20
Gilhus, Ingvild Saelid	71 n. 23
Golb, Joel	33 n. 68
Goldberg, Jonathan	64 n. 5, 87, 88 n. 9, 88 n. 11
Goldstone, Andrew	22 n. 21
Gordon, Avery	94 n. 29, 97 n. 40
Gratton, Peter	111 n. 16
Graybill, Rhiannon	44 n. 8
Gregg, Melissa	7 n. 13, 18–19, 102 n. 61
Grossberg, Larry	65 n. 8
Grosz, Elizabeth	12 n. 21
Grusin, Richard	5–6, 44 n. 8
Guardiola-Sáenz, Leticia	62 n. 2
Guattari, Félix	9–10, 17, 21 n. 21, 28 n. 41, 32 n. 60, 33 n. 67, 43–50, 54 n. 53, 55–58, 99, 107, 114, 116
Guest, Deryn	80 n. 47
Gunkel, Heidrun	100–101 n. 58
Guy-Bray, Stephen	87 n. 5
Habberjam, Barbara	43 n. 5, 99 n. 54
Haggerty, George E.	93 n. 28
Halberstam, J. Jack	64 n. 5, 79, 86, 97 n. 43
Halley, Janet	86 n. 3, 98 nn. 47–48
Halley, Jean	18 n. 10
Halperin, David M.	86 n. 3
Hamilton, Carolyn	91 n. 20
Hand, Seán	27 n. 39
Haraway, Donna J.	5 n. 10, 61, 115–16 n. 26, 125

Index of Modern Authors

Harrill, J. Albert	37 n. 74
Hester, David	80 n. 48
Hezser, Catherine	82 n. 52
Hick, John	108 nn. 4–5
Hird, Myra J.	12 n. 21
Hirsch-Luipold, Rainer	100–101 n. 58
Hoare, R. W. N.	35 n. 70
Hodges, Ames	43 n. 5
Hoorn, Jeanette	75 n. 35
Hornsby, Teresa J.	21 n. 20
Howard, Richard	43 n. 3
Huggan, Graham	75 n. 35
Hulme, Peter	75 n. 35
Humphries-Brooks, Stephenson	77 n. 42
Hur, Ju	100 n. 56
Hurley, Robert	9 n. 18
Irigaray, Luce	110 n. 9
Iversen, Margaret	75 n. 35
Iverson, Kelly R.	6 n. 12
Joughin, Martin	17 n. 7, 28 n. 41
Joyce, James	71 n. 24
Joynes, Christine E.	65 n. 9
Kamuf, Peggy	93 n. 29
Kant, Immanuel	33 n. 64, 70
Kaplan, Edward K.	33 n. 65
Kastan, David Scott	87 n. 4
Keener, Craig S.	89–90, 100 n. 57, 113 n. 17, 122 n. 53
Keller, Catherine	39 n. 77, 112 n. 16
Ketchum, Matthew James	94 n. 29
Klancher, Nancy	77 n. 41, 82 n. 50
Klein, Richard	33 n. 64
Knust, Jennifer	21, 24
Kohn, Eduardo	110 n. 9
Kolnai, Aurel	33 n. 63
Koosed, Jennifer L.	5 n. 9, 6 n. 12, 21, 38 n. 76, 68 n. 15, 69 n. 18, 94 n. 29
Korsmeyer, Carolyn	33 n. 63
Kotrosits, Maia	21, 92 n. 22, 94 n. 29, 97 n. 42, 98 n. 48, 105 n. 71
Kristeva, Julia	4 n. 6
Kurek-Comycz, Dominika	29 n. 45
Kwok Pui-lan	62 n. 2
Lacan, Jacques	4 n. 6, 17
Laist, Randy	110 n. 9
Lamb, David	115 n. 24
Lane, Helen R.	9 n. 18
Latour, Bruno	5, 44 n. 8
Lauretis, Teresa de	85 n. 1
Lavan, Myles	82 n. 52
Lawrence, Louise J.	65 n. 9
Leander, Hans	52 n. 46, 62 n. 2
Leibniz, Gottfried Wilhelm	27 n. 39
Lester, Mark	8 n. 16
Levinas, Emmanuel	109 n. 6
Levine, Amy-Jill	65 n. 9, 77 n. 42
Levison, John R.	100 n. 58
Lewis, Karoline M.	108 n. 3
Llewelyn, Stephen R.	80 n. 48
Lorde, Audre	85 n. 1
Luz, Ulrich	62 n. 3
Lyons, William John	8 n. 15
Macchi, Jean-Daniel	103 n. 67
Mainville, Odette	96 n. 39
Marchal, Joseph A.	64 n. 5, 93 n. 27, 95 n. 36
Marchant, Alicia	91 n. 19
Marcus, Joel	41 n. 2, 53 n. 49
Marder, Michael	110–11, 123 n. 58, 124 n. 64
Massumi, Brian	9 n. 18, 18, 23, 27–28, 109, 111 nn. 13–14, 124 n. 62, 125
Mbembe, Achille	91
McGarry, Molly	93 n. 28
McLean, B. H.	8 n. 15
McLellan, Peter N.	94 n. 29
Menninghaus, Winfried	33
Menon, Madhavi	64 n. 5, 86–88, 90, 93
Michelet, Jules	33 n. 65, 36 n. 72
Miller, Arthur	109 n. 7
Mirguet, Françoise	29 n. 45
Moloney, Francis J.	107–8 n. 3
Moraga, Cherríe	85 n. 1
Morton, Timothy	112 n. 16
Moxnes, Halvor	80 n. 46, 80 n. 48
Muñoz, José Esteban	64 n. 5, 86 n. 2
Naddaff, Ramona	118 n. 36
Nardizzi, Vin	87 n. 5
Nasrallah, Laura	94 n. 29

Nealon, Jeffrey T.	21–22 n. 21, 110–11	Shepherd, William H., Jr.	100 n. 56
Nelavela, Surekha	62 n. 2	Silverstein, Michael	120 n. 49
Nelson, Cary	65 n. 8	Simon, Sherry	7 n. 14
Ngai, Sianne	23	Skinner, Christopher W.	6 n. 12
Olsson, Anders	76 n. 40	Smith, Barbara	85 n. 1
O'Neill, Patrick	28 n. 43	Smith, Barry	33 n. 63
Parnet, Claire	43 n. 5, 44 n. 8, 45 n. 11, 99 n. 54	Smith, Daniel W.	24 n. 27
		Spillers, Hortense	85 n. 1
Patton, Kimberley	71 n. 23	Spinoza, Baruch	17, 28 n. 41
Patton, Paul	52 n. 45	Spivak, Gayatri Chakravorty	65 n. 8, 94 n. 30
Pautrat, Bernard	8 n. 17		
Pellegrini, Ann	19 n. 12	Stark, Hannah	5 n. 10, 12 n. 21, 110 n.9
Philcox, Richard	82 n. 51	Steiner, Gary	71 n. 23
Pinkham, Joan	118 n. 38	Stewart, Kathleen	19, 23
Pippin, Tina	37 n. 74	Stewart, Melissa C.	2 n. 2
Polan, Dana	46 n. 15	Stivale, Charles J.	28 n. 41
Puar, Jasbir	19, 114 n. 20	Stockton, Will	87 n. 5
Rand, Nicholas T.	36 n. 73, 98 n. 49	Stone, Ken	6 n. 12, 21 n. 20
Riches, John K.	35 n.70	Strømmen, Hannah M.	6 n. 12
Ridderbos, Herman N.	30 n. 47	Stulman, Louis	21 n. 20
Ridpath, John Clark	73 n. 33	Sylva, Dennis	30 n. 48
Riley, Denise	23	Talbott, Rick Franklin	80 n. 48
Rivera, Mayra	35 n. 70	Taormina, Mike	43 n. 5
Robinson, Emily	91–92	Taussig, Hal	21 n. 20
Roffe, Jon	5 n. 10, 12 n. 21, 110 n.9	Tazi, Nadia	118 n. 36
Romanow, Rebecca Fine	63–64, 66	Thrift, Nigel	23
Römer, Thomas	103 n. 67	Tiffin, Helen	75 n. 35
Rowland, Christopher C.	65 n. 9	Tomkins, Sylvan S.	15–17, 19, 25
Rubenstein, Mary-Jane	112 n. 16	Tomlinson, Hugh	25–26 n. 35, 43 nn. 4–5, 99 n. 54
Runions, Erin	21		
Ryan, John	110 n. 9	Tompkins, Jane P.	9–10
Sanderson, Bianca L.	80 n. 48	Torok, Maria	98 n. 49
Schüssler Fiorenza, Elisabeth	94 n. 29	Traub, Valerie	86 n. 3, 88 n. 9
Schwartz, Margaret	119 nn. 41–42	Trudinger, Peter	67 n. 13
Sedgwick, Eve Kosofsky	16–18, 24, 63, 90 n. 16, 105 n. 70	Tuckett, Christopher M.	103 n. 67
		Underwood, Ted	22 n. 21
Seem, Mark	9 n. 18	Vander Stichele, Caroline	8 n. 15
Seesengood, Robert Paul	68 n. 15, 69 n. 18	Van der Tuin, Iris	112 n. 16
		Vieira, Patrícia	110 n. 9
Segovia, Fernando F.	2 n. 4, 65 n. 9	Von Gemünden, Petra	29 n. 45
Seigworth, Gregory J.	7 n. 13, 18–19, 28 n. 41, 102 n. 61	Voorwinde, Stephen	29–30, 32 n. 59
		Vriend, John	30 n. 47
Shaviro, Steven	111–12 n. 16	Wainwright, Elaine M.	65 n. 9, 67 n. 13
Sheed, Rosemary	10 n. 20	Waldau, Paul	71 n. 23
Sheldon, Rebekah	7	Waller, Alexis G.	21, 24

Warner, Michael	63 n. 4
Warren, Meredith J. C.	37 n. 74, 117 n. 33
Wearne, Gareth J.	80 n. 48
Weber, Elizabeth	4 n. 7
Weheliye, Alexander G.	119 n. 39
Weil, Kari	6 n. 12
Weissenrieder, Annette	67 n. 13
White, Paul	92
Whitehead, Alfred North	17
Wills, David	69 n. 18
Wills, Lawrence M.	68 n. 16
Wolfendale, Peter	112 n. 16
Woodard, Mitch	78 n. 44
Woodhouse, S. C.	41 n. 2
Yates, Julian	120 n. 46
Zauhar, Francis Murphy	9 n. 18

www.ingramcontent.com/pod-product-compliance
Lightning Source LLC
Chambersburg PA
CBHW031434150426
43191CB00006B/517